TEACHING AND LEARNING SCIENCE

TEACHING AND LEARNING SCIENCE
Towards a personalized approach

Derek Hodson

Open University Press
Buckingham · Philadelphia

Open University Press
Celtic Court
22 Ballmoor
Buckingham
MK18 1XW

email: enquiries@openup.co.uk
world wide web: http://www.openup.co.uk

and
325 Chestnut Street
Philadelphia, PA 19106, USA

First Published 1998

A catalogue record of this book is available from the British Library

ISBN   0 335 20116 4 (hb)   0 335 20115 6 (pb)

Library of Congress Cataloging-in-Publication Data
Hodson, Derek.
    Teaching and learning science : towards a personalized approach /
Derek Hodson.
        p.   cm.
    Includes bibliographical references and index.
    ISBN 0–335–20116–4. – ISBN 0–335–20115–6 (pb)
    1. Science–Study and teaching–Psychology.   2. Individualized
instruction.   3. Cognitive psychology.   4. Motivation (Psychology)
I. Title.
    Q181.H69   1998
    507.1'2–dc21   98–3374
                                                                                              CIP

Typeset by Graphicraft Limited, Hong Kong
Printed in Great Britain by Biddles Ltd, Guildford and King's Lynn

To Susie, for everything

• • •

Contents

Acknowledgements   viii

1   In pursuit of scientific literacy   1

2   Towards a personalized science   9

3   The significance of prior knowledge in science and learning   23

4   Constructivist approaches to teaching and learning science   34

5   The paradox of constructivism   44

6   Prioritizing the affective   58

7   Exploring some social dimensions of learning   74

8   Science education as enculturation   84

9   Problems of assimilation and exclusion   100

10 Authenticity in science and learning   112

11 Walking the line: enculturation without assimilation   127

12 Exploring and developing personal understanding through
    practical work   143

13 Exploring and developing personal understanding through
    language   154

14 Making it work: the role of the teacher   168

References   181
Index   198

• • •

Acknowledgements

This book would not have been possible without the constant inspiration and encouragement of my wife, Sue Hodson, and the unfailing interest and support of Julie, Jolie, Gareth and Paul. My thinking has also been immeasurably sharpened and my ideas have been refined by discussion with numerous OISE graduate students, with whom it has been a pleasure and privilege to work for the past six years.

Thanks are also due to the University of Illinois Press for permission to reproduce Figure 2.1 (from P.B. Porter (1954) Another puzzle picture, *American Journal of Psychology*, 67, 550–1) and the Open University for permission to reproduce Figure 11.1 (from Hodson 1993d).

A society which places such great value on education and schooling that it requires the individual to attend school for long periods of time must find the means to make education attractive and meaningful to the individual learner.

(Benjamin S. Bloom 1976)

• • • 1

In pursuit of scientific literacy

A decade ago, Roberts (1988) posed the question 'What counts as science education?' It is still a pretty good question, though we may be only a little nearer to a satisfactory answer than we were when he suggested that 'it depends!' It depends on what is seen as the overall purpose of science education and, on this question, different stakeholders (students, teachers, parents, scientists, employers, politicians and the like) continue to express significantly different views. For some, school science education is about the selection and education of future scientists; for others, it is about preparation for responsible citizenship. Yet others see it as a means of responding to economic needs, social crises and problems of environmental degradation. As a consequence, says Roberts, science curricula exhibit a range of 'curriculum emphases': everyday coping; structure of science; science, technology, decisions; scientific skill development; correct explanations; self as explainer; solid foundations. Fensham (1994) has extended this list to include 'science for nurturing' (knowledge for improving the quality of life and environment) and 'science for making' (science for technological capability).

In recent years, it has been widely argued that many of these disparate goals are subsumed under the umbrella notion of science–technology–society (STS) education (Solomon and Aikenhead 1994; Yager 1996) and its overarching goal of *scientific literacy*. 'The STS (science, technology and society) concept of curriculum . . . is an opportunity to organize and present *all* the goals of science education in a coherent package' (Ministry of Education (Alberta) 1990: 44, emphasis added).

Although scientific literacy is by no means a new term, it has become established as one of today's slogans or rallying calls, along with the more recent 'authentic science', and is increasingly being used as a substitute term for the goals of science education. The opening paragraph of a decade-old article by Shahn (1988: 42) is typical of much of the rhetoric surrounding the notion of scientific literacy, and is worth quoting at length.

Science illiteracy is a serious problem. At one level it affects nations; because large parts of their populations are not adequately prepared, they cannot train enough technically proficient people to satisfy their economic and defense needs. More basically it affects people; those who are science illiterate are often deprived of the ability to understand the increasingly technological world, to make informed decisions regarding their health and their environment, to choose careers in remunerative technological fields and, in many ways, to think clearly.

While scientific literacy seems to be almost universally welcomed as a desirable goal, there is little clarity about its meaning (Jenkins 1990; Eisenhart *et al.* 1996; Galbraith *et al.* 1997).[1] It seems to mean different things to different people, though many simply assume that others know what it means and so avoid any attempt at clarification. In one early attempt at clarification, Pella *et al.* (1966) suggested that it comprises an understanding of:

- the basic concepts of science;
- the nature of science;
- the ethics that control the scientist in his or her work;
- the interrelationships of science and society;
- the interrelationships of science and the humanities;
- the differences between science and technology.

A quarter of a century later, *Science for All Americans* (American Association for the Advancement of Science 1989: 4) defined a scientifically literate person as 'one who is aware that science, mathematics, and technology are interdependent human enterprises with strengths and limitations; understands key concepts and principles of science; is familiar with the natural world and recognizes both its diversity and unity; and uses scientific knowledge and scientific ways of thinking for individual and social purposes.' Many other definitions, some very similar to these, others strikingly different, can be located in curriculum documents originating in Canada, the United Kingdom, Australia and New Zealand.

The long-standing confusion over the use of terms such as 'literacy', 'illiteracy' and 'literate', where some writers refer to a mere functional competence, while others imply a sensitive awareness of the complexities of language, is mirrored in the use of the term 'scientific literacy'. Thus, some see 'being scientifically literate' as the capacity to read, with reasonable understanding, lay articles about scientific and technological matters published in newspapers and magazines; others regard it as being in possession of the knowledge, skills and attitudes deemed necessary for a professional scientist. The American Association for the Advancement of Science (AAAS) document *Benchmarks for Scientific Literacy* (1993: 322) suggests that: 'People who are literate in science . . . are able to use the habits of mind and knowledge of science, mathematics, and technology they have acquired to think about and make sense of many of the ideas, claims, and events that they encounter in everyday life.' There are strong echoes here of Arons's (1983: 93) emphasis on the ability to 'discriminate, on the one hand, between acceptance of asserted and unverified end results, models, or conclusions, and on the other, understand their basis and origin; that is, to recognize when questions such as "How do we know?" "Why do we believe . . . ?" "What is the evidence for . . . ?" have been addressed, answered, and understood, and when something is being taken on faith.' Similar capabilities have sometimes been included in the notion of *intellectual independence* (Munby 1980; Aikenhead 1990; Norris 1997). Without such capabilities, citizens are 'easy prey to dogmatists, flimflam artists, and purveyors of simple solutions to complex problems' (AAAS 1989: 13) – including, one might add, some otherwise respectable scientists, politicians and commentators, who intimidate through their facility in a mode of discourse unfamiliar to many citizens.

The authors of *Science for All Americans* (AAAS 1989: 12) also direct attention towards scientific literacy for a more socially compassionate and environmentally responsible democracy when they state that science can provide knowledge 'to develop effective solutions to its global and local problems' and can foster 'the kind of intelligent respect for nature that should inform decisions on the uses of technology', without which, they say, 'we are in danger of recklessly destroying our life-support system.' However, they don't suggest that scientific literacy also includes the capacity and willingness to act in environmentally responsible and socially just ways. It is this concern with science education for action which has prompted the Scottish Consultative Council on the Curriculum (SCCC) to adopt the term *scientific capability* instead of scientific literacy. In a discussion document (SCCC 1996), scientific capability is described in terms of five distinct, but clearly interrelated, aspects.

- Scientific curiosity – an enquiring habit of mind.
- Scientific competence – ability to investigate scientifically.
- Scientific understanding – understanding of scientific ideas and the way science works.
- Scientific creativity – ability to think and act creatively.
- Scientific sensitivity – critical awareness of the role of science in society, combined with a caring and responsible disposition.

Becoming scientifically capable involves considerably more than the acquisition of scientific skills, knowledge and understanding. It also involves the development of personal qualities and attitudes, the formulation of one's own views on a wide range of issues that have a scientific and/or technological dimension and the establishment of an underlying value position. In the words of the SCCC (1996: 15), 'a person who is scientifically capable is not only knowledgeable and skilled but is also able to draw together and apply her/his resources of knowledge and skill, creatively and with sensitivity, in response to an issue, problem or phenomenon.' It is interesting that although the document declares that it is action-oriented, sociopolitical action by students is not included in the definition – a characteristic shared with most other STS-oriented curriculum documents.

My own view, elaborated a little in Chapter 2, is that an STS curriculum is incomplete if it does not include preparing for and taking action, a position that Miller (1993) characterizes as transformational education.[2] By deploying the term 'universal *critical* scientific literacy' throughout this book as my overarching goal for science education, I am signalling my rejection of the long-standing differentiation of science education into high-status, academic/theoretical courses for those deemed to be of high ability and low-status courses oriented towards life-skills for the rest (Hodson and Reid 1988). In my view, we should draw later science specialists from a much wider pool (close to 100 per cent, I hope) of successful, enthusiastic students who have already achieved critical scientific literacy through a common science education. I am also signalling my advocacy of a much more politicized issues-based science education, a central goal of which is to equip students with the capacity and commitment to take appropriate, responsible and effective action on matters of social, economic, environmental and moral-ethical concern.

Achieving critical scientific literacy

In a multi-ethnic and increasingly pluralist social environment, there are major problems in achieving such a complex and wide-ranging goal as critical scientific literacy. Clearly it will not be achieved by the traditional means of a subjects-based curriculum presented by transmission methods of teaching or by a shift to a process approach, as some advocates for scientific literacy argue. Many official curriculum documents and textbooks continue to organize subject matter along a 'concepts only' or 'concepts first' approach, despite evidence that even those students deemed to be successful in school science often cannot apply their scientific understanding in real contexts or in ways that enable them to make sounder and wiser decisions in their everyday lives (Furnham 1992; Layton *et al.* 1993). Moreover, it seems that very few students expect it to; they do not see scientific knowledge learned in school as having any currency outside the context of school work (McRobbie and Tobin 1997).

If we really want scientific knowledge and understanding to be used for informing action, it must be taught and experienced, at least in part, in the contexts of use. In this book, I postulate two contexts of use: conducting scientific investigations, both inside and outside laboratories; engaging in social and environmental action. Socially and environmentally responsible behaviour will no more follow directly from knowledge of key concepts than ability to conduct scientific investigations will follow directly from experience of carrying out exercises based on the sub-skills of science (Hodson 1992). In addition, to enable *all* students to achieve critical scientific literacy, we must pay much closer attention to the transitions from everyday understanding to scientific ways of understanding and from everyday ways of communicating to scientific ways of talking and arguing. Increasing access and participation levels also entails paying much more attention to the specific barriers and obstacles experienced by individuals, many of them related to ethnicity, gender and social class. This means addressing the inherent biases of science and science education, creating a more authentic, culturally sensitive and inclusive image of science, scientists and scientific practice, showing science being used and developed by diverse people in diverse situations and establishing and maintaining a school science environment in which all students feel a sense of comfort and belonging. At present, many students in science lessons are bored by content they consider irrelevant to their needs, interests and aspirations. They are uninvolved by the kinds of teaching/learning methods we employ and they find the social and emotional climate of the science classroom uninviting, or even alienating. Some of those who do engage in effective science learning do so at considerable social and emotional cost, sometimes resulting in disaffection, exclusion or ostracization from peers and family.

Considerations like these led me to write this book and to organize its principal arguments around the notion of *personalization*. In my view, critical scientific literacy for an increasingly diverse student population can only be achieved by the personalization of learning, by developing an education that looks not only to the students' cognitive development but also to their emotional, aesthetic, moral and spiritual needs.

The personalization of learning

For convenience, the multi-dimensionality of critical scientific literacy will be considered in terms of three major elements:

- *Learning science* – acquiring and developing conceptual and theoretical knowledge.
- *Learning about science* – developing an understanding of the nature and methods of science, an appreciation of its history and development, and an awareness of the complex interactions among science, technology, society and environment.
- *Doing science* – engaging in and developing expertise in scientific inquiry and problem-solving.

While it will be useful in the early chapters of the book to consider learning science, learning about science and doing science as separate activities, it is important to recognize their interrelatedness and interdependence – matters that are elaborated in later chapters. With respect to these three major elements of the science curriculum, personalization of learning means ensuring that: (a) learning takes account of the knowledge, beliefs, values, attitudes, aspirations and personal experiences of individual students; (b) science and technology are presented as more person-oriented and science/technology education is politicized and infused with sound human and environmental values; (c) every student has the opportunity to conduct scientific investigations and to engage in technological problem-solving tasks of his or her own choosing and design.

Science teachers are just as guilty as other teachers of academicizing their subject, and sometimes more so. We often treat science education as the manipulation of complex, abstract, conceptual schemes that will only later on, if at all, be applied to real situations, events and problems. As a consequence, those who are successful in school science are usually good at remembering and at analysing and tackling academic puzzles, but cannot always use their knowledge in real situations. Many others never 'tune in' to science at all. For them, it constitutes esoteric and abstract game playing, remote from their everyday concerns. For some, it is difficult and forbidding, even intimidating, and remains the province of experts. Few students ever achieve a personal understanding of science; few students ever really own the science they study in school. If we listed the characteristics of science education as it ought to be, or as it needs to be to ensure universal critical scientific literacy, it might look something like this: accessible to all; interesting and exciting; real, relevant and useful; non-sexist (even antisexist) and multicultural/antiracist; personally relevant and humanized; value-laden and caring. Too often, it is more likely to be: elitist and restrictive; boring; abstract, academic and remote from real life; sexist; racist; impersonal and dehumanized; detached, objective and presented as value-neutral. This book is about shifting the balance towards the first list, while recognizing that for teachers working with a highly prescribed official curriculum, as in England and Wales, there is sometimes little room for manoeuvre.

Perhaps something can be done about the twin problems of accessibility and usefulness by paying much more attention to context. One way of setting appropriate contexts, especially for younger students, is to use the old primary (elementary) school tactic of starting with the individual learner and working 'outwards': *science and me* (my body, the senses, growth and development, health, communication, simple genetics etc.); *science and home* (science and technology in the home, food and its preparation and storage, natural and synthetic materials, fuels, dyes and paints etc.); *science and leisure* (sports science, pets, toys, fishing, photography, music etc.); *science and work* (telecommunications, agricultural science, medicine, forensic science, biotechnology, local industries etc.); *science and the environment* (local flora and fauna, weather and climate, geology, astronomy, space science etc.). For older students, it can be helpful to organize at least part of the curriculum around the consideration of issues or problems at local, regional, national and global levels. Such a curriculum has the advantage of being based on the daily experiences of learners and (possibly) would be perceived by them as being more relevant, more important and more useful, both socially and economically. My own research in New Zealand and Canada shows an overwhelming student preference for science and technology to be located in environmental concerns. By focusing on issues rather than concepts, the curriculum can develop a sense of inquiry and investigation, build self-confidence, assist the personalization of understanding and foster decision-making skills – all of which are matters to be discussed in subsequent chapters.

Teachers opting for an issues-based curriculum can adopt either of two strategies: (a) become reactive curriculum developers, responsible for putting together a meaningful, coherent and effective teaching/learning package based on any issue the students identify as important to them; or (b) produce issues-based materials in advance, possibly allowing students a measure of choice among them. The Bangalore conference on Science Education and Future Human Needs (Tendencia 1987) focused on a number of key areas of concern that would, with a little enhancement, provide a convenient overarching curriculum framework for an issues-based curriculum anywhere in the world: food and agriculture; energy resources; land, water and mineral resources; industry and technology; the environment; information transfer; ethics and social responsibility. Perhaps the ideal position is a combination of local, regional, national and global issues identified by the teacher, and some personal ones identified by the students.

There are always problems when teachers allow students to make the choice. If we don't know in advance what they want to study, we don't know whether we have the knowledge and skills, and we don't know whether we can assemble the resources or provide the facilities and support that are necessary. It can be very scary to teach a course with no predetermined content. And adopting an issues-based approach can be scary enough as it is, without the extra dimension of uncertainty. It often requires teachers to venture into areas with which they have little familiarity; it requires them to consider values and to deal with matters where there are no 'correct answers'. Most significantly, it casts them in a very different role: no longer the dispenser of accumulated wisdom; rather, a facilitator of learning, or even a co-learner. It shifts knowledge away from a concentration on abstract conceptual relationships towards a functional understanding of scientific principles and, eventually, towards decision making and action taking.

Chapters 3 to 14 are concerned with aspects of personalization that are central to the design of learning experiences capable of achieving meaningful and useful learning for all students. First, though, it is important to consider ways in which the principle of personalization can be used to address issues related to the image of science and scientists presented in the curriculum.

Notes

1 It is not the purpose of this book to examine and evaluate the literature debate of scientific literacy, or to argue for a particular definition. Rather, its purpose is to discuss how such a goal can be achieved. Clearly, however, some flavour of what is being advocated and whatever emerging consensus there may be is essential if the magnitude of the teacher's task is to be fully appreciated.

2 Miller (1993) outlines three basic positions for analysing and describing curricula: *transmission*, with its focus on traditional subjects taught through traditional didactic methods; *transaction*, in which education is seen as a dialogue between student and curriculum and through which the student reconstructs knowledge; *transformation*, which is concerned with individual and social change.

• • • 2

Towards a personalized science

In many school curricula, science is presented as the meticulous, orderly and exhaustive application of a powerful, all-purpose, objective and reliable method for ascertaining factual knowledge about the universe. Scientists are portrayed as rational, logical, open-minded and intellectually honest individuals who are required to adopt a disinterested, value-free and analytical stance, and who readily share their procedures and findings with each other. In Cawthron and Rowell's (1978: 32) memorable words, the scientist is regarded as 'a depersonalized and idealized seeker after truth, painstakingly pushing back the curtains which obscure objective reality, and abstracting order from the flux, an order which is directly revealable to him through a distinctive scientific method.'

There are several reasons why such a depersonalized image of science and scientists is to be deplored. First, it seriously misrepresents the nature of science and scientific practice. Second, it is immensely offputting for large numbers of students and so discourages them from pursuing science further. Third, by presenting scientific knowledge as a collection of fixed, non-negotiable, authoritative pronouncements by 'experts', it dissuades students from critical scrutiny of the justification for scientific belief. Thus, it contributes to continued intellectual dependence on others and to the disempowerment that results from scientific illiteracy. What I am arguing here is that critical scientific literacy depends on a clear understanding of the epistemological foundations of science and recognition that scientific practice is a human endeavour that influences and is influenced by the sociocultural context in which it is located. The first step in developing a more personalized view of science is to consider the ways in which the knowledge, experience, beliefs, values and aspirations of people influence the kind of science they choose to do and, to an extent, the ways in which they do it.

Figure 2.1 Find the hidden man.

The theory dependence of observation

The traditional school curriculum description of science says two things about observation. First, nothing enters the mind of the scientist except by way of the senses – that is, the mind is a *tabula rasa* on which the senses inscribe a true and faithful record of the world. Second, the validity and reliability of observation statements are independent of the opinions and expectations of the observer and can be readily confirmed by other observers. Neither is true. In reality, we interpret the sense data that enter our consciousness in terms of our prior knowledge, beliefs, expectations and experiences. As Barlex and Carre (1985: 4) say, 'We do not see things as they are, we see them as *we* are' (emphasis added).

Consequently, a change in mental constructs brings about a change in perception. For years, I was unable to see a face in the snowy landscape of Figure 2.1. It remained for me a series of blotches, despite the insistence of colleagues that it reveals the face of Jesus of Nazareth. Earlier this year, confronted by a giant reproduction of the picture at the Ontario Science Centre and urged by my wife to squint, stare hard and think of the familiar picture of Che Guevara, I finally saw the face. Now I can't look at the picture without seeing the face. Similarly, once you have seen the faces hidden among the foliage in those puzzle pictures often found in children's comics, you can no longer see the trees without the faces. However, it is not the image falling on the retina that has changed. Rather, it is the observer that has changed. The observer now has a different perspective, a different view of the world.

Scientific inquiry, and the experimentation and observation that accompany it, is a selective process and requires a focus of attention and a purpose. A scientist needs an incentive to make one observation rather than another. As Peter Medawar (1969: 29) says, 'We cannot browse over the field of nature like cows at pasture.' The traditional view of science as beginning with the open-minded assembly of observational data does not provide that incentive. In practice, making a scientific observation presupposes a view of the world which suggests that particular observations can be made, and are worth making. In other words, it is not innocent and unbiased, it is theory-dependent. Doing science (choosing a focus, designing and conducting an inquiry and communicating findings) depends on who we are, what we know and what we have experienced. Some view of the world, some theoretical perspective, precedes observation. It is simply not possible to observe things which you don't expect, don't know how to look for and are not conceptually prepared for – a position admirably summed up by David Theobald (1968: 26): 'If we confront the world with an empty head, then our experience will be . . . meaningless. Experience does not give concepts meaning, if anything concepts give experience meaning.'

Furthermore, observation statements are expressed in the language of some theory, and such statements are as vague or as precise as the underlying theoretical and conceptual framework allows. Thus, the quality and usefulness of observations depends crucially on the observational language available to the observer. Without an adequate conceptual framework, perceptions cannot be given meaning; without an adequate observational language, they cannot be recorded, criticized and communicated. Even an apparently simple, objective statement such as 'Anhydrous copper sulphate has a solubility of 205 grams per litre at 20 °C' can only be made in the light of a prior theoretical framework involving concepts such as dissolving, temperature, hydration and volume.

Because the collection and interpretation of observational data can only take place within a theoretical framework, it follows that prior knowledge determines the observations that scientists (and students in school science) can make and the meanings they can ascribe to them. Further, because sense data may be interpreted in a variety of ways, it is necessary to learn how to observe 'correctly' – that is, in accordance with the currently accepted paradigm. Thus, the key to good observation in science is a sound theoretical frame of reference. As Medawar (1967: 133) says, what a person sees 'conveys no information until he knows beforehand the kind of thing he is expected to see'. This is in stark contrast to the view usually promoted through the science curriculum, that observation precedes theory. In emphasizing and promoting 'open-eyed' and 'open-minded' observation, many contemporary science curricula miss the essential point that good scientific observation depends crucially on education and training. Without an appropriate theoretical framework, there can be no guarantee that students will observe 'correctly' even the readily observable. They may fail to see the phenomenon under investigation or, indeed, may see something else entirely.

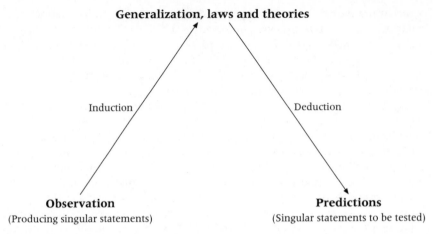

Figure 2.2 Science as induction.

Scientific method

Textbook accounts of science often assert that science proceeds inductively (Figure 2.2) and that inductive generalizations can be relied upon, provided that certain conditions are met.

1 The number of observation statements must be large.
2 The observations must be repeated under a wide variety of conditions.
3 No accepted observation statement should conflict with the derived generalization or universal law.

This model of science has enormous appeal and is seen to lend authority and predictive capability to the knowledge it generates. Observations can be made by anyone, by careful use of the senses. No personal, subjective element is involved. The validity of observation statements, when correctly acquired, is not dependent on the opinions and expectations of the observer. Provided that the three conditions for inductive inferences are met, the generalization will be valid. If the generalization is true, any predictions derived from it are bound to be true.

Quite apart from the matters already discussed, there are several problems with this model of science. One concerns the three conditions for drawing inductive generalizations. What, for example, constitutes a 'large' number of observations? How does one know which variables are significant in attempting to provide a 'wide variety of conditions'? How does one know whether a conflicting observation is merely an erroneous reading or a potential falsifier? The answer in each case is, of course, theoretical understanding, but this has been ruled out from the start by insistence that scientific inquiry is objective, value-free and unprejudiced by theory.

It is important for students to be brought to the realization that objectivity in science does not consist in placing equal weight on all observations (something that children consider to be 'fair' and which the traditional view of science seems to emphasize). Rather, they should be led to an awareness that they need to select relevant and appropriate observations and discard irrelevant and incorrect ones (Hodson 1986). Observations often have to be checked for acceptability by recourse to theory. This is the reverse of what we usually tell children. The usual message is that scientists test their theories for acceptability against reliable observations. In reality, we often reject sense data on theoretical grounds: the Earth is not flat, a stick partially immersed in water is not bent, distant stars are not red. A secure and well understood theoretical perspective is essential if students are to make these decisions. Of course, observations will also be misleading when the theory underpinning them is mistaken, or is insufficiently sophisticated for the task in hand (see later).

There is an interesting paradox with which students can be confronted: unless they know what to look for, they may not see anything; yet if they concentrate only on what they expect, they may miss or seriously misinterpret the unexpected. Students can begin to appreciate this point by considering how they might design an apparatus to detect particular entities. Unless they speculate about their properties, they cannot design instruments to detect them. Moreover, the instruments will fail to detect them if their properties deviate in any significant way from the expected. However, one of the more interesting features of science is that the unexpected often turns out to be theoretically more significant than the predicted. So it is important that from time to time we provide students with experiences that are entirely unexpected by them. Through such experiences, students develop the skills of critical observation, admirably summed up by Pasteur's famous saying that, in scientific observation, chance favours only the prepared mind.

However, the real problem is that inductive generalizations just cannot be relied upon, because they derive directly from a series of single observations. As David Hume (1854: 390) reminds us, 'There can be no demonstrative arguments to prove that those instances of which we have had no experience resemble those of which we have had experience.' In other words, induction is not logically valid. A generalization derived from singular statements, however numerous, may still turn out to be wrong, as Bertrand Russell's tale of the inductivist turkey reminds us (see Chalmers 1980: 13).

Towards an alternative model of science

If there are so many difficulties and absurdities with this traditional model of science, we should discard it in favour of a more realistic account of how science proceeds – an account that starts with existing theory and knowledge, and attempts to explore it, think about it, use it, criticize it, test it, doubt it, modify it, replace it; an account that gives a more faithful description of how new ideas generated during these activities are refined, developed and tested by criticism based on internal consistency and consistency with other accepted theories, and by observation and experiment.[1]

One such account is Karl Popper's hypothetico-deductive model, in which science proceeds by successive cycles of imagination and criticism (Popper 1968). First, a hypothesis is produced by intuition, by inspired guesswork from an existing theoretical background. From the hypothesis, certain conclusions are deduced and compared among themselves for internal consistency. Next, the conclusions are tested by observation or experiment. If the predictions are borne out, the hypothesis is corroborated; if not, the hypothesis must be modified or discarded. Thus, scientific reasoning is a constant interplay among hypotheses, the logical expectations (predictions) they give rise to and experimental or observational evidence; a constant dialogue between 'what might be' and 'what is'. In Popper's language, science proceeds by means of a series of *conjectures* and *refutations* until it arrives at a theory which satisfactorily explains the evidence (or, more precisely, is not refuted by it). This is not a random 'hit or miss' procedure; there is constant feedback for the modification and restructuring of hypotheses. Each conjecture is made in the light of previous experience.

There are several important differences between Popper's view of science and the traditional inductivist view: observation is placed much later; imagination and speculation based on existing theoretical understanding is placed first; falsification, rather than verification, is the central feature of hypothesis testing. In other words, every test of a theory is an attempt to falsify it, rather than an attempt to prove it correct. The significance of falsification in Popper's model is a consequence of the asymmetry between confirmation and refutation: while universal statements cannot logically be confirmed by single observations, no matter how numerous, they can be refuted by a single observation. The observation of one black swan falsifies the hypothesis that all swans are white. In other words, falsification is decisive.

By exposing hypotheses to a fierce struggle for survival, we ensure that only the fittest hypotheses survive. 'Fittest' means those that best fit the facts, the observational evidence. By rejecting hypotheses that fail to stand up to observational and experimental test, scientists make progress towards a truer description of the world, because they have ruled out some possible explanations. Of course, we could never know if we had arrived at the truth; we are all prisoners of our senses, confined by our environment and limited by our imaginations. *Scientific truth* is simply our current 'best shot' at explanation. The theories that we hold are no more than provisional, those that we have not yet managed to falsify.

An alternative to Popperian ideas is presented in *The Structure of Scientific Revolutions*, where Thomas Kuhn (1970) argues that science is not the orderly, systematic and continuous activity that Popper describes. Rather, it proceeds by successive phases of revolution and consolidation. The disorganized and diverse activities that precede the emergence of a particular science become structured and directed when the community of practitioners reaches agreement on certain theoretical and methodological issues; that is, when the disciplinary matrix (the *paradigm*, as Kuhn calls it) becomes established and accepted. Workers then practise 'normal science' in an attempt to explore and develop the particular paradigm they have adopted and whose basic validity they have accepted. Inevitably, unsolved problems and apparent falsifications are encountered. Such anomalies are to be expected and tolerated. However, if they resist solution for a long time, if they strike at the very core of the paradigm or if they have some pressing social or economic significance, then a 'crisis' develops. The crisis is resolved when a new paradigm emerges which can satisfactorily solve the problems and provide guidelines for a new normal science. Thus, according to Kuhn, the path of science is discontinuous; it proceeds through a series of major conceptual revolutions interspersed with periods of stability and consolidation.

There are some interesting features in Kuhn's model of science. First is the tolerance of anomaly and falsifying evidence. Provided that these are not 'serious', they are accepted as normal. The paradigm is given 'breathing space' in which to accommodate anomaly through modification and development. If scientific theories were not remarkably resilient in the face of apparently falsifying data, we would have to live with new theories all the time. Theories *are* resilient because they can accommodate counter observations in many ways. Indeed, according to Lakatos (1978), scientists engage in all kinds of pragmatic intellectual manoeuvres to defend a favoured theory. Second, Kuhn argues that rival paradigms are *incommensurate*. Because they involve different concepts and ideas, they direct attention to different things, and in different ways. Even when the new paradigm uses words from the old, it does so in a new way. Compare, for example, the use of concepts such as 'mass', 'time' and 'energy' in the Newtonian and Einsteinian paradigms, or 'acid' and 'base' in the Lowry–Bronsted and the Lewis theories.

> The proponents of competing paradigms practice their trades in different worlds . . . In one, solutions are compounds, in the other mixtures. One is embedded in a flat, the other in a curved, matrix of space. Practising in different worlds, the two groups of scientists see different things when they look from the same point in the same direction.
>
> (Kuhn 1970: 149)

It follows that direct comparison of rival paradigms is difficult, perhaps even impossible. There are no paradigm-independent concepts that can be used; there are no paradigm-independent observations that can be made or experiments that can be performed. So much for the decisiveness of Popper's falsificationist model! If it isn't possible to perform critical experiments capable of furnishing theory-free data, it follows that there are no purely empirical criteria for establishing the superiority of one paradigm over another. In other words, science is not entirely objective and rational, at least not in the sense that rationality is conventionally portrayed in science education. A message that we do not build into the science curriculum, or into the public image of science, is that scientific theories are empirically under-determined. Empirical adequacy is insufficient, in itself, to establish validity. Consistency with the observable facts does not confer truth status on a theory. Such consistency simply means that a theory may be true. But so may lots of other theories that also correspond with the observations (Duhem 1962). Moreover, empirical *in*adequacy is frequently ignored by individual scientists fighting passionately for a well loved theory, and is often considered subordinate to the 'context of discovery' by the community-appointed validators (Knorr-Cetina 1983). Additional factors that may play a part in bringing about the shift of paradigm allegiance that constitutes a scientific revolution include:

- elegance and simplicity (the aesthetics of science);
- similarity and consistency with other theories;
- 'intellectual fashion', in the sense of compatibility with trends in other disciplines;
- social and economic considerations;
- cultural considerations;
- the status of the researchers;
- the views of 'significant others' – influential and powerful scientists, journal editors, publishers and so on;
- the priorities of research funding agencies.

If one takes the view that science is a communal activity, and that the ideas of particular scientists only become accepted as scientific knowledge when they achieve consensus within the community of scientists, it follows that many of the sociological, psychological, political and economic issues that influence individuals could, and sometimes will, influence the decisions that the community makes. By failing to address these influences, the simple-minded accounts of theory acceptance and rejection presented in some school science textbooks are insulting to students and often flatly contradict what they read, elsewhere, about real scientists like Galileo, Albert Einstein, Barbara McClintock, Francis Crick and Jim Watson. What these accounts omit is *people*, and their views, attitudes, passions and prejudices. By contrast, Fuller (1988) writes about the rather wider issues that influence the ways in which scientists present their own work and evaluate each other's. Prominent among them are strong presuppositions or feelings about the way things work, sometimes before evidence is collected, sometimes despite the evidence that has been collected (Holton 1978; 1986).

It would be more appropriate for the school curriculum to emphasize the ways in which knowledge is *negotiated* within the community of scientists by a complex interplay of theoretical argument, experiment and personal opinion, than to try to project the view that science is independent of the society in which it is located. Criteria of judgement include factors outside pure logic and empirical adequacy, including the social, economic, political, moral and ethical factors that impact on the decision-makers. In other words, science is not value-free and 'people-proof'. As Robert Young (1987: 18) says:

> Science is not something in the sky, not a set of eternal truths waiting for discovery. Science is a practice. There is no other science than the

science that gets done. The science that exists is the record of the questions that it has occurred to scientists to ask, the proposals that get funded, the paths that get pursued ... Nature 'answers' only the questions that get asked and pursued long enough to lead to results that enter the public domain. Whether or not they get asked, how far they get pursued, are matters for a given society, its educational system, its patronage system, and its funding bodies.

What is important is that we achieve a sensible balance between the view that science is absolute truth ascertained by value-free, disinterested individuals using entirely objective and reliable methods of inquiry – a view that, unfortunately, is still quite widespread in school science curricula – and the dangerously relativist view that 'scientific truth' is that which is in the interests of those in power or, as Slezak (1994: 269) lampoons it, 'truth is what you can get away with'. While we should reject the notion that science is entirely determined by a combination of scientists' self-interests and political expediency, we should recognize that it is profoundly influenced by social, economic and moral-ethical considerations and so is, to a large extent, a product of its time and place. While it would be absurd to claim that scientific knowledge is less reliable or valid simply because it is developed in furtherance of particular interests, or that the products of scientific inquiry and theory building cannot be understood apart from their socio-historical contexts, appreciation of the sociocultural milieu within which particular scientists work (or worked) provides the context for understanding their priorities, working styles and criteria of judgement. This applies just as much to a full understanding of the elegant rationalist work of Isaac Newton as it does to understanding the theory of phrenology, a set of beliefs and values held by many prominent scientists and non-scientists in Victorian England (Hodson and Prophet 1986).

The role and status of scientific knowledge

Rather than being a collection of well established facts, strict definitions and non-negotiable rules and algorithms, scientific knowledge is a network of interrelated concepts and propositions that stand or fall on their ability to describe, explain and predict a range of observable phenomena, without being dependent on any single observation. Moreover, these complex structures are tentative and temporary. History shows us that they grow and develop over time in order to meet the various purposes of science. Consideration of these purposes is beyond the scope of this book, save to say that what needs to be established clearly in the minds of students is that:

• conceptual structures are designed for diverse purposes;
• role and status are inextricably linked.

At the very least, students should be made aware of the crucial distinction between explanatory theories and instrumentalist models. Theories can be described as our 'current best shot' at explaining 'how things are' in the physical world. They should not be regarded as 'true' or as 'proven'. Rather, they should be taken as a more tentative *scientific truth*: knowledge that has been subjected to, and has survived, critical scrutiny by other scientists using the distinctive procedures and criteria legitimated by the scientific community. Inevitably, theories will change as a consequence of the complex interactions among theoretical speculation, experiment and observation. Models are imaginary conceptual devices for predicting, calculating, manipulating events and generally achieving a measure of control of the environment. Models have no pretentions towards 'truth'; they merely have to work (i.e. to do their job satisfactorily). Whether they correspond to reality or not is irrelevant.

An intriguing feature of science is that models which are initially introduced as predictive devices are sometimes elaborated and developed into theories. On occasions, scientists discover that the entities they had earlier created for instrumental purposes actually exist. Put another way, and somewhat more cautiously, they accumulate observational support for the existence of these entities.[2] More frequently, explanatory theories that are superseded by better theories revert to the status of model and continue to fulfil a useful predictive function. It is not illogical or unscientific to retain a falsified or superseded theory in an instrumental capacity, provided that its status is recognized and acknowledged. Within a restricted domain of application, and this applies particularly to school science, it may be simpler to use than current theory. Nor is it illogical or unscientific to use alternative (even seemingly incompatible or contradictory) instrumental models for different aspects of the same phenomenon if all that is sought is a prediction or calculation of a numerical quantity. In a school context, it is common for conflicting wave and particle models to be used side-by-side in accounting for different properties of light.

Understanding and successfully using scientific knowledge entails knowing something about the justification for and status of different conceptual structures, and knowing when their use is appropriate and inappropriate. Just as it is important for students to learn that in day-to-day life the appropriateness of language and behaviour is dependent on the social context, so it is important for them to recognize that the appropriateness of scientific models and theories is dependent on the kind of issue or problem being addressed. It is important, also, to recognize that the variety of specific purposes that motivate theory building and model building within the sciences ensures that the precise meaning attached to a concept will depend on the specific role that it has within a particular knowledge structure. As suggested earlier, the differences in meaning of *mass* and *energy* in the Newtonian and Einsteinian views of the world, and the shift in meaning of *acid* and *base* between the Lowry–Bronsted and Lewis theories, illustrate this point very clearly.

Achieving a balanced view of science and scientists

The purpose of this chapter is to show how a more personalized view of science and scientific inquiry might be promoted in school. Replacing inductivism by Popperian methods puts imagination and creativity back into what is still a rigorous method, but a method driven by people and their particular interests, knowledge and values. Including the Lakatosian notion of rival 'research programmes', each with its particular protagonists, puts passion back into science; acknowledging Kuhn's views about the revolutionary nature of scientific progress opens the door for a consideration of sociocultural forces. Finally, Feyerabend's so-called 'anarchic view of science' recognizes the significance of intuition and tacit knowledge in scientific expertise or connoisseurship. Scientific inquiry is not the simple application of an all-purpose algorithm comprising a series of content-free, generalizable and transferable steps, as advocates of the so-called process approach to science education allege (see Wellington 1989). Real science is an untidy, unpredictable activity that requires each scientist to devise her or his own course of action. In that sense, there is no method. In approaching a particular situation, scientists choose an approach they consider to be appropriate to the particular task in hand by making a selection of processes and procedures from the range of those available and approved by the community of practitioners. Further, scientists refine their approach to a problem, develop greater understanding of it and devise more appropriate and productive ways of proceeding all at the same time. As soon as an idea is developed, it is subjected to evaluation (by observation, experiment, comparison with other theories etc.). Sometimes that evaluation leads to new ideas, to further and different experiments or even to a complete recasting of the original idea or reformulation of the problem. Thus, almost every move that a scientist makes during an inquiry changes the situation in some way, so that the next decisions and moves are made in an altered context. Consequently, scientific inquiry is holistic, fluid, reflexive, context-dependent and idiosyncratic, not a matter of following a set of rules that requires particular behaviours at particular times. It is best summed up by Percy Bridgman's (1950: 351) remark that 'the scientific method, as far as it is a method, is nothing more than doing one's damnedest with one's mind, no holds barred.'

In making their choices and in implementing their chosen strategy, scientists make use of a kind of expertise that has been variously labelled tacit knowledge, scientific intuition and scientific flair. It is the kind of knowledge, often not well articulated, or even consciously applied, that can be acquired only through the experience of doing science. It constitutes the central core of the art and craft of the scientist. It is not distinct from the possession of laboratory skills, on the one hand, and the possession of conceptual understanding, on the other. Rather, it is the capacity to use both in a purposeful way, in order to achieve particular goals. It combines conceptual understanding and bench skills with elements of creativity, experimental flair (the scientific equivalent of the gardener's 'green fingers') and a complex of affective attributes that provide the necessary impetus of determination and commitment. With experience, it develops into what Polanyi (1958) and Oakeshott (1962) call 'connoisseurship'. Thus, scientists proceed partly by rationalization (based on their theoretical understanding) and partly by intuition rooted in their tacit knowledge of how to do science (connoisseurship): 'A practising scientist is continually making judgments for which he can provide no justification beyond saying that that is how things strike him' (Newton-Smith 1981: 81).

It is not my wish to portray all scientists as self-serving, cynical opportunists, and it would be a disaster if the science curriculum did so. There is no doubt that scientists' personal, political and religious views impact on the kind of science they choose to do; there is no doubt, either, that intuition, luck (both good and bad), self-interest, personal ambition and academic and publishing pressures will, from time to time, influence the way they do it. The key question, as Loving (1997: 436) reminds us, is 'whether these are the predominant factors driving good science or factors that make science simply a human (and thus imperfect) endeavor.' Above all, I want to remind students that science is carried out by people, and that these people, like everyone else, have views, values, beliefs and interests. I want the curriculum to show students that these people (scientists) can be warm, sensitive, humorous and passionate. More importantly, I want them to realize that people who are warm, sensitive, humorous and passionate can still become scientists, though they are required to conduct their work in accordance with codes of practice established, scrutinized and maintained by the community of scientists.

Once we put people back into science, we open up the possibility that science can be and has been different. Different groups of people have different priorities, they identify different problems, which they approach in different ways, using different theories, instruments and methods. They may even have different criteria of validity and acceptability. If science has different goals, methods and criteria of judgement, it is inevitable that it will generate different knowledge and different theories. This new curriculum message is that science is not propelled exclusively by its own internal logic. Rather, it is shaped by the personal beliefs and political attitudes of its practitioners and reflects, in part, 'the history, power structures, and political climate of the supportive community' (Dixon 1973: 71). This can be highlighted by historical studies, by studies of non-Western science and by studies of the misuse of science for social and political purposes (Hodson 1993a). By emphasizing that current ideas are no more than the latest in a series of views shaped and influenced by personal and social conditions and attitudes, historical case studies can reinforce understanding of the mechanisms of scientific practice and imbue students with a healthy scepticism regarding scientific claims – an important element in developing critical scientific and technological literacy. When reinforced by consideration of some current thinking concerning feminist science and ethnoscience, for example, these activities will help to impress on students that we can reorient, reprioritize and redirect *our* science and technology towards more socially just and environmentally sound practices.

The politicization of science education

One of the absurdities of some current curriculum initiatives is that they attempt to teach that science is a value-laden activity (the STS emphasis), but try to do so in a value-free way. Many teachers studiously avoid confronting the political interests and social values underlying the scientific and technological practices they teach about, and seek to avoid making judgements about them or influencing students in particular directions. This makes little or no sense. First, it asks teachers to attempt the impossible. Values are embedded in every aspect of the curriculum: content, teaching and learning methods, assessment and evaluation strategies are selected using criteria that reflect and embody particular value positions, whether we recognize it or not (Layton 1986). Second, it mistakes the very purpose of education in science, which, in my view, is to ensure critical scientific and technological literacy for everyone. That goal requires that school science addresses 'not only the traditional question of whether the science is good science but also the newer question of who benefits and who loses' (Jenkins 1992: 232). In other words, critical literacy necessitates the politicization of the curriculum.

My own view is that politicization of science education can be achieved through an issues-based curriculum comprising four levels of sophistication.[3]

Level 1: Appreciating the societal impact of scientific and technological change, and recognizing that science and technology are, to some extent, culturally determined.

Level 2: Recognizing that decisions about scientific and technological development are taken in pursuit of particular interests, and that benefits accruing to some may be at the expense of others. Recognizing that scientific and technological development is inextricably linked with the distribution of wealth and power.

Level 3: Developing one's own views and establishing one's own underlying value positions.

Level 4: Preparing for and taking action.

As argued elsewhere (Hodson 1994), a central goal of this issues-based curriculum is to equip students with the capacity and commitment to take appropriate, responsible and effective action on matters of social, economic, environmental and moral-ethical concern. The keys to this translation of knowledge into action are *ownership* and *empowerment*. Those who act are those who have a deep personal understanding of the issues (and their human implications) and feel a personal investment in addressing and solving the problems. Those who act are those who feel personally empowered to effect change, who feel that they can make a difference. At level 1, students are encouraged to recognize the societal and environmental impact of science and technology. At level 2, they are sensitized to the socio-political nature of scientific and technological practice. At level 3, they are encouraged to become committed to the fight to establish more socially just and environmentally sustainable practices. But only by proceeding to level 4 can we ensure that students acquire the knowledge and skills to intervene effectively in the decision-making processes and ensure that alternative voices, and their underlying interests and values, are brought to bear on policy decisions. What is being argued here, of course, is that education for critical scientific literacy is inextricably linked with education for *political literacy* and with the ideology of education as social reconstruction. As Kyle (1996: 1) puts it: 'Education must be transformed from the passive, technical, and apolitical orientation that is reflective of most students' school-based experiences to an active, critical, and politicized life-long endeavour that transcends the boundaries of classrooms and schools.'

Unfortunately, there are many students who feel disempowered by their experiences in school and are increasingly alienated from science. There are many who feel no sense of ownership and certainly no feelings of empowerment, and who continue to regard science as a body of fixed, authoritative knowledge located in textbooks. It is these students who are the principal focus of attention throughout this book.

Notes

1 What follows is a very brief account of several alternative views of scientific method. It is not intended to be a rigorous treatment; its purpose is to indicate some points that collectively constitute a more personalized view of science and, hence, a more appropriate image of science for the school curriculum.

2 This more cautious phrasing recognizes the theory dependence of experiments and correlational studies, and of the interpretation of evidence provided by them.

3 By reference to four levels I am not suggesting a sequential teaching programme, nor that teachers proceed to level 4 on every topic/issue. The level for any particular issue should be determined by the topic and the learning opportunities it presents, the current knowledge and experience of the learners, what was attempted 'last time' and so on. In short, students should have the experience of reaching level 4 on some (i.e. the most appropriate) topics/issues.

••• 3

The significance of prior knowledge in science and learning

Many school science curricula insist that a clear distinction can be drawn between raw data (and their manipulation) and our theoretical interpretation of them – that is, between facts and theories or observation and inference. Thus, Abruscato (1988: 33) claims that 'nothing is more fundamental to clear thinking than the ability to distinguish between an observation and an inference'. Superficially, this distinction sounds fine, and seems to relate to what we usually consider to be a major aspect of good scientific inquiry: that scientists should have respect for the evidence and not claim more from their investigation than the facts will support. However, I do not believe that such a distinction exists in any absolute sense. Indeed, when a new theory appears, or when new instrumentation techniques are developed, our notion of what is a theoretical statement and what is an observation statement may change. As Feyerabend (1962) points out, observation statements are merely those theoretical statements to which we can assent quickly, relatively reliably and without calculation or inference, because we all accept, without question, the theories on which they are based. In other words, the demarcation between observation and inference shifts with experience, and where particular individuals 'draw the line' depends on their knowledge, level of experience and familiarity with the phenomena or events being studied.

When theories are well understood and taken for granted, they provide an observation language. Thus, terms like *reflection* and *refraction, suspension* and *solution, contraction* and *expansion* all carry with them an inferential component rooted in theoretical understanding. Unless some theory is taken for granted and theory-loaded terms are used for making observations, we cannot make progress. We would forever be trying to return to simpler terms that are allegedly theory-free – but mistakenly so. In the familiar exercise of observing a burning candle, for example, all but very young children *know* that the liquid on the top of the burning candle is molten wax because they have no doubts about the theoretical assumptions that impregnate such an observation. To insist that they regard it as an inference is to be pedantic to a degree that can be counterproductive to good science (Geddis 1992).

Secure conceptual understanding is the 'trigger' for changing the language and for making progress towards more sophisticated understanding. With the general acceptance of a theory of solubility, for example, students see things *dissolve*, where previously they saw them disappear. In addition, once they understand that there is an important conceptual difference between *dissolving* and *melting*, they see why it is important to be careful in their use of the terms. Young children, without this conceptual knowledge, will continue to refer to sugar and salt 'melting' in water. They have no reason to do otherwise. This conceptual-linguistic shift can be readily demonstrated to students on those occasions when an observational exercise from earlier in the course is repeated: the new description employs observational language that includes previously unknown theoretical notions. Perhaps solids can now be observed to melt, sublime or decrepitate on heating, whereas previously they just 'changed'. All three of these new terms include theoretical inference. By reflecting on these matters, students can be made aware of the ways in which their own observational skills change and develop as their theoretical understanding becomes more sophisticated. Discussion of the theoretical assumptions underpinning the design of common laboratory instruments (ammeters, voltmeters, pH meters and the like) can also help students to appreciate that the supposed distinction between objective observation and theoretical inference is less clear than some science textbooks would assert, and is more a characteristic of their own stage of conceptual understanding, and their confidence in that knowledge, than a demarcation between two processes of science.

Arguments similar to those for the theory-ladenness of observation extend to all the other processes of science, such as classifying, measuring, hypothesizing and inferring. One has to classify and measure something, rather than something else; one has to hypothesize about particular entities or events. It simply is not possible to engage in these processes independently of content. Moreover, the way one classifies, measures and hypothesizes, and one's level of sophistication in doing so, depend crucially on one's theoretical understanding. Science education is not about teaching students to observe, classify, measure and hypothesize *per se*. They can already do that perfectly well, and have been doing so since long before they came to our science lessons. Moreover, they continue to do so every day in their lives outside the laboratory. What school science is concerned with is *scientific* observation, *scientific* classification and *scientific* hypothesizing. What makes these processes scientific is the utilization of relevant and appropriate science concepts in pursuit of scientific purpose.

Scientific classification, for example, is not just a matter of noting similarities and differences – or it would be sufficient in science lessons to classify banknotes and postage stamps, using criteria such as country of origin, colour, size and style of illustration. Rather, it involves the application of scientifically significant and appropriate categories suited to the purpose for which the classification is being carried out. Different purposes demand different criteria and may involve different theoretical understanding. Consequently, successful classification is a matter of recognizing and using appropriate theory-based categories. It depends crucially on the knowledge, experience, assumptions and expectations about purpose that the classifier brings to the task. Any classroom activity involving classification or 'looking for patterns' is, therefore, inextricably linked with theory (appropriate concepts for classification) and purpose.

So it is with measuring, predicting, collecting data, recording data and all the other processes of science. None of them can be carried out without a substantial measure of theoretical knowledge. The notion that predictions can be made independently of content, for example, is just too absurd to be seriously contemplated. What can possibly constitute the basis of a prediction other than some good understanding of the phenomenon or event under consideration? Without theoretical understanding, predictions are no more than 'blind guesses', and there is little of educational value in encouraging children to make those. McNairy (1985) says that whether a prediction is correct or not does not matter. I agree. But what does matter is that the student has good (scientific) reasons for making a particular prediction, can establish a chain of argument from her or his current understanding to the prediction and knows enough about the methods of scientific inquiry to know what would constitute an appropriate test of that prediction.

Nor can the control of variables be achieved without substantial knowledge of the phenomenon being studied. How would a theory-free experimenter know what the variables are likely to be? In a state of ignorance, no variables can be controlled, except fortuitously. Clearly, the planning of any experiment in which variables are to be carefully and systematically varied is a theory-driven and theory-impregnated activity. Without an appropriate conceptual framework, meaningful observation, experimentation and interpretation are impossible. Without appropriate conceptual understanding, students may fail to see the phenomenon under investigation or, on occasions, may see something else entirely. During classroom experiments, they may find patterns in observations, as demanded by process-oriented courses, but the patterns they find may differ substantially from those intended by the teacher. Students can only find patterns that reflect the views they hold. Moreover, they may reject alternative explanations that 'see' the data differently or may reject observations that conflict with their beliefs (Gunstone 1991). The bottom line is that learners do not organize their knowledge around processes. Rather, they do so around ideas. In other words, students do not acquire new concepts by observation, or by any of the other sub-processes of science; rather, they use concepts to make sense of observations and the other sub-processes of scientific activity. Of course, in doing so, they test and develop that understanding. Through observing, classifying, designing experiments, comparing and contrasting ideas and so on, conceptual understanding is necessarily articulated, tested and challenged.

Ascertaining children's views

Just as existing knowledge determines the kind of scientific activity that students can engage in, so it determines the way in which they respond to new ideas and information. Ausubel (1968: 337) expresses it as follows: 'If I had to reduce all of educational psychology to just a single principle, I would say this: "Find out what the learner already knows and teach him accordingly".' Once we know the kind of understanding learners already have, we can begin to design learning strategies to ensure that they shift in the direction we desire (see Chapter 4), but the necessary first step would appear to be: find out where they currently are. After all, if you want to ensure that someone reaches a particular destination, you start by asking where he or she is now.

Ascertaining children's views in science has been a very active and very fruitful area of research during the past decade and a half. It is significant – and, perhaps, fortunate too – that there appear to be certain kinds of understandings held in common. Imagine the task facing a teacher if there were no common elements in children's understanding. The beliefs that children hold prior to instruction have been variously termed: alternative frameworks, alternative or prior conceptions, mini-theories, naive theories, children's science and so on. Each term has its adherents and its particular justification, but, as yet, there is no universally accepted term, beyond a general concern to avoid the use of *misconceptions*, a convention to which I am strenuously opposed, as will become apparent later.[1]

Research strategies for ascertaining children's views are as varied as the terminologies, and include the use of interviews, classroom observation, multiple choice tests, word association methods, concept maps, essays, student diaries, repertory grids and questionnaires. Driver and Erickson (1983) distinguish between methods which generate data of a verbal nature and those producing behavioural data, claiming that such a distinction defines the positions of the various data collection methods along the conceptual–phenomenological continuum. Situations framed by conceptual constraints generally produce linguistic data and, therefore, are more suitable for eliciting the structure of children's propositional knowledge; situations framed in actual events or phenomena (i.e. contextual constraints) are more likely to elicit behaviours which would inform the student's knowledge-in-action. The significance of this distinction, and the relationship between the methods, will become apparent in later discussion.

This is not an appropriate place to enter into a lengthy consideration of the nature of children's alternative understandings[2] and, for present purposes, one example (in this case, children's understanding of electricity) is perhaps sufficient to give a flavour of the variety of understandings that is possible within a class.

Electricity is a topic that abounds with all kinds of theoretical terms: *current, voltage, energy, power* etc. Many students have difficulty differentiating among them, and frequently use them as synonyms. Many also have difficulty understanding the nature of electric circuits. An idea that is very common before teaching, and also persists after teaching, is a one-way flow of electricity from a source (the cell) to a consumer-device (a lamp or motor, for example), where it is used up. At first, what is 'used up' is unclear. Because there is considerable emphasis on electric current in much of the early teaching of electricity, students often come to believe that it is current that is stored in cells and used up in bulbs and motors. Shipstone (1985: 35) quotes a German study showing that about 85 per cent of 'a very large sample' of 13–15-year-olds, who had recently completed an introductory physics course, agreed with the statements: 'in every new battery is stored a certain amount of electric current . . . [and] . . . the current contained in a battery will be consumed by electric appliances in the course of time.' Research in New Zealand (Osborne and Freyberg 1985) showed that 8–12-year-old students subscribe to one of four models in explaining electric circuits. In model A, current flows from the upper terminal of the cell to the bulb. Since no current returns, only one wire is needed. In model B, current flows to the bulb through both wires – positive electricity in one direction, negative electricity in the other. As one 11-year-old explained: 'the currents clash in the bulb'. Current flows in one direction only in model C, but because some has been 'used up' in lighting the bulb, the current in the 'return wire' is smaller. Model D (the scientists' view) states that current is in one direction only and is uniform around the circuit. The prevalence of these four views changes over time, with model D steadily increasing in popularity and model C rising to a peak at age 15, and then declining sharply. What is particularly interesting, and relates to the discussion on *personal frameworks of understanding* in Chapter 5, is that children may change models as the situation-to-be-explained changes. It should also be noted that not only do many children have views other than scientists' views (even after exposure to teaching), but that they often strenuously resist scientists' views as absurd. Supposedly conclusive demonstrations with ammeters have even failed to change students' views that electric current is consumed by a lighted bulb.

It has already been asserted that students who lack a theoretical framework will not know where to look, or how to look, in order to make observations appropriate to the task in hand, or how to interpret what they see. Consequently, much of the activity will be unproductive. Bearing in mind the foregoing discussion, it can be readily appreciated that, in practice, the situation can be much more complex and considerably more damaging. When children have a different theoretical framework from that assumed by the teacher, they may look in a different (wrong?) place, in a different or wrong way, and make different or wrong interpretations, sometimes even vehemently denying observational evidence that conflicts with their existing views. More frequently, children will adjust or modify their observations to conform with the expectations their existing theories give rise to. In other words, they 'see' what they expect to see. As a consequence, students may go through an entire laboratory-based activity misunderstanding the purpose of the activity, the procedure and the findings, and compounding whatever misconceptions they brought with them to the task. It is not too much of an exaggeration to say that, because predictions, perceptions and explanations are all strongly influenced by prior conceptual understanding, students who hold different frameworks of meaning conduct different investigations, with correspondingly different learning outcomes. The alternative conceptions research literature provides many such examples.

Where do children's ideas come from?

As George Kelly (1955) says, we are all searching for personal meanings that enable us to make sense of the world and to establish a measure of control. Since we cannot know reality directly, we have to construct theories about it.

> Man looks at his world through transparent patterns or templets which he creates and then attempts to fit over the realities of which the world is composed. The fit is not always very good. Yet without such patterns the world appears to be such an undifferentiated homogeneity that man is unable to make any sense out of it. Even a poor fit is more helpful to him than nothing at all.
>
> (Kelly 1955: 8)

Students have been engaged in this process since long before they come to school science lessons. Consequently, they may already have ideas and theories about many of the things that we attempt to teach them in the science curriculum. They form their ideas and beliefs in response to everyday experiences, including the kinds of contrived experiences that we provide in school, through talking with others, through interaction with the media (particularly television) and through visits to zoos, museums and recreational areas. In all these interactions, language is the key mediator.

Many words (like *force, energy, plant, animal* and *cell*) have meanings in science that differ from or are specialized refinements of their common everyday usage. It would be surprising, therefore, if everyday language use did not influence children's understanding of what these terms mean, sometimes in contradiction of the meanings emphasized in science lessons. Bell's (1981) work on children's understanding of the term *animal* illustrates very clearly how persistent everyday meanings can be: 78 per cent of 11-year-olds and 35 per cent of primary teacher trainees did not classify a spider as an animal. It seems that, in common with everyday usage, 'animals' are relatively large, have four legs, live on land and probably have fur or hair.

A common turn of phrase or everyday expression can play a significant role in children's theory building about phenomena. For example, simple everyday usage attributes an active role to the eye (we 'look daggers' at people, our eyes 'flash', we 'look *for* things', and sometimes it is as though 'looks could kill'); it assigns a passive role to the object that is seen, 'looked at' or apprehended. Not surprisingly, young children have views about vision that are consistent with this kind of language use: something comes from the eye, hits the object and bounces back – rather like a bat's 'sonar'. Children acknowledge that we need light in order to see, but they are reluctant to accept that light enters the eye, because that would dazzle us (Guesne 1985). It is this kind of interaction between everyday experience and common language use that produces what some have termed lay science (Furnham 1992) or just plain common sense (Hills 1989). While this knowledge is certainly not correct from a scientific point of view, it is perfectly capable of enabling us to function adequately on a day-by-day basis.

> The 'naive' or 'fuzzy' theories of physics that most of us carry in our heads are undoubtedly ill conceived and, in many respects, patently wrong from the point of view of the physicist. For the most part they are not *so* wrong as to put us at great risk in the day-to-day world ... In other words, for the most part, our models of physical reality are, in spite of their deficiencies, sufficiently accurate to permit us to make the kinds of decisions that survival in our day-to-day world requires.
>
> (Nickerson 1986: 352)

What Nickerson is illustrating is the point made earlier: that the level of sophistication of a theory employed by a particular individual or group is in direct relation to the tasks that have to be accomplished. If a theoretical structure at a low level of sophistication will enable the task to be carried out successfully, there is no need to employ a more sophisticated view.[3] It follows that the level of theoretical sophistication in the school curriculum should be determined by the overall goals of science education. While this may not be a novel idea, it seems to be one that eludes many curriculum designers. Of particular relevance here is the potential conflict between science education for responsible citizenship and science education as pre-professional preparation. It would be absurd if our desire to establish proper scientific meanings and to promote the use of forms and styles of communication employed within the community of scientists led us to extinguish a student's capacity to access everyday meanings and to use lay discourse. This conflict is examined in later chapters, where enculturation into scientific discourse and scientific practice is identified as the essence of science education.

Chapter 13 examines some of the ways in which language-based activities can be used by teachers to promote and develop scientific understanding. We should not forget, however, its potential for building misunderstanding, especially when presented in the seductive forms of advertising. In Kirkwood's (1989) study of children's understanding of energy, there are numerous striking parallels with the ways in which chocolate bars and natural gas heaters are advertised, and the marketing slogan 'living gas fires' may be partly responsible for the curious finding that almost 50 per cent of 12-year-olds interviewed in Stead's (1980) study of New Zealand children asserted that *fire* is 'living'. The entertainment industry may play a prominent role, too; there are few children in Western schools who have not seen and been influenced by the 'science' in TV shows such as *Star Trek*, *Dr Who* and *The X-Files*, and movies such as the *Star Wars* series, *Jurassic Park* and *Contact* (see Gough (1993) for an account of how science fiction might be used advantageously in the curriculum). Children's everyday conversation is littered with scientific and pseudo-scientific terms; the teacher's job is to help students to use this vocabulary critically and appropriately, while enriching it with a more scientifically useful one.

Common everyday experience is, of course, another major stimulus to theory building, and it is this influence that no doubt explains the often striking parallels between children's views in science and the theories held by scientists in previous centuries.[4] It also explains both the similarities and some of the differences revealed in cross-cultural studies. For example, experience tells us that objects only move when you apply a force to them. As soon as you stop pushing or pulling, the object stays at rest. Consequently, 'at rest' means *no force acting*. Everyday experience also 'tells us' that heavy objects fall faster than light ones, the Sun moves across the sky (and, therefore, around the Earth), when you burn something there is less afterwards than there was before and electricity gets used up in lighting a bulb (which is why batteries run down). Some of the scientific theories we expect children to learn are counter-intuitive and often flatly contradict these commonsense views. They are also sometimes pitched at a level of abstraction that can be problematic for young children. It is difficult for them to understand the existence of something which has no immediate physical manifestations. Consequently, substances dissolving or evaporating are regarded by young children as having disappeared. Even some 15- and 16-year-olds will say that when water is boiled it first gives steam (which you can see, of course) and then splits into its component gases, hydrogen and oxygen, which are invisible (Osborne and Cosgrove 1983). The notion that light is all around us, not just coming from a torch or other light source, is also a strange and uncomfortable one for many children. Consequently, when teachers identify real world examples of scientific principles they may sometimes be reinforcing students' misconceptions. There may be occasions when it is more politic to leave the citing of real world examples until the abstract concept is better established.

It is not uncommon for children to attribute a physical reality or objective existence to physical sensations such as *cold*. For them, coldness is something that comes into the house from outside, through windows and doors. We wear bulky clothes in winter to 'keep out the cold'. Sometimes these entities are animized or anthropomorphized, so that cold *tries* to squeeze in through the cracks and heat *forces* the air out of things. As a personal aside, I must say that, having experienced several Canadian winters, I now have much sympathy with views that portray 'cold' as an essentially malignant entity. Watts and Bentley (1994) point out that there is an implicit anthropomorphism in the very language of science: light *interferes*, electrons become *excited*, poor conductors *resist*, magnetic poles *attract* and *repel* and so on. And, on occasions, teachers encourage it: students are told that alkali metals *want* to lose an electron, while halogens *want* to gain one, an electric current *chooses* the path of least resistance and so on. There are situations in which animism and anthropomorphism may assist understanding by giving things a graphic personal quality, but there can be some very real problems. If we don't make it clear to students that we are using metaphors and similes, some of them may be led to accept these accounts as explanations and incorporate them as such into their personal understanding of phenomena. There can be even more serious problems when the language of the anthropomorphic metaphor runs counter to good scientific understanding. For example, it can be counterproductive for chemists to talk about elements *wanting* to lose electrons and then proceed to a consideration of ionization energies – that is, the energy *required* to remove an electron. An essentially similar point is that careless language use by science teachers can also cause learning problems for students, as in the case of biology teachers accounting for the release of energy in the ADP–ATP system in terms of the breaking of 'energy rich bonds'. And, of course, there are those cases (hoped to be rare) when student misunderstandings are directly attributable to errors passed on by teachers or textbooks (Barrass 1984; Cho *et al.* 1985).

Alternative conceptual understanding and alternative theories and explanations are sometimes held in common within particular social groups, giving rise to superstitions, folk wisdom and what, in less politically correct times, we called old wives' tales. For example, it was once common practice to draw the curtains (close the drapes) during an electrical storm, so that metal objects such as cutlery could no longer attract the lightning. Many of these notions deal with the same kinds of issues and problems addressed by science, such as food, health and child care. But they conceptualize and rationalize matters in significantly different ways, as George and Glasgow (1988) show in their study of the folk beliefs (which they call 'street science') common to Trinidad and Tobago. The literature of situated cognition abounds with examples of specialized communities developing alternative explanatory frameworks and alternative problem-solving strategies that are unique to the contexts in which they are deployed (Lave 1988; Hennessy 1993; McLellan 1996). If conceptual structures (theories) reflect the problems, priorities, experiences, insights and cumulative wisdom of the cultures in which they arise, as this literature asserts, it follows that cultural identity can be a very significant influence on learning.

Towards a more personalized theory of learning

The views that students hold will influence the questions they ask, the way in which they interpret results from teacher demonstrations or laboratory investigations of their own, the meaning they extract from text, the variables they consider important to control in designing their own experimental work, how they interpret and answer test questions and so on. In laboratory-based activities, observations may even be selected or rejected on the basis of whether they 'fit' with students' expectations, and explanations proffered by teachers may be rejected because they conflict with students' firmly held commonsense views. An impressive body of research findings of this kind has been amassed during the past decade and a half, and points to the need to develop an approach to the teaching and learning of science that takes account of students' existing views and the ways in which they interact with and are modified by experience.

There are a number of key elements in such a view of learning. First, learners are not passive recipients of knowledge; rather, they are active constructors and reconstructors of their own understanding. Mental representations are continually being confirmed, rejected, adapted, reformed or developed in response to experiences, both inside and outside school. Second, learning depends as much on what the learner brings to the task as it does on what the teacher builds into it. In other words, students relate new observations, activities and text-based information to what they already know, and so generate new meanings. The way students engage in classroom activities and how they interpret events and experiences are shaped by prior ideas, though not entirely determined by them. Clearly, students change their views, on occasions, in response to what they experience and their attempts to make sense of it. Otherwise, no new learning would ever occur. However, there are also occasions when students' views are uninfluenced or are influenced in unanticipated ways by the teaching they experience (Osborne *et al.* 1983).

Third, the restructuring that constitutes learning is a continuing process; there never comes a point at which we stop learning. Moreover, learning is a purposeful activity. Although we can seemingly learn 'by accident', the restructuring process entails an evaluation and judgement phase and a commitment to accept the new or modified view. In the absence of this commitment, a new idea will be rejected. The internal reflection and decision-making stage, swift and tacit as it may often be, is a key to designing more successful learning opportunities in class. It should be emphasized that the word 'opportunities' is not used carelessly here; it carries with it an implication of student responsibility for learning that is explored further in Chapter 6.

These elements of a theory of learning, which are often clustered under the umbrella term 'constructivist views of learning', are well summarized by Shuell (1990: 540):

> Meaningful cognitive learning is an active, constructive, and cumulative process that occurs gradually over a period of time. It is a goal oriented process best characterized in terms of problem solving. Learning is not merely an additive process – qualitative, as well as quantitative, changes occur, and qualitative differences are evident in both the substance of what is being learned and in the learning processes most appropriate for acquiring additional knowledge.

Strong parallels are evident between constructivist views of learning as conceptual change brought about through encounters with experience and Piagetian notions of assimilation and accommodation. However, constructivism takes a more domain-specific view of learning than the more global, formal structures and operations of Piagetian theory.

Notes

1 It will also become apparent that my 'strenuous opposition' is related to context.
2 A number of review articles and books provide ready access to the extensive research literature: Driver and Erickson (1983), Gilbert and Watts (1983), Driver *et al.* (1985, 1994a). Cheek (1992) and Pfundt and Duit (1994) also provide extensive bibliographies.
3 Hawkins and Pea (1987) refer to this principle of sufficient sophistication for purpose as *pragmatic precision*.
4 It should be noted that although children's explanations of common everyday phenomena often do resemble past ideas in the history of science, their ideas often lack the conceptual coherence of scientific theories.

• • • 4

Constructivist approaches to teaching and learning science

A constructivist theory of learning does not necessarily entail a constructivist approach to teaching. As Millar (1989: 589) points out, the 'process of eliciting, clarification, and construction of new ideas takes place *internally*, within the learner's own head. This occurs whenever any successful learning takes place and is independent of the form of instruction.' Nevertheless, the ideas outlined in Chapter 3 provide some useful pointers to teaching strategies that might assist students in the task of conceptual reconstruction. They suggest, for example, that the most powerful stimulus for the extension, modification or rejection of a particular idea is its failure to cope with circumstances encountered. Consequently, teachers can initiate or stimulate learning by setting demanding tasks, issuing challenges or presenting counter experiences. However, because learning is a process of personal development, it is important that each learner is given and accepts a degree of responsibility for her or his own learning. Students need to explore their own ideas and understanding, to make choices among them, to justify and test different ideas and to evaluate them for themselves, in both familiar and unfamiliar situations.

A number of constructivist approaches to science teaching have been developed (Cosgrove *et al.* 1982; Biddulph and Osborne 1984; Driver 1989; Harlen 1992; Appleton 1993). While they differ a little in detail, they can be usefully summarized as follows:

- identify students' ideas and views;
- create opportunities for students to explore their ideas and test their robustness in explaining phenomena, accounting for events and making predictions;
- provide stimuli for students to develop, modify and, where necessary, change their ideas and views;
- support their attempts to rethink and reconstruct their ideas and views.

Acknowledging and exploring students' ideas

Constructivist approaches generally involve creating opportunities for students to make their own ideas explicit, share them with others, subject them to critical scrutiny and test their robustness by observation and/or experiment. To provide an initial focus for thought, a teacher might begin a topic by posing a question, stating a problem, conducting a demonstration, showing a video or involving students in a laboratory-based or outdoor/field activity of some kind. Students' responses and interpretations can be elicited by a variety of means, including skilful teacher questioning, use of art work, group discussion and writing activities of various kinds. Fensham (1989) suggests that students keep individual learning diaries in which to record their ideas, reactions and questions. Other written methods include constructing diagrams, making notes with self-generated headings and subheadings, drawing flow charts and using Venn diagrams, concept maps and Vee diagrams. In effect, any of the research methods used to elicit students' understanding can be used as teaching tactics. Indeed, Gunstone (1988) and Abdullah and Scaife (1997) even suggest that teachers use individual interviews-about-instances and interviews-about-events (the methods developed by the University of Waikato's Learning in Science Project). Sadly, the practicality of such an approach for classes of the size that many teachers are required to manage is doubtful. Nevertheless, it is a method that teachers can keep in reserve for use with specific students who, for a variety of reasons, may have been unable to make their ideas explicit in other, more easily administered, ways.

Of course, there are topics, phenomena and events concerning which students may have no prior experiences and so will not have formed any prior views. Not all matters studied in science lessons are open to common everyday experience. In these circumstances, it will be necessary to provide further practical experiences in order to build up a student's stock of personal experience. This is what Woolnough and Allsop (1985) call 'getting a feel for phenomena' and White (1991, 1996) refers to as building up 'episodic knowledge' or 'recollections of events'. Throughout these activities, students might be encouraged to pose their own questions as a stimulus for further inquiry (Biddulph and Osborne 1984; Faire and Cosgrove 1988; Watts and Alsop 1995). This approach creates two focuses of attention for teachers: first, creating a classroom climate within which children will be stimulated to ask questions and supported in their attempts to ask *scientific* questions; second, ensuring that questions are expressed in operational form (that is, they are in a form that supports investigation). Thus, there are both affective and cognitive dimensions: we have to show that questions are welcomed and we have to ensure that students know what constitutes a good or productive question.

Many of the questions asked by young children are best characterized as 'correct answer seeking', and are often in the form of a simple 'why' question. They need extensive practice in converting them into a form that is likely to stimulate a scientific inquiry. Indeed, some fairly explicit teaching, during which different kinds of questions and their functions are defined, described and modelled, may be required in the early stages. Encouraging students to use words such as *which, where, when* or *what if,* instead of why, is an early step in this direction. As many opportunities as possible should be taken for stimulating children to ask operational questions. Watching a demonstration, reading an article, listening to a speaker, viewing a video and so on are all valuable opportunities for students to formulate questions, as well as for taking notes and answering the teachers' questions. As a first step, Elstgeest (1985) suggests that teachers classify their own questions into five categories: attention-focusing (What do you notice ... ?); measuring and counting (How many ... ? or How long ... ?); making comparisons (What are the differences ... ?); prompting action (What happens if ... ?); and problem-posing (Can you find a way to ... ?). But teachers need to do more than just ask these kinds of questions; they also need to describe them (and their purposes) and encourage students to ask them.

Because students often ask questions that teachers wouldn't usually ask, question sessions can play a crucial role in gaining student involvement and developing the sense of ownership essential to building intellectual independence. Moreover, when teachers are working alongside students in trying to answer *everyone's* questions, they are cast in the role of learner, another element contributing to students' self-esteem and intellectual independence. While the child-centred thrust of constructivism might incline teachers towards encouraging students to explore phenomena and events individually, and to design and conduct their own investigations with the minimum of teacher direction, there is also enormous value in all students attending to the same phenomena and events in order to generate a wider range of ideas from which to begin to criticize and challenge.

Presenting challenges for restructuring ideas

Through further laboratory activities, role play, games and simulations, talking, reading and writing, students continue to explore their own understanding and begin to gain an appreciation of the views and understanding of others. Through various group activities, students learn to acknowledge and criticize the views of others, accept and value criticism and recognize discrepancies, conflicts, contradictions and inconsistencies, as well as points of similarity and agreement. In teaching the particle model of gases to seventh grade classes, for example, Nussbaum and Novick (1982) implemented a strategy based on individual drawings, which were subsequently made 'public' within the class. Students drew the conditions they believed pertained in a flask before and after the use of a vacuum pump. After moving around the classroom, the teacher asked students associated with each type of drawing to reproduce their sketches on the blackboard and to give reasons for their particular representation. In a subsequent lesson, each student was provided with copies of the drawings for discussion and criticism purposes. Driver (1989) describes a similar teaching sequence involving comparing and contrasting pictures produced during group activities.

In the 'classroom profile' strategy devised by Shapiro (1988, 1994), different student-generated explanations of a phenomenon are recorded on a public chart and rank ordered by popularity.[1] Shapiro comments that this strategy often results in students providing a further description rather than an explanation, which provides an opportunity for this crucial distinction to be clarified. In addition to the benefits associated with assisting students to articulate their own views, become aware that others may see things differently, learn the skills of comparing and contrasting different viewpoints and evaluate the robustness of particular explanations in relation to observational and experimental evidence, this strategy helps students to recognize that the most widely held view is not always the most productive or the one closest to the accepted scientific view. Champagne et al. (1985) describe the 'ideational confrontation strategy', in which students share their personal views with the specific intention of generating controversies. Students come to a clearer understanding of their position as they are required to defend it, and gain a keener appreciation of the views of others by being required to oppose it. It is at this stage that the teacher might introduce the ideas identified by the curriculum as appropriate learning – unless, of course, some students have already done so.

In addition to comparing, contrasting and criticizing the different views that have been presented, there may be an opportunity to test their robustness with respect to external evidence – that is, to subject them to observational and experimental test. Teachers may challenge students to find the limitations of their views or may deliberately present them with surprising or discrepant events through hands-on experiences of various kinds (Hewson and Hewson 1984; Fensham and Kass 1988). For example, students might describe their understanding of a concept, use their understanding to make predictions, observe a discrepant event presented by the teacher and then explain how these new observations confirm or refute their initial understanding. Alternatively, in the predict–observe–explain (POE) tasks developed by Gunstone et al. (1988), which are perhaps better described as predict–explain–observe–explain (PEOE) tasks, students are asked to provide a written prediction, with reasons, for what will happen in certain situations. During the subsequent teacher demonstration, students record what they observe, and any discrepancies between observation and prediction can be confronted. In both these approaches, it is assumed that feelings of surprise, puzzlement, uneasiness or curiosity occasioned by the inadequacy of existing ideas to explain the new event or phenomenon act as both a motivating factor and a stimulus to conceptual change. It is further assumed that the 'collision' of existing ideas with new experiences precipitates what Piaget calls 'cognitive disequilibrium', the resolution of which is achieved by cognitive restructuring, or what Ausubel et al. (1978) call 'integrative reconciliation'.

A necessary condition for cognitive restructuring is an opportunity for repeated, exploratory, inquiry-oriented behaviors about an event or phenomena in order to realize that the intact schema option is no longer tenable, and that the only reasonable option is to revise one's cognitive structure so as to be more consistent with one's experience (data, measurements, or observations).

(Saunders 1992: 138)

Resistance to restructuring

Despite Saunders's optimism that the 'only reasonable option' is to restructure one's cognitive schema, many students don't take it! Research shows that restructuring does not readily or easily occur. Existing ideas are often strongly resistant to change (di Sessa 1982; Eylon and Linn 1988). If an idea has served its purposes well in the past, there will be little urgency to replace it. Instead of replacing their views, students may retain them by denying the new data, or reworking the data in a way that is consistent with their existing views (Gunstone and White 1981; Nussbaum 1985). Another strategy is to distort the new idea until it can be regarded as compatible with the old (Chinn and Brewer 1993). Many individuals exhibit a 'confirmation bias' and look for evidence to confirm rather than disconfirm their ideas (Hashweh 1986). In such circumstances, the existing notion is likely to prevail. This probability is heightened when students are responsible for designing the inquiry: they will only subject to critical scrutiny those aspects of their understanding which they have reason to doubt. More importantly, in designing an experiment, they can test only those variables they believe to be involved. Put simply, it isn't possible to generate data about something of which one is unaware.

Variations in personality traits make some students more open to new ideas than others. Some students may simply disengage from the struggle to resolve cognitive disequilibrium. Rather than accepting responsibility for understanding the nature of the discrepancy and for rationalizing it, they may simply declare that the matter is not worth bothering about, of no interest whatsoever, and irrelevant to their needs – in effect saying, 'I may not understand, but I don't care.' Some may be reluctant to consider alternatives through fear of change, uncertainty and unfamiliarity. Furthermore, students may be much more tolerant of inconsistencies than Saunders anticipates. As Claxton (1991: 86) points out, there is often very little consistency and coherence in a student's thinking about phenomena:

Far from being the neat, coherent unitary sort of theory to which science proper aspires, the mind-scape of the child is patchwork and piecemeal. It consists not of a single integrated theory but of an assembly of 'minitheories', each generated to provide successful engagement with a particular kind of scenario.

As a consequence, what may be a significant discrepant event for the teacher may not be recognized as such by students. Thus, while cognitive disequilibrium may be a necessary stimulus to learning, it is not sufficient to ensure that learning will occur. Only when learners recognize that there is a conflict, and are sufficiently concerned about it, will they attempt to resolve it. Therefore, the teacher who uses this strategy must endeavour to provide exactly the right form and extent of discrepancy. Too little, and there is no stimulus for change; too much, and students may be overwhelmed.

The conditions for conceptual restructuring

Posner *et al.* (1982) argue that a new conceptual scheme will be accepted only if learners are dissatisfied with their current belief/understanding and have access to a new or better idea with which to replace it. To gain acceptance, the new idea must meet certain conditions.

- It must be *intelligible* (understandable) – that is, the learner must understand what it means and how it can and should be used. Additionally, the student should be cognizant that scientists are concerned that it should be coherent and internally consistent.
- It must be *plausible* (reasonable) – that is, it should be consistent with and be able to be reconciled with other aspects of the student's understanding. In simple terms, it should be believable and should make sense, though 'making sense' in scientific terms may be rather different from what it is in commonsense terms.
- It must be *fruitful* (useful) or seem that it will become fruitful – that is, it should have the capacity to provide something of value to the learner, by solving problems, making valid and reliable predictions or providing new insight (making sense of the world) and suggesting new areas for investigation and study. It could also be fruitful in the sense of gaining marks in tests (but see Chapter 6).[2]

Conceptual change is made possible when students understand the limitations of their current views and recognize the need to replace them. Dissatisfaction with an existing idea may reside in its failure to predict correctly or to control events beyond its previous restricted context (i.e. it is no longer fruitful). It may also be located in its failure, when confronted with vigorous alternatives, to meet satisfactorily the conditions of intelligibility and plausibility. Hewson and Thorley (1989) describe the conceptual change approach to teaching and learning science as a matter of changing the status of rival conceptions – that is, of changing the extent to which they meet the three conditions of intelligibility, plausibility and fruitfulness. Put simply, the teacher's task is to lower the status of the existing idea and raise the status of the new one. Having promoted conflict between existing understanding and the new observation, experience or text, the teacher strives to resolve the conflict in the desired direction by 'status adjustment'. Such a strategy necessitates that the rival theories/understandings are unambiguously described and satisfactorily discriminated.[3] In the absence of these conditions, no meaningful debate is possible and there is no rational basis for choosing. Two points should be made. First, a student's existing idea may be poorly articulated, incoherent and imprecise, so that no decisive debate is possible. For all kinds of reasons, this is often the case, especially among young children. Second, the very misconception that is supposedly 'under attack' may cause a student to misinterpret the counter examples, thus eliminating the intended cognitive conflict.

It should also be recognized that an individual's ideas are linked in complex and idiosyncratic ways. Concepts are not isolated cognitive artefacts; they have syntactical and semantic relationships to other concepts. They are not just related, they are interrelated: they depend on each other for meaning. Hence, changing one idea may entail changing, modifying or rearranging others. It takes time; it is uncertain. It is unlikely that a concept will be readily changed if it is embedded in a set of relationships that is otherwise sound (in terms of intelligibility, plausibility and fruitfulness). It is also likely that a single example of a discrepant event or cognitive conflict may be identified by students as no more than a 'rogue case', a special exception for which an *ad hoc* explanation can be used while the rest of the complex of ideas remains unchanged. Hence, lots of hands-on experiences, group discussions and language activities are necessary to assist students to clarify the nature of conflicts, to test new ideas in a variety of contexts to see how robust, versatile and useful they are, and to ensure that the new idea is fully appreciated and integrated into their view of the world. Rowell *et al.* (1990) make a case for a systematic critique of 'old way versus new way of thinking' based on predictive and explanatory capability.

Burbules and Linn (1988) show that even when students do change their views in response to counter experiences, they don't rush to do so. They cling to existing ideas as long as possible. They need time to deal with threatening, disconcerting or confusing data; they need a period for reflection, preferably with teacher guidance and support. These authors also show that individual learners differ quite substantially in their 'learning histories' and that knock-on effects can cause confusion with ideas that students thought they already had clear in their minds. Interestingly, Hynd *et al.* (1994) show that a well designed and carefully used 'refutational text' is often more effective in changing student conceptions than is teacher demonstration, laboratory exercise or group discussion. Moreover, these authors state that when misconceptions are located in commonsense knowledge and everyday experience, peer group discussion may actually consolidate existing ideas. By contrast, perhaps because of the authority that the written word is perceived to carry, refutational texts that state clearly that particular commonsense views do not explain the phenomena under consideration, and provide a sound argument and good supporting evidence for the scientific view, are often successful. Explicit confrontation of misconceptions through video presentation may also have considerable potential (Muthukrishna *et al.*

1993). Chapters 12 and 13 provide additional perspectives from which this research can be considered, but clearly there is a need for much more research in other areas of science (the Hynd *et al.* study concerned a fairly restricted aspect of Newtonian physics).

Teachers making extensive use of cognitive conflict and discrepant events should be cognizant of the hidden curriculum message: that, even in learning, something (or someone) wins and something (or someone) loses. Howe and Thompsen (1989: 6) ask whether extensive use of cognitive conflict will 'lead to a contentious classroom, with the possibility of injured feelings and personal insult'. There is also the matter of who is in control. Cognitive conflict strategies require the teacher to create dissatisfaction for students. The result, says Clark (1985), can be 'a kind of "cognitive assault" in which students are *forced* to confront and abandon a part of self that has been, and is, serving them reasonably well.' In a multi-ethnic or cross-cultural situation, it could be argued that assertive forms of cognitive displacement might serve 'as an agent of Western cultural imperialism by devaluing the integrity of students' non-Western world views' (Baker and Taylor 1995: 700).

The overall purpose of these strategies is, of course, to move from the personalized, context-specific understanding that particular students already possess towards the more abstract, universalistic understandings that science is concerned with, a transition from children's minitheories to the science community's macrotheories. Herein lies a major problem: learning science is recognized as a personal process, in which individual learners attempt to reconcile for themselves any disparities between and among their existing ideas, the expectations they give rise to, the views of others and their observations and experiences both inside and outside school; yet, at the same time, we expect students to acquire a specific body of public, consensual scientific knowledge.

Reviewing progress

Many constructivist approaches include a phase of review or reflection on the changes of understanding that have taken place. For example, Faire and Cosgrove (1988: 26) say: 'Encouraging children to reflect on their findings, on how they reached them and on how their findings compare with their previous ideas and the ideas of others, is a central part of interactive teaching.' Three points should be made.

- Comparing before and after views, keeping learning logs, arguing and debating points of view and presenting ideas to others in oral and written form are activities that assist students in gaining an understanding of how ideas are related.
- Without such reflection, whatever conceptual development has occurred may not be maintained. As White and Gunstone (1989: 579) say, 'It is all too easy for an apparent change to slip away or to be no more than a

shallow, casual adoption of a principle without real belief in it or commitment to it.'
- Reflecting on their own learning helps students to appreciate that conceptual change is involved in learning. It is not just a case of remembering or of 'being clever'; one can learn how to learn.

Gunstone (1994) sees reflection and metacognition as the key to meeting Posner et al.'s (1982) conditions for conceptual change because the learner has to recognize his or her existing ideas and views, evaluate them in terms of what is being presented as an alternative and then decide whether or not to reconstruct or change existing understanding. Through metacognitive activities, and the increased awareness and understanding of their own learning processes that results, students gain more control over their learning. In other words, knowledge of cognition can translate into regulation of cognition.[4] By learning how to monitor and reflect on their own processes of conceptual change, students are encouraged and enabled to become responsible for their own learning, and may become sufficiently aware of their own learning habits and characteristic patterns that they can identify and correct their own errors as they proceed (an idea developed in Chapter 6). As Osborne and Wittrock (1985: 66) maintain: 'When students accept that they, rather than their teachers, their parents, other people, or other factors, are primarily responsible for constructing the meanings that represent their success or failure in school, their learning is likely to increase.'

There are a variety of strategies available to the teacher for helping students to develop an understanding of how to monitor their own learning. For example, they can provide checklists of questions which encourage students to consider and comment on their understanding and how it is changing during a particular curriculum activity: 'What do I know about this topic?'; 'Do I understand this idea as well as I would like?'; 'How does this idea compare with what I used to think?'; and so on (Baird 1986; Hewson and Thorley 1989). A variation of this approach is for student and teacher to share in the upkeep of an interactive learning/thinking log, each taking time to comment on the entries of the other. The aim is to compile an ongoing critical dialogue about the relative status of ideas in terms of intelligibility, plausibility and fruitfulness. Teachers might ask, for example: 'What do you find difficult about this idea?', 'Could you use this idea to explain the data from experiment X?', 'Is this idea useful in solving the problem posed earlier?' What I am arguing here is that we introduce students to Posner et al.'s (1982) conditions for conceptual change – that is, consciously encourage them to weigh the merits of rival ideas in terms of intelligibility, plausibility and fruitfulness.

Shapiro (1988) suggests that students read stories and view tapes of other students using learning strategies found to be effective in the science classroom; Novak (1990) has written at length on the use of concept maps and Vee diagrams; Paris et al. (1984, 1986) have recommended an explicit programme of 'informed strategies for learning', involving direct instruction in learning strategies, frequent practice and immediate feedback via peer group discussion and criticism. Many of the techniques to encourage good information processing to be found in study skills books can be usefully employed: devising appropriate sub-headings for text and teacher-produced notes; deleting surplus data from text or unnecessary instructions from problem-solving activities; reordering scrambled text; setting a test on a topic; and so on. Significantly, teachers involved in the Project to Enhance Effective Learning (PEEL) (Baird and Mitchell 1986; Baird and Northfield 1992) found that no one technique will sustain reflective action by students or maintain their personal motivation. After a while, almost any method becomes routine. There is also evidence that students can fake good learning behaviour by devising and then following algorithms for supposedly reflective activities (White and Mitchell 1994). Clearly, what is needed is frequent variation in methods (White and Gunstone 1989).

There are two further problems. First, students are often unwilling to change their views of learning, especially if their current strategies are successful (in whatever terms the school recognizes success). Second, if there is no immediate pay-off from the school system, students will continue with existing, familiar methods – unless there is very powerful alternative motivation. Clearly, this has implications for assessment and evaluation practices. It is worth noting that portfolio-based assessment creates opportunities for engagement in more authentic learning tasks and provides a valuable resource for metalearning. Student portfolios include tangible evidence of conceptual changes that have occurred and reinforce recollections of changes undergone, thereby providing a powerful stimulus for reflective thought.

Notes

1 Whether the names of students are included should depend, Shapiro reminds us, on the prevailing 'classroom climate'.
2 From the perspective of science itself, fruitfulness might also be interpreted in terms of elegance, parsimony and economy (the aesthetics of science).
3 It also requires that teachers have a clear understanding of what these terms mean (in a scientific context) and a repertoire of methods to enhance them through linguistic expressions, emphasis on criterial attributes, use of analogies, metaphors and exemplars (Thorley and Stofflett 1996).
4 Metacognition is a recurring theme in this book, and is cited a number of times as a decisive factor in learning of all kinds.

• • • 5

The paradox of constructivism

Among others, Matthews (1993a, 1994, 1997) has argued that in its pursuit of personal understanding of phenomena and events, the constructivist approach is open to the charge of neglecting and trivializing scientific understanding. In a vigorous and highly publicized attack on the constructivist base of the New Zealand science curriculum,[1] he described constructivism as a 'loony doctrine' which is leading New Zealand into an educational and scientific abyss. At the heart of his criticism is a concern that constructivist approaches imply that students who construct their own understanding of the world are also constructing scientific understanding. Anything is allowed to count as science, he says, because the criteria of scientific truth and the explicit teaching of established scientific knowledge are disregarded in favour of 'ensuring equity for all students, creating a friendly learning environment, listening to students, ensuring students communicate, challenging sensitively the ideas of students and providing resources' (Matthews 1993b).

Absurdly, some constructivist writers assert that *everyone* is a scientist, even children. In New Zealand, as Matthews points out, the Ministry of Education states that 'we are all scientists' (Ministry of Education 1989: 5), and science is described as 'an activity that can be carried out by all people as part of their everyday life' (Ministry of Education 1992: 8).[2] Similarly, Raper and Stringer (1987: 26) assert that 'thinking scientifically comes naturally to children'. Nothing could be further from the truth. Not all investigations and inquiries are *scientific* and not all knowledge and explanations resulting from them are equally valid from a scientific point of view. Some ideas have more scientific credibility, validity and reliability than others precisely because the inquiries that produced them adhere to well established criteria for judging and evaluating knowledge claims and to rigorous standards for conducting and appraising scientific investigations. These standards and criteria have to be learned; they are not natural, commonsense and child-like.

A view that a child has, for reasons that satisfy him or her, is not necessarily good science. Scientific knowledge is more than personally held belief reinforced by personally gathered observational confirmation. It is an attempt to explain and account for the real nature of the physical universe (science has realist goals), regardless of whether it 'makes sense' in the everyday meaning of that expression. Indeed, much scientific knowledge flies in the face of common sense: the physics of Galileo, Newton and Einstein compare unfavourably with Aristotelian views if common sense is to be the arbiter. Lots of beliefs that make sense are simply not true, or are otherwise undesirable. What science seeks is rationally justifiable abstract knowledge about phenomena and events in the real world, using whatever existing knowledge, procedural expertise and technical tools are available and appropriate. This realist perspective is essential for science because it provides the impetus for further exploration and investigation, and it is essential for science education because it provides the justification for attempting to develop or change students' everyday commonsense views about phenomena and events.

The reluctance of some science educators to identify any element of a student's understanding as a misconception, or to state that a particular view is wrong, stems from the laudable motivation not to 'blame' students for any inadequate understanding they may possess, and not to risk damage to self-esteem or to denigrate knowledge and belief located in other socio-cultural contexts in which students are located. However, if we are unwilling to evaluate students' views, if we are unwilling to judge some ideas as better than others (in the sense of being more accurate, more general, more coherent, more consistent with other views, more useful or whatever), we do students a gross disservice. We give our students no incentive to change or develop their views; we give ourselves no incentive to design good curricula, or even to teach science at all. Why struggle to design good and effective curricula if we don't have a commitment to the notion that some ways of understanding are more desirable or useful than others? If we take the relativist position regarding the 'quality' of knowledge, any curriculum content will suffice, and no curriculum is better than any other. However, we also need to take account of what other purposes knowledge and understanding may serve, and how they relate to other social contexts (see later discussion).

Radical constructivism and its critics

Central to the charge of relativism that Matthews (1994) levels at constructivists is his assertion that because constructivists acknowledge that science cannot know reality in an absolute sense they necessarily believe that scientific knowledge is no more than a human construct and could, therefore, be otherwise; and presumably would be otherwise if different people were involved. His concern is that this leaves the door open for any views to be accepted as science and for the disregarding of scientific truth. He points out that in building his theory of radical constructivism, von Glasersfeld (1989: 122) quotes Ludwik Fleck's claims that the 'content of our knowledge must be considered the free creation of our culture', and that 'every thinking individual, insofar as it is a member of some society, has its own reality according to which and in which it lives.' Passages such as these lay constructivists wide open to charges of relativism, and rightly so. While we may wish to recognize that different people see the world in different ways, and that much of our knowledge is a product of our social structure, we should reject Fleck's (and, it seems, von Glasersfeld's) view that 'objective reality can be resolved into historical sequences of ideas belonging to the collective' (cited by Matthews 1994: 229). Scientific knowledge is a 'free creation' in the sense that scientists created it (theory building is a creative activity), but it is not free in the sense that it is unrestrained. It is restrained by the nature of the universe (scientific knowledge has to be consistent with observational evidence of real phenomena and events) and it is restrained by the professional practice of scientists and its attendant standards and criteria of acceptability. Were it not so, any knowledge would, indeed, be as good as any other, and it wouldn't matter what we taught in science classes. Most science teachers, including many who would identify strongly with constructivist pedagogy, believe that it matters very much what we teach. Among other things, we teach those ideas in science that we believe best represent our understanding of how the natural world functions. In other words, we teach 'scientific truth' (Chapter 2), or at least a version of it that we consider appropriate to school age students.

Scientific knowledge is a human construct, but scientists have confidence in the knowledge they generate because of the distinctive nature of scientific inquiry and the agreed practices of the community of scientists. The personal constructions of individual scientists have to be seen by others to be reasonable, convincing and productive in some way. Otherwise they fail to gain admission to the corpus of scientific knowledge. An individual scientist's claim to knowledge is adjudicated by the scientific community in accordance with strict criteria. Although some scientists may work alone, the products of their inquiries must be recorded and reported in appropriate form and language for critical appraisal by other scientists. Nothing is accepted into the corpus of scientific knowledge on the authority of a single individual. 'Scientific knowledge' is a status that is accorded to ideas which have been subjected to, and have survived, critical scrutiny by members of the community of scientists, using whatever methods and criteria have been deemed appropriate to ensure the necessary degree of validity and reliability. Of course, the community comprises individuals, too, so its criteria are also human constructs. However, acknowledgement of the social construction of knowledge within the scientific community does not necessitate the view that scientists can legitimate any knowledge they wish or that science is no more than the views of those in power. We should have no greater enthusiasm for the Edinburgh school's so-called 'strong programme' in the sociology of science[3] than for von Glasersfeld's radical constructivism.

Several points are worth making. First, saying that knowledge is actively built by a cognizing subject does not lead to the conclusion that it is merely a personal construct, in the sense that *anything* is admissible. Second, although our inadequate perceptions do not capture real parts of the external world, and observations have to be interpreted via our theoretical knowledge, it does not follow that we need always to doubt our constructions. Personally constructed knowledge isn't necessarily untrue or unreliable. In other words, recognizing that scientific inquiry is driven by our own inadequate and fallible human constructs does not entail the conclusion that science is both unfounded and relativist. Third, recognizing the socially constructed nature of scientific knowledge does not necessitate an abandonment of the realist thrust of scientific inquiry.

When von Glasersfeld (1989) states that cognition is adaptive and serves the personal organization of the experiential world, not the discovery of ontological reality, and when he asserts that knowledge exists only in the minds of cognizing beings and cannot reside in books, for example, he is ignoring the social world (and the construction of meaning within social groups), the specific social world of science (and its cumulative consensus-based knowledge) and the realist thrust of science. Quite rightly, radical constructivism seeks to avoid claims to absolute truth, but it is so anxious to do so that it claims we are unable to be sure of anything. Paradoxically, however, anything is considered *viable* if it works for the individual.[4] Theory becomes merely an instrumental device – a useful fiction with no claim to represent ontological reality. Thus, radical constructivism doesn't provide any criteria for why one idea is better than another. Truth, even the modified version of 'scientific truth' discussed by Hodson (1982), is simply 'how you see it'. Just as importantly, radical constructivism provides no mechanism by which students can construct new ideas about the world. How would they start? What would they do? The counter-intuitive, non-commonsense ideas of science have to be presented – by teachers or other curriculum materials. As Osborne (1996) states, unassisted students will not arrive at the notion that the Earth spins, inherited characteristics are transmitted through coded information and all matter is composed of a limited number of elements.

While the act of constructing is a crucial part of learning, the nature of what is constructed and the reasons for that particular construction are equally crucial. In other words, science education needs to consider the socially agreed constructions of the community of scientists.

> If knowledge construction is seen solely as an individual process, then this is similar to what has traditionally been identified as discovery learning. If, however, learners are to be given access to the knowledge systems of science, the process of knowledge construction must go beyond personal empirical inquiry. Learners need to be given access not only to physical experiences but also to the concepts and models of conventional science.
>
> (Driver *et al.* 1994b: 7)

Learning science is not simply a matter of 'making sense of the world' in whatever terms and for whatever reasons satisfy the learner. Learning science involves introduction into the world of concepts, ideas, understandings and theories that scientists have developed and accumulated (that is, *what* science knows). It is concerned with understanding and being able to use appropriately the meanings developed by the scientific community – notions such as *molecule, gene, magnetic field* and *electron*. While these notions relate to the real world, they are not just copies of it. Science doesn't just describe events and phenomena; rather, it uses mental models and theories to go beyond mere description, in order to explain, interpret and predict. The transition sought by science teachers is from students' commonsense, empirical descriptions of phenomena and events to the abstract, idealized and mathematical descriptions of science. When we teach science we should emphasize that we are not presenting true facts about the world, but theoretical constructions which are subject to further refinement and development, and may eventually be falsified and discarded in favour of better alternatives. Moreover, scientific theory neither creates the objects being studied nor derives from the naive observation of them. Rather, it is an enabling device by means of which we idealize, model and interpret. Recognizing this is central to understanding the distinctive nature of scientific knowledge and, therefore, is a crucial aspect of science education (see Matthews (1994) for an elaboration of these points).

Understanding scientific concepts necessitates an appreciation of the role and status of scientific knowledge and its means of production. In the absence of an awareness of the relationship between hypothesis and evidence, students are unable to distinguish a theory from a simple belief. Without an appreciation of the relationships among theory, observation and experiment, they have no incentive to progress beyond commonsense everyday levels of conceptual understanding. Gil-Perez and Carrascosa-Alis (1994) draw a parallel between the historical development of science, which necessitated a shift away from 'common sense' towards scientific ways of proceeding, and science education, where conceptual change of the kind demanded by contemporary science curricula can only be effected by a similar kind of methodological change. In other words, learning in science is as much an epistemological issue as it is a cognitive one. In teaching science and teaching about science, and for doing science, the questions 'How do you know?' and 'Why do you know?' are just as important as 'What do you know?' Students need to learn the criteria by which knowledge claims in science are judged, and they need to know how these compare with knowledge claims and their criteria of validity in other disciplines and in commonsense understanding. These matters are explored further in Chapters 8 to 11. When constructivist teaching strategies concentrate solely on personal understanding, and pay scant attention to methodological and epistemological issues, it is not surprising that children maintain the 'methodology of superficiality' (Gil-Perez and Carrascosa-Alis 1985) that produced their commonsense understanding in the first place. Common sense is not enough!

Personal frameworks of understanding

One of the intriguing paradoxes of constructivist writing is that it sometimes neglects the rationality of science but over-emphasizes the rationality of learning, especially in its assertions that conceptual change can be precipitated through cognitive dissonance (conflict of ideas). As discussed earlier, research conducted over the past decade and a half has revealed convincing evidence that children's commonsense and intuitive views about everyday phenomena and events are not only strongly held, but are remarkably persistent, even in the face of direct attempts by teachers to effect change. Put simply, children are often very reluctant to relinquish views that have served them adequately in the past. There is evidence that two views (the children's and the curriculum's) can coexist, with children using their own science in everyday life and reproducing 'official' science when required to do so by teachers' questions in class, homework assignments, examinations and so on. Even when teachers point out inconsistencies among students' views, there is no guarantee that they will seek to eliminate them.

Driver and Bell (1986) describe an incident in which students did not think that a weight had potential energy when they carried it upstairs, but did have potential energy when they hoisted it up to the ceiling using a pulley and rope. For them, it depends on the circumstances! Similarly, young children attempting to explain floating and sinking will readily shift from explanations based on differences in weight to those based on differences in size or texture, depending on the particular problem context. As a consequence, it is difficult to use conflict between existing views and 'official views' as an incentive to change. First, students may not recognize that conflict exists. Second, even if they do, they may be tolerant of it. If children do not expect consistency, then inconsistency is not a reason to change one's views. They may see no need to resolve conflict; conflicting notions are simply compartmentalized.

According to Claxton (1990), we all build up 'minitheories' about the world around us. As we gain experience of the world, we are continually testing, refining and replacing them. Inconsistencies among minitheories are tolerated because we *laminate*: we have levels of explanation that are appropriate to different contexts. When presented with a challenge or problem, we access whatever chunk or 'package' of knowledge, set of operations or manipulative techniques we consider will help us to respond appropriately to the situation. These packages function as 'tool kits' with specific purposes, hence no overall coherence and consistency is required. It doesn't matter if there are inconsistencies because they are used for different purposes. Scientists laminate all the time, using theory A to explain x, y and z and model B to explain p, q and s. Moreover, they may employ an entirely different, non-scientific package of knowledge when presented with an everyday problem. It shouldn't surprise us, then, if students deploy different knowledge in school contexts and everyday situations.

What each of us does when presented with the need to respond is to make a rapid assessment of the context/situation and come to a judgement about the situationally appropriate language, behaviour and theoretical explanation. There is no single, all-purpose right answer. What is appropriate depends on the circumstances: Who is asking the question? Why do they wish to know? What do they already know? And so on. With regard to children and their science knowledge, much depends on whether the questioner is a teacher (and, moreover, which particular teacher it is), a parent or similarly perceived adult, a friend or another student. This raises all sorts of interesting questions about the research methods employed by constructivist researchers into children's alternative frameworks of understanding. Which version of their understanding did students give to the researcher? Would different responses be produced by interview, written examination and undirected reflective writing? Different contexts are likely to be perceived differently by students and different responses are likely to be made. The situation is similar to that with the draw-a-scientist test (DAST) (Chambers 1982), where it isn't always clear whether students are consciously portraying a stereotypical scientist (the comic book or movie image) or giving researchers insight into what they really believe. It may even be that older students present a stereotyped picture in order to make a political point – for example, that women have fewer opportunities in science than men, or that certain ethnic groups are excluded from science. At the very least, students have three images of scientists at their disposal: the comic book/movie image, the approved school version and their own view. It isn't always clear which one DAST is accessing (Hodson 1993b).

There is abundant research evidence to show that students select different knowledge for different purposes. For example, Galili and Bar (1992) found that students who successfully employed a Newtonian theoretical framework to solve force and motion problems set in a familiar school physics context sometimes reverted to pre-Newtonian reasoning of 'motion implies force' in less familiar contexts. And the literature of situated cognition abounds with examples of children and adults using significantly different knowledge and problem-solving strategies in different circumstances. To date, most science educators have regarded this as a problem, as something to be overcome. Over the course of the next several chapters, I intend to build a case for regarding it as both inevitable and able to be exploited in assisting students to develop a more sophisticated scientific understanding. If it is recognized as normal for individuals to hold more than one explanatory structure, the focus for the science teacher shifts to ways of assisting students to recognize the contexts or circumstances in which a particular conception is appropriate.

As discussed previously, science seeks universal explanations (coherent and consistent) when it is acting in its realist mode (that is, when scientists are engaged in theory building), but is tolerant of discrepancies, inconsistencies and even contradictions when acting in its instrumentalist mode (that is, when scientists are merely seeking a measure of predictive control through the use of convenient models). Moreover, a complex and sophisticated scientific theory or conceptual model has several layers of meaning, some of which only become apparent through continued use in practical contexts. It follows that scientists will differ among themselves in terms of their understanding and use of scientific knowledge, and will conduct their activities at different levels of sophistication. If science accepts a variety of meanings, because each is suited to a different purpose, why should science educators expect students to have only one coherent and consistent set of explanations (i.e. those specified in the curriculum plan)? Do learners not also have a variety of purposes? If so, is it not the case that only some of those purposes are met by the official scientific explanation? It is more reasonable to expect every student to have a unique *personal framework of understanding,*[5] compounded of a variety of meanings accumulated for different purposes.

A number of writers have described meaning as comprising a central core of *denotative* meaning and a wide-ranging periphery of *connotative* aspects (see Sutton (1992) for an extended discussion). Thus, our understanding of a term such as *water*, for example, comprises denotative elements such as covalent molecule (formula H_2O), with intermolecular hydrogen bonding, H–O–H bond angle = 105°, BP 100 °C and so on, together with all the other non-scientific associations it has for us: runny, wet, cold, used for making tea and washing the car. Often, this framework of associations and connotations will include attitudinal and emotional elements located in previous experience. *Force* may arouse feelings of anxiety, fear or anger; *water* may conjure up happy memories of windsurfing or distressing ones of nearly drowning; *spider* may trigger feelings of revulsion. For any individual, the meaning of a word or phrase is the current array of denotative and connotative aspects. It will necessarily vary from individual to individual; it will change over time in response to experience; and it will be strongly influenced by the sociocultural contexts in which the individual moves. Learning is a matter of adding to, modifying and sometimes deleting elements from this complex of meanings and understandings.

In teaching science, it is the teacher's task to assist students in modifying and developing their personal framework of understanding in order to incorporate the desired scientific aspects of meaning and an appreciation of when their use is appropriate. Of course, these 'approved meanings' jostle alongside a wide range of personal, idiosyncratic meanings and associations. It is the capacity to select and use appropriate aspects of our personal framework of understanding in response to different circumstances that is at the core of learning: knowing, for example, when to use a model and when to use a theory, or which particular aspects of a concept's meaning to use for different tasks. Moreover, it is often the array of personal, idiosyncratic and emotional connotations that render the scientific aspects more meaningful to us.

It has been traditional in science education to ignore these 'other' aspects of meaning, even to attempt to suppress or eliminate them: hence the use of specialized scientific terms and the insistence on a formalized linguistic code. Students are instructed not to use 'fizzing', much less to use 'a seething frothing turmoil' (as I recently saw in a 12-year-old's notebook), to describe the reaction of dilute hydrochloric acid with zinc. *Effervescence* is the approved term, precisely because it is not an everyday term. Similarly, Greek and Latin terms are often employed in science with the specific intent of eliminating 'unwanted' associations. While the increased explanatory power of specialized terms such as *photosynthesis* is sometimes a sufficient argument for their use, it is also the case that jargonization can increase difficulty and decrease interest for some children. It may even alienate some children from science. By contrast, it is likely that these 'other' aspects of meaning, with their everyday associations, can provide the key anchoring points for new learning, and so render it more meaningful. We should be encouraging rather than discouraging the connotative aspects of understanding.

Similar arguments extend to the formalized language of conventional instruction and the even more ludicrous formalized writing style often demanded of students, where they are dissuaded from saying that 'Julie and I did such and such' in favour of 'Procedure *x* was performed on . . .'. Lemke (1987) criticizes teachers for emphasizing the formal language of science to the exclusion of everyday ways of speaking and writing, arguing that too great an insistence on careful and precise language may help to promote an ideology of authority concerning science and lead students to believe that scientific knowledge is fixed and certain. By contrast, he says, more familiar vocabulary and language forms help students to see the relationship between science and the real world and to appreciate how scientific knowledge derives from everyday, commonsense knowledge (but see later discussion). A related point is that we need to draw a distinction between language as a means of exploring understanding and language as a means of transmitting knowledge to others – another matter to be discussed in Chapter 13.

Other factors influencing conceptual change

When Posner *et al.* (1982) assert that conceptual change occurs when a student becomes dissatisfied with an existing idea and recognizes a new idea as intelligible, plausible and fruitful, they seem to imply that conceptual change is an entirely rational process. Indeed, it has become common practice to interpret these conditions for change as a matter of learners simply making a choice based on compelling evidence and argument. However, decisive decisions based on a rational appraisal of evidence for and against particular ideas may be impossible. Concepts cannot be 'evaluated' separately from their relationships with other concepts and the roles they play within conceptual structures (theories and models). As a consequence, no theory-independent means of appraisal is available. Moreover, conceptual change or modification often has a 'knock-on' effect, requiring a change to other, well established understanding that some students may resist for complex emotional and social reasons.

If the community of scientists changes its views (or not) for all kinds of 'non-rational' reasons, as discussed in Chapter 2, why should it be any different for individuals? Surely one cannot assign non-rational motives to a group without also doing so to the individuals that comprise it. Other factors that might influence an individual learner's acceptance or rejection of an idea include: interest; perception of relevance; self-interest; feelings of anxiety, uncertainty, satisfaction, confidence and pride; aesthetic, political, economic and moral-ethical concerns; and so on. When teachers make the assumption that a clear understanding of the evidential justification of an idea will result in its ready acceptance, they fail to account satisfactorily for why some students who seem to have the requisite prior conceptual knowledge, and the intellectual capability to appraise the evidence, fail to engage in cognitive restructuring. They also tacitly accept the obverse: that when students decline to incorporate a particular idea into their personal framework of understanding it is because they don't understand the scientific evidence that supports it. As a consequence, they may misdirect their teaching efforts and, in doing so, may reinforce the student's reluctance to accept it.

By contrast, the view that learning in science should be regarded as the development of a personal framework of understanding, within which multiple meanings (some contradictory) can coexist, acknowledges the realities of scientific practice and the realities of ordinary daily life. Because it acknowledges that personal meaning includes an array of highly personal experiential and affective elements, it also recognizes the significance of these same factors in bringing about conceptual change and development. Posner *et al.* (1982: 215) admit something along these lines when they refer to the influence of 'epistemological commitments' to 'elegance, economy, parsimony, and not being *ad hoc*'. West and Pines (1983: 38) extend this line of argument to include four 'feeling components of conceptual change': feelings of power (which makes learners feel good), simplicity in complexity (which is emotionally satisfying), aesthetics (principally beauty, harmony and balance) and personal integrity (without which 'humans feel uncomfortable'). Students are also likely to have strongly held intuitive feelings about what can and cannot be true and what counts as a valid and reasonable explanation, similar to the feelings that Holton (1978, 1986) acknowledges as legitimate for scientists (Chapter 2).

Not least among the non-rational factors influencing learning is social pressure: other students who hold a particular view, especially students who are important, either in a personal sense or with respect to the student power hierarchy, may create massive social pressure to conform, so precipitating and legitimating a change of view. Perhaps, then, reaching consensus within the class should be regarded as an important teaching strategy (Meyer and Woodruff 1997). Exactly the same forces are at work, of course, within the scientific community, where opinion is led and strongly influenced (even determined) by major figures whom we might call the 'gatekeepers' of community opinion. It is also the case that each individual is a member of several social groups, each of which will exert social pressures to conform. The personal framework of understanding view of learning allows for the proliferation of meaning in response to entry into additional social groups. Another important part of this complex of non-rational factors is one's self-perception. If successful learning depends on learners exploring and developing their store of personal knowledge, and if a significant part of that personal knowledge is experientially determined and includes powerful affective components, then social and cultural identity become significant factors affecting learning. In other words, one's gender, ethnicity, religion and politics, as well as one's emotional well-being, impact very considerably on learning.

Put simply, how students feel about the ideas being presented to them, for whatever reasons, influences their learning. Feelings of wonder, delight, amusement, interest, disinterest, boredom and disgust will clearly impact in different ways on a learning task – sometimes favourably, sometimes unfavourably. Bloom (1992) shows how emotions, values and aesthetics can influence not only students' willingness or reluctance to engage in a learning task, but also the kinds of meanings that they construct – in the case of the data he presents, about earthworms. Clearly, students will have a strong emotional commitment to ideas that are well established and have been used successfully by them in contexts they regard as personally and/or socially important. Indeed, some ideas are so much a part of the student's everyday life that they are used automatically and unconsciously. Changing them is not easy, especially when they continue to be used by their peers and within family groups, and are promoted by religious teachings or the practices of other sociocultural groups to which the student belongs. Abelson (1986) describes some views as being like 'possessions': they have become so much a part of the student's view of self and sense of identity, held in the face of otherwise substantial changes, that if ever they were abandoned it would only be with the greatest reluctance and an acute sense of loss and discomfort. Similarly, accepting views that are in opposition to views accepted within other groups to which the student belongs or wishes to belong may be so emotionally stressful that it becomes virtually impossible. What I am suggesting is that Posner et al.'s (1982) conditions for conceptual change need to incorporate a new element: that students feel *comfortable* with the new idea, in the sense that it meets their emotional needs and is 'culturally safe'. Mulkay (1979: 41) points to the existence of these kinds of culturally determined predispositions, socialized values, unquestioned assumptions and emotional commitments within the practice of science when he says: 'Most scientific research is carried out in a context in which a whole series of assumptions are so firmly entrenched that their revision or refutation is virtually unthinkable.'

It is also the case that some students seem to be more open to new ideas than others, and that these differences are present from an early age (Rokeach 1960). For some, reluctance to change ideas stems from a deep-seated fear of uncertainty. Such students are distrustful of new ideas unless they are presented with authority. Consequently, they seek certainty in knowledge, rather than the ambiguity, fluidity and context-dependence that is characteristic of learning viewed as the development of a personal framework of understanding. A very supportive classroom environment is essential if these students are to accommodate to a learning style in which they are encouraged to proffer their own developing ideas and to regard current ideas (including misconceptions) simply as potentially useful steps on the path to better understanding. Watts and Bentley (1987) discuss the kinds of changes that are essential, most of which can be summed up as having a teacher with warmth, sensitivity and humour.

Learning conceptualized as the continuous development of personal frameworks of understanding involves taking risks. Asking questions, expressing one's ideas and criticizing and challenging the views of others are all risk-taking activities which can be too much for some children, at least in the early stages. Learning to debate, to give and accept vigorous and rigorous criticism and to negotiate shared meaning all require a substantial measure of self-confidence and tolerance of uncertainty. Fear of ridicule and the risk of losing status when one's ideas are rejected by others might be sufficient to dissuade some students from engaging in these tasks. Again, it is vital that teachers develop the kind of emotional climate in which everyone feels free enough, safe enough and confident enough to participate.

In addition to making students feel comfortable within the classroom, teachers must also strive to ensure that students feel comfortable within science itself. Moje (1995) points out some of the ways in which teachers' use of language can promote a sense of belonging within the classroom that extends to a sense of belonging within the scientific community. It is also important to recognize that if particular forms of language and language use can influence the thinking and attitudes of students in a positive way, they can also act to exclude or alienate students, or contribute to their feelings of frustration and inadequacy. Adopting appropriate forms of language is just as much a part of curriculum decision making as choosing among theories of learning.

We should also bear in mind that when students are presented with a learning task they may perceive it in a way that is in marked contrast to the way in which the teacher saw it during the planning stage. Consequently, their actions may be somewhat different from those anticipated. Rather than attending to the rational appraisal of competing explanations in order to extend their understanding, for example, students may be actively engaged in any number of other pursuits, including: seeking teacher approval for compliant behaviour; trying to look busy, thereby avoiding unwelcome teacher attention; ascertaining the 'right answer' (that is, the one that gains marks in tests); trying to maintain feelings of self-worth; attending to their 'classroom image'. These other agenda may lead students to adopt behaviour and make responses that are not helpful in bringing about better scientific understanding.

One final point is worth making: teachers often stop teaching at the point where they feel they have helped students to appreciate the essence of the topic under consideration, at the point where they feel students can recall the basic points of a theory and cite its use in a single, simple context. This doesn't enable students to penetrate the deeper layers of meaning of the theory or to make their personal frameworks of understanding more like those of scientists by using theory in varied contexts. The skilled use of conceptual and procedural knowledge that constitutes scientific connoisseurship only results when formal knowledge can be adapted rapidly and appropriately to specific contexts and problems. The capacity to respond in this way is, in part, a product of a framework of personal understanding in which key concepts are located in a rich and varied array of contextual referents. Much school science learning stops well short of providing opportunities for students to acquire this richness. As Weck (1995: 1290) comments: 'Our very attempts to condense and distill out the essence of our disciplines as an aid to student learning helps reinforce a cultural habit of representational short-cutting (i.e. sound-bites, acronyms, and catch phrases).' By trying to ensure the completion of the syllabus, in what is often an unrealistically brief time allocation, teachers sometimes encourage partial understanding. Often, students are rewarded for simply being able to repeat verbatim a collection of phrases from textbooks. Little attempt is made to probe for deeper levels of understanding or to ascertain whether students can utilize their supposed knowledge in novel situations. By not checking, and by not ensuring that knowledge is properly appropriated and personalized, teachers maintain a classroom culture in which misunderstanding flourishes.

Notes

1 A series of articles in *The New Zealand Herald, The Dominion* and other provincial newspapers, two symposia at the University of Auckland and the publication of a book under the title *Challenging New Zealand Science Education* (Matthews 1995) generated nationwide controversy about constructivism and precipitated the publication of a detailed rebuttal of the Matthews arguments by other New Zealand science educators (Bell 1995).

2 In the final version of the curriculum (Ministry of Education 1993: 9), this is modified to read 'an activity that *is* carried out by all people as part of their everyday life' (my emphasis). The change may represent an even more worrying position.

3 A term used to identify those views in the sociology of science influenced by and following in the tradition of David Bloor's (1976) *Knowledge and Social Imagery* (London: Routledge and Kegan Paul).

4 The essence of radical constructivism is that 'knowledge' refers to the conceptual structures that 'epistemic agents' consider 'viable' (work for them). Thus, science does not provide truth about the natural world (or anything that aspires to it). Instead, it provides a way to interpret and cope with the natural world that will vary substantially from person to person. These central tenets are captured in these two quotations: 'Knowledge does not reflect an "objective" ontological reality, but exclusively an ordering and organization of a world constituted by our experience' (von Glasersfeld 1987: 199). 'The basic elements out of which an individual's conceptual structures are composed and the relations by means of which they are held together cannot be transferred from one language user to another ... they must be abstracted from individual experience' (von Glasersfeld 1989: 132). A

detailed critique of von Glasersfeld's views can be found in Suchting (1992), Matthews (1994) and Kelly (1997), with a response in von Glasersfeld (1992). In addition, a special issue of *Science and Education* (1997, 6(1–2)) includes ten articles and a lengthy bibliography dealing with philosophical aspects of constructivism.

5 While I acknowledge Sutton's (1992) concerns that 'framework' can suggest something that is fixed, I find the term *personal framework of meaning* useful for my purposes. What I have in mind is a network of relationships that is subject to continuous modification and development, and within which different aspects are prominent on different occasions.

• • • 6

Prioritizing the affective

It is fundamental to the personalized view of learning being developed in this book that the behaviour and eventual attainment of students in science lessons can only be properly understood as the response of a 'whole person' to a complex educational situation involving other 'whole people' (teachers and other students). The cognitive nature of the task is only part of the cluster of variables that influence learning. There are many other elements, including personal concerns and feelings, issues from other lessons and from outside school (some unresolved or only partly resolved), competing priorities and ambitions, self-assessment of personal capabilities and limitations (accurate or not), social mood and structure of the class, feelings and assumptions about the teacher and so on. In other words, a complex of items comprises the social and emotional context in which the learning task is located. A crucial part of that learning context is the view of themselves as learners that students hold.

Within a particular lesson, students will adopt a stance (as Claxton 1990 calls it) that they believe will maximize their goals, whatever they might be, and minimize threats and sanctions. Now, because the range of goals and threats is as much social and emotional as intellectual, a selected stance sets parameters for both academic endeavour and other kinds of classroom behaviour. As well as accessing (or not) the appropriate scientific concepts and generally adopting a 'scientific mind set', students are cued to a particular view of learning (learning by rote, searching for deep understanding, exploring the personal significance of the topic or whatever) and to a particular classroom demeanour (quiet, sociable, enthusiastic, disruptive etc.). Although each learner's set of stances, from which she or he chooses a response to a particular situation, will be idiosyncratic, depending on his or her particular hopes, fears and experiences, there are some common, generalized stances that all teachers recognize. Claxton (1990) lists swot, boffin, socialite, dreamer and rebel; others might include jocks, jokers and no-hopers. He describes how students select a classroom stance on the basis of an intuitive, largely unconscious decision-making process that may take into account any or all of the following considerations:

- What is my current portfolio of priorities (academic, vocational, emotional, social)?
- Which are compatible and which incompatible? Which are more urgent at this time?
- What opportunities (intellectual, behavioural, social) are presented by this situation?
- What sacrifices and penalties are associated with a particular choice?

Previous experience of the teacher, the curriculum and other students is brought to bear in a rapid analysis of the benefits and costs of adopting a particular stance. In addition to the more obvious questions of whether successful learning is likely and whether it is worth the effort that is judged necessary, this analysis includes all manner of complex emotional and social issues: What is my standing with this class, or this teacher? What is the impact on my self-esteem if I try and fail, or simply say something silly or wrong? If I try and I am successful, will too much be expected of me in future? If I decide to work hard, will the socialites and rebels make my life miserable? Will family members be disappointed or angry if I adopt the socialite or rebel stance? Do I care? Is it my intention to upset them? Will my friends disown me if I am successful in school? These are just some of the questions that students may ask – consciously or unconsciously – in deciding how to behave in class. Clearly, individuals will differ in the particular questions they ask, the answers they consider and the relative weighting afforded to the answers, and it almost goes without saying that all this will be impacted by a student's social class, gender and ethnicity.

Some students may shift stances from lesson to lesson, from topic to topic or even within a lesson. As Claxton (1989) says, swots may become socialites or dreamers if they think the lesson is no longer on track; socialites and rebels may 'tune in' when the teacher introduces something they consider relevant or provocative; socialites may become rebels if they consider they have been treated unfairly; swots may become no-hopers in the face of failure or frustration. Sometimes considerable differences are evident between subjects, so that teachers are wont to say, 'We can't be talking about the same Debbie Jones!' Those who are swots in high-status subjects (English, maths and science) may take 'time out' to attend to their social image during what they perceive as less important subjects – music, art, religious education, for example. Sadly, some students become locked into a particular stance all the time; Stipek (1993) refers to Defensive Dick, Hopeless Hannah, Safe Sally, Satisfied Sam and Anxious Amy, though she doesn't list Bullying Bernard, Wise-cracking Wilfred and Rebellious Rita.

Building a view of self as learner

If Claxton, Stipek and others are right, students are constantly appraising the educational situations in which they are located, constantly making decisions based upon their estimates of competing priorities, opportunities, demands, resources and risks. Only when the emotional and motivational factors considered in the cost–benefit analysis and decision making result in a decision that permits or encourages involvement in learning will students engage in the task. So it is only in those cases that significant attainment is possible. Moreover, all kinds of social forces, including sexism and racism, may act to restrict an individual's freedom for choice, creating the kinds of injustices that prevent those from particular subcultural groups having proper access to science education. Those who utilize crude notions of intellectual ability or intelligence to account for academic attainment seriously misjudge the nature of the learning enterprise. Capacity to learn cannot and should not be inferred from current levels of attainment and current classroom behaviour. Such crudeness fails to take account of the complexity and sub-tlety of the decision making that underpins a learner's classroom stance. And it fails to take account of the considerable variations in emotional climate between classrooms and, from student to student, even within a classroom.

Just as one's ability to do science and to learn science depend on prior knowledge (of science), so one's response to a particular situation, including classroom events, depends on one's previous experience (good and bad) of similar situations. How we act and react to the world depends on how we perceive it, and how we perceive it depends on what has gone before and the understanding we have constructed about it. In one sense, then, there is no 'reality', merely our various perceptions of it. Consequently, one's learning behaviour depends on one's 'learning knowledge', and this is built up through experience of other learning situations and their outcomes. How a student responds to a learning task is largely driven by recollections of previous encounters and the feelings of satisfaction or dissatisfaction that resulted. Everything that happens in the classroom (presentation of information, giving of instructions, personal interactions, use of individual versus group work etc.) can have emotional impact, and this can vary considerably from individual to individual. Each student reacts at a personal level to both the personal characteristics and professional practices of her or his teachers.

In learning something new, one moves away from the familiarity and safety of the known into the uncertainty of the unknown. Mistakes are inevitable. Occasional feelings of confusion, apprehension and loss of confidence are inevitable. It would be surprising if learners didn't sometimes feel anxious, frustrated, distressed or even angry. An effective learning environment is one that develops each student's ability to anticipate and cope with these feelings. Unfortunately, many schools do a poor job in this respect. Claxton (1991) lists some of the more destructive beliefs about the relationship between learning and self-worth that schools often promote:

- worthwhile people do not make mistakes;
- worthwhile people always know what is going on;
- worthwhile people live up to, and within, their images of themselves;
- worthwhile people do not feel anxious, apprehensive or vulnerable.

Because of these falsehoods, the inevitable experiences of incompetence, being confused and feeling nervous that attend any difficult and uncertain learning task can induce feelings of guilt and shame, and can seriously impair some students' self-esteem. Learning becomes threatening and students defend themselves by avoiding it, becoming aggressive or excessively dependent on the teacher, or identifying themselves as failures. It is important that a clear distinction is drawn between the capacity to learn and the performance of learning. What students normally achieve in school and what they can achieve under more ideal circumstances are quite different. Many students can learn, but do not learn. What they lack is appropriate motivation and appropriate support from the teacher and the school.

Some elements of motivation

Motivation to engage in a learning task is composed of a cluster of factors internal to the learner, including: students' interests, needs, goals and aspirations; beliefs about their own worth, abilities, competencies and expectations of success; positive and negative feelings about the particular classroom environment and the kinds of activities that take place there. Motivation is also impacted by a cluster of factors external to the learner, including the responses of others (teachers, peers, parents) and the use of rewards, incentives, penalties and punishments.

According to Maslow (1970), basic human needs are arranged as a hierarchy. Needs at a lower level must be satisfied before we can attend to those at a higher level, and progress at higher levels is enhanced when lower level needs have been thoroughly met. Once basic physiological needs have been met, safety must be attended to – the learning environment must be made physically safe and emotionally secure for students. The need for 'love and belonging' comes next in priority: all children need to give and receive affection and to feel that they belong. At the next level, Maslow identifies two sets of needs associated with self-esteem: the desire for competence (adequacy, independence, personal autonomy and freedom) and the desire for recognition (reputation, prestige, importance, appreciation). He is reminding us that self-esteem has both internal and external dimensions. The final stage of Maslow's hierarchy is self-actualization, or fulfilling one's potential. Of course, part of self-actualization is self-realization: we have to know what we are capable of before we can know whether we are achieving our potential. Each of us needs to clarify our personal ambitions and gain an understanding of the extent to which they are achievable. Among the characteristics of those who have achieved self-actualization, Maslow

(1970) lists the following: a better perception of reality; acceptance of self and others; spontaneity, simplicity and naturalness; problem-centredness (the individual has some mission in life or task to fulfil); autonomy; openness to new experiences and understanding; sympathetic understanding of others; deeper and more profound interpersonal relations; democratic in outlook; sense of humour; creative; resistant to assimilation. In a later work, Maslow (1971) also talks about the further goal of self-transcendence, in which reflection and contemplation give rise to deeper and richer levels of intuition.

It is central to Maslow's theory that the affective needs lower in the hierarchy must have been thoroughly met before any significant progress in the cognitive domain can be made. The point is clearly made: a stable emotional climate is essential to cognitive growth. In a trusting and supportive environment, learners are willing to take the intellectual risks that are the key to developing more sophisticated understanding. When they feel threatened or insecure, or feel that they are not loved and valued, they may withdraw. Further, if we are to reach higher levels of the cognitive hierarchy, we must foster each child's self-esteem and self-actualization. Of course, Maslow's work can be seen either as a way of identifying learning problems (through diagnosis of inadequately met needs) or as a guide to more effective curriculum building, depending on our penchant for 'deficiency models' of education versus 'growth models'. As an aside, it is worth mentioning that teachers have these same needs, and a school intent on creating a better learning environment for all students should also pay attention to meeting the needs of its teachers – an aspect of school life that is often woefully neglected.

While subsequent research and theorizing about motivation have generated many areas of dispute and controversy, there is an emerging consensus on which teachers can draw. First, all of us (students and teachers) have a need for experiences that generate feelings of competence, accomplishment, recognition and self-esteem, and a need to avoid those that generate feelings of failure, worthlessness and disapproval. Second, all individuals have a natural tendency to be intrinsically motivated when enabled to focus on personal learning goals without fear of failure, and when learning is perceived as personally meaningful and relevant, and meets the needs for autonomy and self-determination – that is, when we can make decisions and have some control over the learning process.

Some years ago, Vroom (1964) conceptualized motivation as the product of *value* and *expectancy*:

$$motivation = value \times expectancy$$

We are only motivated to learn when we value, in a personal sense, that which is to be learned. If we don't care about it, if we don't see it as relevant to our needs, interests, aspirations and experiences, we are unlikely to have the necessary commitment to learn. This is a strikingly clear message about the importance of both content and context in science curriculum design (see Chapter 1). It also reminds us to ensure clarity of learning task, so that students perceive it in the way it was intended.

The other factor in Vroom's equation tells us that in order to be motivated to learn we have to expect that we can learn successfully. In school, students' expectation of success would normally come from evidence of past success, or lack of it, and from the teacher's expectations, as communicated to them in all manner of explicit and implicit ways. In Rosenthal and Jacobson's (1968: 180) classic study *Pygmalion in the Classroom*, the researchers conclude:

> By what she said, by how and when she said it, by her facial expressions, postures, and perhaps by her touch, the teacher may have communicated to the children of the experimental group that she expected improved intellectual performance. Such communications together with possible changes in teaching techniques may have helped the child learn by changing his self concept, his expectations of his own behavior, and his motivation, as well as his cognitive style and skills.

Presumably, the reverse effect – inadvertently depressing a child's performance through implicitly transmitted messages – is also possible and, tragically, perhaps this is more common. Lengthy and detailed research by Dweck *et al.* (1978) revealed startling and disturbing gender-related differences in teachers' verbal interactions with students, which resulted in differences between boys' and girls' views of the reasons for success and failure in class. Teachers tended to interact positively with boys and negatively with girls with regard to the intellectual quality of their work, while interacting negatively with boys and positively with girls regarding non-intellectual aspects. In addition, in cases of failure, they referred directly to lack of motivation more frequently with boys than they did with girls. As a consequence, girls tended to place less emphasis than did boys on effort (or lack of it) as a cause of failure and were more likely than boys to attribute failure to a lack of ability.

Vroom's work suggests two sites for curriculum intervention. First is providing a curriculum that students value – there is evidence, for example, that students put higher value on social considerations, environmental issues and aesthetic and humanitarian aspects of science than on more traditional science content (Aikenhead 1994). Second is raising students' expectancy levels by ensuring that everyone experiences successful learning. Unfortunately, most students expect science to be difficult and, too often, teachers reinforce this expectation by making science in schools difficult. It doesn't have to be that way! We can set reasonable and achievable targets, we can locate essential science learning in contexts that are interesting and meaningful to students.

What seems beyond dispute is that the greater the success of the learner, the stronger the tendency to raise levels of aspiration, provided that success doesn't come too easily. For example, Solomon (1996) shows that when students are assisted in performing better in examinations by the provision of 'revision sheets', even if they employ rote learning methods, self-esteem is enhanced and better learning follows. By contrast, unexpected and continued failures tend to lower students' levels of aspiration. Moreover, persistent failure prevents students from making a reasonable estimate of their capabilities, and so prevents them setting realistic goals for themselves. However, failures can sometimes be useful learning experiences, both cognitively (provided there is productive feedback) and affectively (perhaps everyone needs to experience failure once in a while, but in a supportive emotional climate). It seems that a judicious use of success and (limited) failure could form a productive classroom strategy. It is worth noting, however, that highly valued goals may sometimes trigger a lowering of levels of aspiration, as students strive to ensure some measure of success.

Of particular interest to teachers, of course, is why some students persist in their efforts to learn, even when the task is complex and difficult, while others do not. There is evidence that even some high achieving students, many of them girls, have surprisingly low expectations of their future performance in science and are easily debilitated by any failure to learn. As a consequence, they tend to avoid difficult or challenging tasks or give up as soon as things begin to get tough. Nicholls (1984, 1989) calls these strategies *maladaptive* motivational patterns. By contrast, *adaptive* motivational patterns are those that lead students to engage positively in challenging tasks and to gain satisfaction from doing so. Students exhibiting these characteristics are often very persistent, even in the face of obstacles. Dweck (1986) argues that a key factor in determining motivational patterns is the student's view or theory of intelligence. Those who believe that intelligence is fixed (and genetically determined) tend to be oriented towards 'providing evidence' of that intelligence, and gaining the teacher's favourable judgement of it through the successful completion of tasks – that is, they have *performance* goals. Those who believe that intelligence is a more malleable or developmental quality tend to be oriented towards developing that quality and acquiring or developing understanding – that is, they have *learning* goals. Different goals initiate different patterns of learning behaviour, patterns that are reinforced by teachers' educational priorities, views of learning, expectations of student attainment and beliefs about intelligence.

Students who consider intelligence to be a fixed quantity regard cognitive tasks as occasions during which their intelligence will be assessed and, possibly, their weaknesses exposed, while those who consider intelligence to be a malleable and acquired skill see cognitive tasks as opportunities to 'become smarter'. It follows that these latter students are much more favourably inclined towards challenging cognitive activities. Moreover, students who consider intelligence to be an acquired skill probably believe that successful learning has resulted in a significant change in their ability to think, whereas students who believe intelligence to be fixed will simply see it as further evidence of a capability they knew they already had.

Promoting good and bad habits

In a situation where teachers convey to students, either implicitly or explicitly, that they regard intelligence as a fixed quantity, those students who are oriented towards performance goals will make an early decision about their capacity to complete any task that is set. If they estimate that they cannot succeed, they will attempt to conceal their perceived lack of ability, protecting themselves by task avoidance behaviour. Whenever choice of task is possible, they will choose personally easy tasks, where success is assured, or will opt for excessively difficult tasks, where failure doesn't matter because no one would be expected to succeed. In either case, they are protected from further external judgements concerning their ability and from the trauma of having to revise their self-estimates. Even individuals with high estimates of their ability may sacrifice valuable learning opportunities that involve risks of making mistakes in exchange for opportunities to 'look smart' on easy tasks. In other words, performance goals promote defensive strategies and avoidance of challenge. For these students, maintaining confidence is difficult. Errors and difficulties are readily interpreted as evidence of low ability and likely failure in the future. As a consequence, these students may give up. They withdraw from the very activities that would promote growth of understanding. Dweck (1986) points out that withdrawal is more common in science and mathematics than in other subjects because they are generally perceived by students as difficult subjects and, therefore, are seen as a greater threat to self-esteem.

By contrast, students oriented towards learning goals are encouraged by challenge and are willing to risk displaying their ignorance in order to acquire skills or knowledge through experience. Instead of estimating their ability level in relation to the task in hand, and wondering how they will be judged by teachers and peers, these students concentrate on what they will learn, how they will benefit from engagement in the task and how interested they will be in it. Even when they estimate their ability as relatively low, such students will choose challenging tasks (that foster learning) because they believe they will learn from the experience. Maintaining confidence is not nearly so problematic for these students. They can, and do, exploit and use difficulties and errors; they learn from their mistakes, and use them to analyse performance and modify future strategy. As a consequence, performance improves.

Many of the traditional practices of science teachers serve to reinforce the bad habits of performance-oriented students and to penalize the more productive strategies of those who are learning-oriented. For example, while learning-oriented students are more likely to seek understanding through what Entwistle (1981) calls 'deep processing', performance-oriented students, with their tendency to seek affirmation through marks and grades, may be content to seek superficial recall through 'surface processing', because simple recall is what tests and examinations usually reward. Often, maximum marks are gained by reproducing material from text and class notes in exactly the form in which the teacher presented it. To do that, the student does not have to think very deeply about it, or to reorder or restructure the ideas. Many of these students don't even recognize how superficial their understanding is, and so don't take steps to improve it. Moreover, learning-oriented students, who do engage in restructuring in order to personalize their understanding, don't gain sufficient extrinsic reward for having done so. In many schools, self-directed effort to understand the material is wasted effort as far as tangible reward is concerned.

A learning orientation is likely to be encouraged or discouraged by the extent to which the teacher requires, encourages, accepts, tolerates or actively discourages idiosyncracy and the expression of personalized meaning. Detecting and pointing out errors in students' work, and providing informative and corrective feedback quickly, and within a stable and supportive emotional climate, are further steps a teacher can take. In a sense, this speaks to the charge of relativism levelled at some constructivists in Chapter 5. When students pass tests by simple recall of previously given notes, as in traditional learning situations, there is little incentive to engage in the difficult and emotionally challenging business of making personalized meaning. However, when constructivist-oriented teachers accept student explanations and answers that are inappropriate, incomplete or wrong, as Matthews (1993a, 1995) suggests they often do, student misunderstanding is compounded, science is trivialized and bad learning habits are reinforced. Teachers need to be demanding in the quality of response they expect, as otherwise performance-oriented students will be content with giving sloppy and ill-considered answers. They also need to be flexible enough to recognize interesting and worthwhile responses that don't simply reproduce textbook language, as otherwise learning-oriented students will be discouraged and performance-oriented students will be further encouraged to engage in simple recall. It is also important to provide vigorous, personalized and informative feedback on student errors. When students are wrong, they need to know that they are wrong, and why.[1] It is here that I part company with those constructivists who carefully avoid labelling any student idea a misconception. Self-esteem and motivation are not well served by pretence of success. Students also need to know how they can avoid similar errors in future.

The commitment to positive reinforcement methods, particularly the use of frequent praise in response to small units of approved behaviour or fairly minimal correct responses, can be counterproductive. Presenting performance-oriented children with very easy tasks in familiar contexts does nothing to help them deal later on with challenging and unfamiliar tasks. If anything, it serves to make them even more afraid of them. Instead of rewarding success in trivial tasks, we should be encouraging students to regard learning problems differently. Rather than attributing their failure to learn or understand to lack of ability, we should encourage students to attribute it to the selection of an inappropriate learning strategy (which can, of course, be readily changed). We should be assisting students to expect difficulties and obstacles, rather than to avoid them, to see them as 'bugs' or 'glitches' that can be overcome by rethinking or replanning. Thus, failure to solve a problem can be taken as a further learning opportunity, a chance to reorder one's ideas. While some might regard this suggestion as hopelessly idealistic and pie-in-the-sky, it is worth reflecting that virtually identical shifts in students' perceptions of errors and mistakes in writing activities have been brought about by more extensive use of wordprocessing activities.

As with other aspects of motivation, it may be helpful to think of students' beliefs about their capacity to complete a task as situation-specific. Sometimes confidence can be productive, sometimes not. For example, when students have confidence in their existing knowledge they may be unwilling to change or develop their ideas. The more confidence they have in their understanding, the more resistant to change those ideas may be. What is more productive of good learning is not so much a confidence in one's understanding (though there are occasions when this is important, too) as confidence in one's ability to reconceptualize and reorganize that understanding, confidence in one's ability to think, gather evidence and consider rival arguments in order to bring about change and development in oneself and others. This kind of confidence is rooted in metacognitive awareness and is fostered by the kinds of activities discussed in Chapter 4. Students can be given more explicit guidance in how to restructure and expand their personal framework of understanding in specific science contexts through modelling and scaffolding (see Chapters 8 and beyond). There may also be a role for peer group tutoring. Seeing others experiencing difficulties, which they subsequently overcome, can have positive effects on students' beliefs in their own ability to perform these tasks.

Classroom language is another important focus for attention. Implicit teacher expectations are conveyed to students through the wording of class assignments. Careless phrasing can inadvertently promote a performance orientation. So, too, can the use of 'simplified theories', convenient models, analogies and metaphors to 'get the point across' without making clear to students their limited instrumental role. Students already inclined towards a performance orientation may thereby be encouraged to recall and repeat these pedagogical devices as explanations or solutions to a problem, instead of using them, as the teacher intended, to develop a deeper understanding.

Kruglanski (1989) accounts for different patterns of student involvement in learning tasks in terms of what he calls a theory of *epistemic motivation*. He posits two general dimensions of epistemic motivation: seeking or avoiding closure and specificity/non-specificity of closure. 'Seeking closure' refers to an individual's desire to obtain an 'answer', thereby ending further cognitive engagement; 'avoiding closure' is the tendency to delay settling on an answer in order to continue thinking. Setting time limits will generate a need for closure, while stressing the costs or penalties of being wrong will lead to a need to avoid closure. The need for specific or non-specific closure depends, of course, on the extent to which a teacher demands clear and unambiguous answers. These two motivational elements interact with a student's prior knowledge, which may be extensive or sparse, to produce different epistemic motivational responses. For example, when students with little relevant knowledge are presented with a need for non-specific closure, they may work well until they find an answer, any answer, at which point they will stop. Those with extensive knowledge may not even begin the task, because they believe they already have an answer that will suffice. Creating the need for specific closure will motivate both groups of students to persist longer in order to find an answer that meets the specificity criteria. However, if there are high costs associated with being wrong, students may avoid closure altogether. Those students with low levels of knowledge will adopt an 'ignorance-is-bliss' approach and avoid reaching an answer at all; those with extensive knowledge may try to find as many feasible answers as possible to avoid being 'pinned down' and judged right or wrong.

Teachers who reinforce students' bad habits may contribute to what some psychologists call 'learned helplessness', a condition in which individuals believe that they are unable to surmount negative outcomes. The most striking characteristic of 'helpless students' is their tendency to view failure as predictive, while discounting their successes. The tendency to discount success cannot help but have adverse impact on students' persistence on a complex or difficult task. Thus, helpless students, who explain their failures in ways that make failures seem uncontrollable, persist less (regardless of their actual ability level) and resort to progressively less effective strategies for problem-solving following failure. Those teachers who reinforce their students' good habits assist them to become learning-oriented or mastery-oriented. In contrast to helpless students, mastery-oriented students tend to interpret failure as a cue to escalate their efforts. They view feedback about failure as useful information they can use in altering their strategy or reconsidering the effort they expend. As a consequence, they often respond to failure with increased persistence or improved problem-solving efficiency (Diener and Dweck 1978). They also appear to be able to tolerate a lapse from perfect performance and still regard themselves as successful (Diener and Dweck 1980).

The foregoing discussion suggests three major targets for intervention: the student and his or her views of self as learner; the curriculum; the overall emotional climate of the classroom.

Helping learners to help themselves

I have suggested already that a learning or mastery orientation is likely to be assisted by explicit teaching of metacognitive strategies. Students who have more useful knowledge about learning strategies, and the circumstances in which they are and are not successful, have a greater sense of control of their learning and greater confidence in their capacity to deal successfully with difficult or novel problems. Bad learning habits can be cured or avoided altogether, good learning techniques can be taught and students can become habituated into monitoring and developing their learning behaviours. Gunstone (1994) reports that even students as young as 8 years old can be made 'learning conscious', a vital early step on the path to intellectual independence. However, what I now propose is a much more ambitious role for metacognition, and the crux of this chapter's argument for prioritizing the affective: assisting students in reconstructing themselves as learning-oriented, intrinsically motivated students. There are two major steps: (a) understanding the ways in which thinking can influence one's moods and behaviour; (b) recognizing that these thoughts can be brought under more conscious control.

Knowledge and beliefs about oneself built up over the years, such as 'I am no good at science', play a crucial role in motivation and classroom behaviour only if we are unaware that we can change the influence and control these thoughts have on our feelings and behaviour. Just as our conceptual and procedural knowledge store changes and, thereby, enables us to learn new science and to do more and different science, so our perception of classrooms and learning environments can change and, thereby, can lead to different learning behaviours. By understanding and controlling one's thinking, it is possible to proceed beyond a conditioned belief system.[2] In other words, if feelings come from thoughts and thoughts are generated by ourselves, then each of us can control our feelings by controlling what we think. Feelings originate inside our thinking minds! Once you understand how your own mind works, the negative belief 'I am no good at science' can be overridden by the alternative understanding that 'I can control the thoughts and emotions that feed these beliefs and, therefore, I can act differently.' The argument I am presenting is that students are capable of understanding the relationships among their beliefs, feelings and motivational levels; they can gain personal control (agency) over their thinking and acquire the ability to be self-motivated. It is possible for students to identify (some of) the factors that may hinder their learning and to recognize that it is how they feel about these things that disrupts positive feelings and the motivation to learn. By choosing to redirect their thoughts – in essence, by gaining a different perspective – they can overcome them and redirect their efforts in more positive directions.

Some easy-to-use strategies for helping students to understand their psychological functioning, build self-esteem, enhance autonomy and maximize intrinsic motivation can be found in Timm (1992), Raffini (1993) and McCombs and Pope (1994). Early stages include increasing students' awareness of being actively engaged in creating thoughts, beliefs and attitudes. This is the first step in helping them to feel in control of their own development and their own 'reality'. By understanding their own thinking and knowledge building, they are empowered to control it and, in turn, to *choose* their emotions, motivation and behaviour. By recognizing the ways in which different people construct different 'realities', students can reach awareness that their own reality could be different and, perhaps, should be different. The next stage – identifying sources of insecurity and anxiety, developing feelings of empathy with others, recognizing sources of interpersonal conflict and devising ways of peacefully resolving conflicts – has much in common with the strategies of peace education (Hicks 1988) and humane education (Selby 1995). It is followed by helping students to relate personal needs, interests and aspirations to learning goals and to shift from what Nicholls (1989) calls an *ego involvement* (concern with enhancing and protecting judgements about one's ability) to *task involvement* (concern with learning goals). Effecting this shift is largely a matter of judicious design and selection of learning activities to maximize intrinsic motivation and the adoption of appropriate assessment and evaluation strategies.

Some implications for curriculum

Learning activities can be classified in a number of ways in relation to their potential for fostering intrinsic motivation. Clearly, comprehension and evaluation tasks are more useful than simple memory tasks or routine, procedural exercises; personally meaningful tasks with strong sociopolitical overtones are more useful than sanitized, remote, abstract academic tasks. For Deci and Ryan (1985: 32), the desire to meet challenges is at the core of all intrinsically motivating activities, as is the need to feel competent and autonomous.

> The intrinsic needs for competence and self-determination motivate an ongoing process of seeking and attempting to conquer optimal challenges. When people are free from the intrusion of drives and emotions, they seek situations that interest them and require the use of their creativity and resourcefulness. They seek challenges that are suited to their competencies, that are neither too easy nor too difficult.

Almost any activity can become intrinsically motivating if it meets the following conditions.

- It provides an appropriate level of challenge and is perceived by students as challenging, meaningful and authentic (relevant to life outside the classroom).
- Informative feedback is provided on current levels of performance and advice is given concerning future learning strategy.
- The activity is free from other distractions and constraints.
- Learners are acting under their own volition.
- Orientation in assessment moves away from a concern with competition and comparison, and towards a focus on giving insight into the personalized framework of understanding of individual students, a move which may entail giving students some measure of choice regarding style of assessment.

Kruglanski's work points to the need for teachers to consider the motivational elements of a particular task for a particular learner. Blanket assumptions

of what motivates and what doesn't, and which students are motivated and which are not, are no longer appropriate. There are occasions when open-ended activities with no time constraints are appropriate, and there are situations in which time pressures and/or a demand for specific answers will be the wiser choice. It depends on the particular educational situation, and so is yet another case of the need for skilled teacher judgement by someone who knows the students well, and who knows the curriculum content well. In general, however, activities that are open-ended and create a need to avoid premature closure are more likely to facilitate conceptual restructuring. What is not clear is whether, given sensitive teacher intervention, the epistemic goal of avoiding closure on a particular task can override the much more general performance goal orientation of a particular student that demands closure in order to gain marks. Much may depend, of course, on the nature of the assessment scheme.

Hidi (1990) makes a similar point about generalized versus situation-specific motivation with regard to the motivational effect of interest. In addition to students' more general personal interest in science and learning science, which influences their overall levels of attention, involvement, effort and persistence in class, we need to consider the 'situational interest' of a particular activity. Although situational interest may not result in more time being spent on a task, it may result in better learning. It seems that high levels of situational interest lead to deeper processing and deployment of metacognitive control strategies, which are features of a mastery orientation. A situation could arise in which a student has a high level of interest in a particular topic, but also values it in a general sense because of its perceived long-term importance (for example, in entering a career). These circumstances give rise to both mastery goals (a desire to understand) and performance goals (a generalized concern for good grades) for the same activity. In such a case, it may be difficult for a student to decide how best to proceed. As before, resolution of the dilemma may come from a shift in assessment practices.

Since, in general, strong situational interest leads to a learning orientation, while generalized personal interest may not be sufficient to encourage students to proceed beyond a performance orientation, there are clear messages to teachers about the need for enlivening every topic in the programme, even for the supposedly 'good students' – that is, those generally interested in science and learning science, who consistently gain good grades. Features that increase students' situational interest include challenge, choice, novelty, fantasy (a much neglected aspect of science education), surprise and, of course, personal, social and environmental relevance. Clearly, there are optimal levels of challenge: too easy and there is no incentive; too difficult and students will soon give up. The key is to locate difficult problems in a context where students have the necessary knowledge already or where it is reasonable to expect them to be able to acquire it relatively easily. Vygotsky's (1978) notion of a *zone of proximal development* (see Chapter 8) is relevant here.

Confidence in one's ability to accomplish a task, no matter how well placed that confidence may be, does not necessarily translate into good learning behaviour. Students also need to feel a sense of control. First, they need to feel that they have personal control of their actions and are empowered to act in the way they consider appropriate; second, they need to feel that their actions will influence the eventual outcome and its consequences in the way they predict (Ames 1992). Choice of what to study, how to study and how to organize and present work increases students' perceptions of control, and often translates into deeper levels of processing and cognitive engagement and fosters the adoption of more effective metacognitive strategies. Achieving one's own goals is clearly more motivating than achieving someone else's! Project work is ideal for giving students a feeling of greater control, though there may be dangers in giving students too much choice too soon. It can be overwhelming for inexperienced students, who are unable to make responsible and productive decisions. Questions about choice of topic, whether to promote individual projects or group efforts and how much control of the various elements in the project to give to students are clearly a matter of teacher judgement, taking into account the particular circumstances and the particular students. Inexperienced students may be unable to exercise their control wisely. They may be tempted to spend more of their time on those topics where they already possess extensive knowledge, thus reinforcing their existing views, rather than changing or developing them.

One tactic is for teachers to retain control of content (directing students to new areas, as appropriate) while ceding control of learning methods or learning style to students. Riding *et al.* (1995) regard learning styles as distributed in a two-dimensional space defined by an *x*-axis from *verbalizing* to *imaging* and a *y*-axis from *analytical* to *holistic*. Science education has traditionally favoured analysts over holists and verbalizers over imagers, despite the fact that (a) individual preferences are developed early (often prior to 10 years old), and (b) it is reasonable to assume that learning would be assisted and motivation increased by allowing students to exercise their preference. Since Riding and colleagues argue that preference among learning styles can be changed by explicit teaching of alternatives, there is a case for providing a much wider range of teaching and learning methods than has been traditional in science education, together with much more explicit guidance on how to benefit from them. In this way, students' 'learning capabilities' as well as their 'learning consciousness' would be enhanced and they would be better equipped for those all too frequent occasions when choice is not allowed or not possible.

In their analysis of student control over learning strategies, Pintrich *et al.* (1993: 190) distinguish two aspects of metacognitive control: *tactical control* ('the students' ability to monitor and fine-tune thought as they work through the details of particular tasks'), which helps students to sustain the mental effort to remain on a specific task; and *strategic control* ('the ability to engage in purposeful thought over what might seem to be disconnected elements'), which helps them to coordinate and maintain efforts over longer periods of time. Both tactical and strategic control beliefs are necessary for successful engagement in problem-solving, project work and other complex learning tasks. Moreover, both categories of belief are fostered by engagement in these activities. In other words, students learn 'on the job' and, crucially, by critical reflection on it. As with all aspects of motivation, the issue of what counts as appropriate assessment is raised. Withdrawal from science learning and the fostering of performance-oriented students is often a direct consequence of our ego-oriented, competitive assessment practices. Even rewarding students for high levels of attainment can be problematic. Rewards can be perceived by students as a control device, thereby undermining their sense of autonomy and self-determination. Conversely, they can be perceived as external recognition of a developing competence and a signal of transition from novice to expert, thereby enhancing self-esteem. Considerable teacher judgement is involved in striking the proper balance.

In general, in most traditional forms of learning, intellectual challenge, personal interest and learner control are low, and teacher control is high. Good learning is fostered by a shift to high levels of learner control and personal interest, an appropriate level of intellectual challenge and minimal teacher control, but accompanied by lots of teacher guidance, support, encouragement and feedback. Teacher modelling can also play a significant role in bringing about the desired shift: modelling enthusiasm for learning, modelling expertise and the value of competence, showing that learning is valued in relation to personal goals,[3] modelling the processes of monitoring thoughts and moods in order to avoid and resolve conflicts. Teacher modelling is a matter on which more will be said in subsequent chapters.

Notes

1 It is also important that science teachers reconsider their views of what is right and wrong, appropriate and inappropriate, as subsequent discussion will clarify.
2 This 'escape from conditioned belief' is a key point in the underlying rationale of this book's arguments for the personalization of learning, and appears several times in different guises.
3 Discussing one's own professional development with students, and talking freely about attending conferences, enrolling for courses and writing for journals and newsletters, can send a very powerful signal to students.

• • • 7

Exploring some social dimensions of learning

Previous discussion has addressed some of the ways in which the feelings, beliefs and personal aspirations of students interact with the processes of cognitive restructuring. It has been argued that incorporation of a new idea into one's personal framework of understanding involves more than a rational appraisal in terms of its intelligibility, plausibility and fruitfulness. The idea also has to 'make sense' in affective terms. In other words, knowledge doesn't just have to make logical sense, it also has to feel right; students have to be *comfortable* with it. Being comfortable with an idea also has a social dimension. Each of us, whether adult or child, needs the agreement of others if we are to feel comfortable with our ideas, and each of us needs the approval and support of someone else if we are to feel personally validated. Thus, we often talk as much to get reassurance from others about our ideas as we do to convince others of our views. As Solomon (1987: 67) says, 'We take it for granted that those who are close to us see the world as we do, but, through social exchanges, we seek always to have this reconfirmed.'

These social exchanges also serve to establish what others think and so assist the learning of knowledge that has been validated and approved by the social groups to which we belong. Of course, we don't simply accept the views of others in the group unquestioningly, no more than others accept our views without question – though teachers, parents, priests, family physicians and the like may need to be constantly on their guard lest this should happen, especially with young children. Within most social groups, participants make tentative remarks to invite discussion and to seek consensus, making use of the comments of others to extend and modify their own understanding before reaching a firm conclusion. Thus, meaning is negotiated through social interaction. Within these groups, members also negotiate the social relationships with which they are comfortable, adopting a role as leader, tireless questioner, patient explainer, social facilitator and so on, though these roles may, of course, change over time. If meaning is, in part, socially constructed, it follows that different social groups can negotiate and construct different meanings. Moreover, since individuals have member-ship of more than one social group, they need to be familiar with more than one framework of understanding and to be able to access the knowledge, language and codes of behaviour appropriate to each group quickly and reliably, as the social situation changes. Furthermore, within any social group, individuals are continually adjusting their hopes, aspirations, attitudes and intentions in response to complex interpersonal interactions. They are also engaged in a continuing modification of their thoughts, ideas, codes of behavi-our, language usage and even their value positions, in response to the words and actions of other group members. Thus, there is a constant shifting of social roles, understandings and meanings in response to patterns of social interaction.

In terms of school science, this means that we have to pay attention to socially constructed meaning, and the ways in which it changes over time and with experience, as well as to individual understanding – an issue given more significance by the science teacher's extensive use of small group work, especially during practical work. It is during these activities, where students have to comprehend the instructions, collect and assemble apparatus, assign sub-tasks for manipulation of equipment and the taking and recording of readings, agree on the results to be presented, organize the return of the apparatus and the cleaning of the bench and so on, that the social dimen-sions of learning are writ especially large. The outcome of these activities depends on the quality of the social interactions within the group to an extent equal to its dependence on cognitive understanding of the task.

If we include social factors in our theories of how scientists build know-ledge (Chapter 2), it seems reasonable to include them in our theories about how students build knowledge. The same questions that sociologists ask about the ways in which scientists construct consensible and consensual knowledge from their experiences in the science laboratory, teachers should ask about the ways in which students construct a usable and personally meaningful scientific understanding from their experiences in the science classroom. Individuals learning science in school are not 'free agents', any more than scientists are. Both are constrained and driven by social pressures and group aspirations. Consequently, the adoption of some ideas and the rejection of others are likely to be influenced by the extent to which they are consistent with the image students hold of themselves or wish to have others hold of them. Students have many social goals – making friends, impressing others, attracting a girlfriend or boyfriend and so on – all or any of which can interfere with the supposedly rational process of learning. These 'goals for classroom life' will have significant impact on learning as individuals negotiate for themselves a role that maximizes personal benefits and minimizes risks and threats to feelings of personal well-being.

Many of the constructivist strategies discussed in Chapter 4, such as involving students in expressing their own ideas, criticizing and challenging the views of others and reflecting through discussion on changes in concep-tual understanding that have occurred, raise complex social issues relating to the nature of student–teacher and student–student interactions. In class discussion involving the teacher, there is an asymmetry in terms of knowledge, authority and linguistic skills, which usually results in the teacher's ideas prevailing and dominating, unless extraordinary measures are taken. However, in group-based cognitive conflict strategies, agreement has to be reached out of disagreement by negotiation within the group. In such circumstances, intra-group and inter-group interactions are complex and difficult to predict. Sometimes, a generalized group pressure can cause students to change their views and even their data in order to reach early and easy consensus, thus truncating discussion. Sometimes, a particular individual can exercise a powerful influence on the group's 'findings' that is disproportionate to its scientific value. As in science itself, authority and prestige can play an important role, with the views of the most insistent and prestigious group member being likely to prevail – although, of course, one can only be persistent and insistent if the rest of the group permit it. Social context is rarely a unidirectional influence: individuals contribute to and change the social contexts in which they find themselves. Thus, interaction between each individual member and the group as a whole is a dynamic, mutually facilitating and constraining one. The 'direction' of the net influence depends, of course, on the particular nature of the group, its composition and the kinds of internal rules and procedures it develops.

Learning interactions within and between groups

Within the classroom, individual students, groups of students and the teacher interact to forge a complex classroom culture which sets parameters for all aspects of classroom life, determining what counts as normal or deviant behaviour. In elaboration of this point, Solomon (1989) suggests that all student behaviours be regarded as 'social acts', in that they have both meaning and purpose for the actor and for others. These acts build into overall 'moral careers' (similar to Claxton's stances) that establish the reputation and direct the behaviour of individual students and student groups. Social acts may have different meanings for different groups, and so the group response to a particular act may vary from group to group. Moreover, the group response to a particular act may change over time, in accordance with changes in the composition of the group, or as group members gain experience and maturity. For example, most teachers and parents are uncomfortably aware of the power of peer group pressures during adolescence, when the need to feel grown-up frequently makes students dismissive of adult views, opinion and advice (especially from parents and teachers), while eager for peer group approval and support. However, this support is given only under certain conditions – namely, that group norms are obeyed and particular approved roles are adopted and maintained. In other words, the individual's need for peer group approval creates a powerful system of social rules that ensures peer group loyalty and engenders a large measure of compliance. Often, then, the price of admission to the group is conformity

– although, of course, the nature of that conformity varies from group to group. Solomon (1991) remarks that increasing demands for loyalty and conformity within groups of girls during adolescence engenders an increasing degree of personal intimacy that is unrelated to science and science education, while among groups of boys, she says, perception of science as a masculine pursuit works to the teacher's advantage and creates a drive for conformity through 'being good at science'. Simply put, boys who do well in science are conforming to stereotypes, and so find the social climate of the classroom supportive or, at least, non-threatening; girls who do well in science are running counter to stereotypes and so must withstand considerable social pressures and overcome additional obstacles.

In a series of articles, Solomon (1987, 1989, 1991, 1993) describes how individuals establish a role for themselves within a group and, more particularly, how groups interact with the teacher and with other groups to establish and maintain their different characters and reputations. Some groups may work to establish their reputation by seeking teacher approval, others by conscientiously seeking understanding, acting as critics of other groups, making a fuss and being noticed, being 'no good at science', ostentatiously not trying and so on. Two further points should be made. First, over time, groups may change their overall stance as they build up favourable/unfavourable experiences and have their needs met or not met. Second, teachers are part of this reputation building, too. Teachers are keen to adopt particular stances towards their students, towards school and towards science itself. However, these stances may vary from class to class. In one class, teachers may act as a source of authority, in another as a friend or facilitator. Just as students feel comfortable in some groups and some classes, but not in others, so teachers feel more comfortable with some student groups than others. Consequently, they may have substantially different relationships with different groups of students. Interestingly, teachers' pedagogical practice seems to be strongly influenced by the social composition of the school. Those in schools with a low socio-economic status (SES) population tend (probably unconsciously) to lower the level of cognitive demand of learning tasks and the level of abstraction of science content (Domingos 1989).

Over time, group rules emerge that determine (a) the amount of dissension with which the group can cope without losing its cohesion, and (b) how the group organizes the management of the tasks it is allocated – collecting and setting up apparatus, interacting with the teacher, allocating sub-tasks to group members, negotiating with other groups and the like. Within the classroom as a whole, and within the individual groups, space itself becomes a matter of great social significance. Where students sit in whole-class or individual activities is related to their seeking (or not) teacher approval and involvement in the lesson, and the amount and location of space occupied by different groups during group-based activities reflects the group's aspirations and sense of group identity. Both individual and group space are governed by complex conventions, transgression of which causes offence. Thus, teachers who approach an individual or group too closely may be resented and, as Solomon (1991) says, individual students who venture into the space of another group may be regarded as 'spies' and may be treated in hostile fashion. Interestingly, some students are allowed to move from group to group, acting as inter-group collaborators and messengers. Solomon (1989) suggests that these are often low status and generally unsuccessful students who are both unimportant to the group's sense of identity and easily manipulated to serve the group's immediate needs. On the other hand, some groups might be flattered to be 'visited' by high status individuals, especially those whom Claxton (1990) refers to as 'socialites'. Indeed, Shapiro (1994) describes a high status, well liked and high achieving student (Melody) who moved freely from group to group, finding out what other groups had done and what they were currently thinking about as explanations for the phenomena under investigation. Melody, whose actions were in contravention of the teacher's instructions, seemed to learn some difficult concepts in science precisely because she was able to move from group to group. Had she conformed to teacher directives, says Shapiro, she might not have learned so well. Sadly, there are also individuals who are unwanted by all groups and those whose social skills are such that they seem unable to function at all in a group setting.

There can, of course, be conflicts between an individual's personal goals and the group's goals. For example, an individual's need for competence and self-esteem may be in conflict with the group's goals of non-cooperation with the teacher. In these circumstances, seeking the approval of friends is likely to prevail, though it will vary with age. It can also happen that groups become locked into a role that none of the individual members any longer wishes to have, but feel compelled to maintain for the sake of protecting their hard-won group reputation. Effecting radical change in group stance may require major intervention by the teacher. Changing the group composition is the obvious first strategy, though this can build up resentment against the teacher. Texts on group learning (for example, Johnson and Johnson 1994; Slavin 1995) have much useful advice for teachers faced with this kind of problem.

Motivating groups

Given that the extent to which an individual student participates in group discussion will be determined by that individual's personality variables, attitudes to learning and stock of relevant content knowledge, and by the overall 'climate' of the group – which, in turn, is dependent on the group composition and the nature of the interpersonal relationships within it – it might be possible to predict the factors that lead to successful and productive group-based learning. As might be anticipated, research attention has often been focused on the influence of differences in ability level among students. Within heterogeneous ability groups, it seems that both high and low ability students benefit, especially when the former are encouraged to act as tutors to the latter, while middle range students seem unaffected or even uninvolved

(Webb 1984). The gender composition of the group can also be significant, with girls being disadvantaged when they are heavily outnumbered by boys (because they tend to be ignored) and also when they are present in much larger numbers than boys (because they are inclined towards social rather than on-task behaviour).

Interestingly, Kempa and Ayob (1995) found that extent of learning is sometimes unrelated to within-group behaviour. Even those students seemingly inactive in the group benefit from their membership and from the activities therein, activities in which they appear to have no more than a spectator role. The authors conclude that even though some students appeared to be uninvolved, they must have been listening and engaging in some kind of internal dialogue because they, like other more overtly active students, produced independently written work in which some 40 per cent of information items had been contributed to group discussion by other students. While personality variables (at the crude introvert versus extrovert level) did not seem to determine the extent of group involvement in Kempa and Ayob's (1995) study, they did influence the nature of the involvement. It was apparent that extroverts were more likely than introverts to engage in off-task behaviour. They were also less inclined to incorporate the ideas of others into their written work.

Hofstein and Kempa (1985) assert that students respond to particular learning tasks in ways that reflect their 'motivational pattern', a characteristic that is, they argue, compounded in various ways from four basic needs:

• the need to achieve;
• the need to satisfy one's curiosity;
• the need to discharge a duty;
• the need to affiliate with other people.

If Hofstein and Kempa are correct in their typology of motivation, it might be expected that those with a high need to achieve will prefer competitive learning environments, while those driven mainly by social needs will prefer non-competitive or cooperative ones. Similarly, those with a high need to satisfy curiosity may incline towards self-directed learning and open-ended problem-solving, whereas those who are more duty-oriented (characterized as 'conscientious students' by the authors) may prefer learning situations in which there are clearly defined goals and clear instructions about how to reach them. Some empirical support for these speculations has been provided by Kempa and Diaz (1990).

While this work has some important messages for teachers concerning the design of teaching and learning activities and the composition of groups, and reinforces the argument for giving students a significant measure of choice concerning the ways in which they study (see Chapter 6), it should be remembered that these four basic needs (and, hence, overall motivational levels) will vary over time and in relation to the task and the composition of the working group in which students find themselves. Further, as Gayford (1992) shows, motivational levels are strongly influenced by group dynamics

– in particular, by leadership style. Students in groups with more 'democratic' or 'negotiated' styles of working often have higher motivational levels and gain greater all-round understanding than those in groups where an individual student assumes a leadership or directive role. Furthermore, Kempa and Ayob (1991) have shown that even when confronting the same task, groups vary enormously in the amount of verbal interaction and in the distribution of contributions. Considerably greater consistency between groups is found in the form of interactions (most tend to be dialogues, even in groups with more than two members) and in the 'content' of discussion, which is predominantly concerned with reducing interpersonal tension, maintaining group cohesion and establishing working procedures (see also Pugh and Lock 1989).

Wallace (1986) identifies six different kinds of talk, each with a different purpose, occurring at different stages of a learning activity. These purposes are:

1 Negotiating and managing the various tasks.
2 Removing tensions.
3 Giving help and tutoring.
4 Non-task talk concerned with social relations.
5 Negotiating perception (agreeing/disagreeing about observations).
6 Constructing meaning.

While, at first sight, it might be tempting to believe that students should spend all or most of their time in category 3 and category 6 talk, it is clear, on further reflection, that without substantial talk in categories 1, 2 and 4 no work at all would be possible. Category 5 talk is particularly interesting. It seems that students need confirmation of what they have observed, and reassurance about what they have measured, from peers and/or from teachers. New effects are sometimes difficult to perceive, even to see, and are often difficult to relate to an existing scheme of understanding. Without social reinforcement, none of us knows whether to 'believe our own eyes' (Solomon 1991: 103). Significantly, category 6 talk is the rarest, and seems to decline further when groups are unsupervised for long periods (Kempa and Ayob 1991).

Even when talk is directed towards cognitive matters, it is generally at a fairly low level of sophistication – simple recall and transmission of information, for example. Effective discussion and the free exchange of ideas and criticism that help to build and develop understanding are both rare and uncertain events. Sometimes meaning is established tentatively and hesitantly, sometimes by bold assertions, as group members talk directly and indirectly about the topic in hand. Sometimes the hoped-for understanding doesn't emerge, because of the group's need for reaching early and easy consensus. Teachers can help matters by better structuring of tasks and by assisting students to acquire the skills to participate more effectively in group activities (see texts on group learning). What is clear above all, however, is that much more research in this area is needed before our knowledge is secure enough to inform a theory of pedagogy. It is also clear that this research must be sensitive to what may be very significant cultural differences.

For example, as Krugly-Smolska (1995) states, Native Americans are less willing to participate when required to speak alone in front of others, take a leadership role or answer direct questioning by the teacher. They are more willing to participate in group activities which don't distinguish between speaker and audience. Durojaiye (1980: 12) comments on this issue from an African perspective:

> Whilst the school encourages talking, the exchange of ideas, questioning and curiosity, the home may put a premium on being seen but not heard as a hall-mark of good behaviour. The child's school experience often belongs to an entirely different world from his home experience.

Many girls brought up within an Islamic tradition experience difficulty in challenging the authority (as they see it) of an adult, male teacher – a problem for many students in Canadian and British schools. Similar problems may exist for Polynesian students in New Zealand. 'Many have learned from their parents that the teacher, like the priest or pastor, holds valuable knowledge and as such is to be respected, not questioned by mere students. Indeed, to ask a question can be a sign of lack of attention and disrespect' (Jones 1985: 21). In addition, there may be conflict between the traditional Polynesian emphasis on cooperation and the attitudes and aspirations required for success in an education system based on the Euro-American values of competition and individualism. While these kinds of distinctions seem to verge on stereotyping and may, therefore, be considered potentially racist in themselves, there does seem to be some validity in the claim that there are culturally determined preferences in learning style (Pomeroy 1994). In New Zealand, for example, radical Maori educators have used this notion to articulate a set of guidelines for a preferred Maori pedagogy based on a *whanau* (extended family) structure (May 1994). The wide age range present within each classroom enables teachers to employ a form of peer tutoring based on the traditional *tuakana-teina* (elder–younger relatives) relationship. Cooperative learning is expected, and recognition of group efforts and achievements replaces the more usual Western principle of rewarding individual accomplishment. The strong oral tradition of Maori culture is reflected in the extensive use of story-telling and song.

Within the classroom, there can be all kinds of 'negative messages' conveyed to particular ethnic groups by teachers' remarks and actions. Certain styles of teacher–student interaction may be culturally inappropriate, or even unconsciously and inadvertently racist. In this respect, teachers need to pay attention to language (especially forms of address, tone and inflexion), gesture and body language, eye contact, question type and distribution, allocation of tasks and responses to children's work and contributions in class. For example, how closely a teacher approaches a child, who sits and who stands, whose head is higher, whether eye contact is maintained, are all of significance in Polynesian society.

Cross-cultural studies of children's conceptual understanding reveal the powerful influence of the student's first or preferred language, regardless of the language of instruction (Ross and Sutton 1982; Baker and Taylor 1995).[1] Even more significant is the influence of local knowledge, custom and ritual. In some instances, the concepts of science seem almost incompatible with knowledge acquired by the student through membership of other social groups. For example, Kawasaki (1996) describes the difficulty for Japanese students in reconciling the Western concept of 'nature' with its closest (but significantly different) Japanese equivalent of '*shizen*'. In elementary school, the goal of fostering a love of nature is consistent with the Japanese *shizen*, but secondary school biology, which regards the natural environment as an object of study and mastery, is not. On occasions, differences between local knowledge and scientific knowledge are located at the level of fundamental beliefs about the nature of the external world and humanity's place in it, discussion of which is continued in Chapter 11.

Personal learning contexts

Accepting the notion of a personal framework of understanding (developed in Chapter 5) means accepting the view that each learner is in possession of a unique array of ideas, beliefs, feelings, values and expectations, within which, of course, are elements held in common with others. As discussed earlier in this chapter, the social contexts in which learners find themselves, including classrooms, create additional opportunities for extending this personal framework of understanding, while simultaneously imposing constraints and limitations on individual action. Just as each student's personal framework of understanding is unique, so also is each student's complex of social group membership and perceptions of what that membership entails and requires. In other words, in addition to building a personal framework of cognitive understanding, students construct and reconstruct their own social reality as they move and act in various social settings. Bronfenbrenner (1979) describes an individual's social settings in terms of four nested and mutually interacting systems.

• A micro system – the individual's immediate social settings of family, friends and school.
• A meso system – the relationships among these micro systems (e.g. parent–school interactions).
• The exo system – a set of social systems that facilitate or constrain activities within and between the micro and meso systems (e.g. local regulations and guidelines for practice, media and religious influences).
• The macro system – the overarching regulatory institutions (educational, legal and political systems).

Families, peers and school groups provide different contexts for social interaction. Because these groups are embedded within other, wider, social and subcultural groupings and institutions, which are, in turn, influenced by still higher order cultural contexts, a complex network of influence, feedback and control is established that both creates and restricts opportunities for learning. Moreover, the ways in which an individual perceives and feels about these four interacting systems become significant factors in determining learning behaviour, contributing to what Shapiro (1992) calls a 'personal orientation to science learning'.

Among the many elements contributing to this personal orientation to science learning are: the student's views of school, science and the activities associated with learning science; relationships with peers, teachers and family; learning preferences and other aspects of metacognitive awareness; self-image, aspirations and values. Some elements are wide-ranging and stable over time; they govern the student's overall attitude and commitment to learning science. Others are topic-specific, even lesson-specific, and influence short-term decision making about learning behaviour. As discussed in Chapter 6, students presented with a learning task engage in a kind of cost–benefit analysis, much of which is tacit or intuitive, and through which they decide how to proceed. A number of questions are asked, and answered. Is the task interesting? Is it likely to meet my long-term or short-term needs and aspirations? What are the costs in terms of time and restriction of opportunities for other activities? How will success be determined? In other words, what am I expected to do? If I make the effort, am I likely to succeed in reaching the target? How will success or failure affect my relationship with teachers, parents, friends? Do I care? Which learning group will I be placed in? Do I get on reasonably well with the other group members? Are there other demands, such as a requirement to change values or to conform to new conventions? In short, is it worth the effort?

What is being argued here is that when students, each with a distinctive personal framework of understanding, are presented with a particular learning task set within a distinctive educational context (involving a particular class or learning group), a unique *learning context* is created for each individual. Understanding the factors contributing to its uniqueness in order to intervene in ways that facilitate successful learning is the complex task facing the teacher. Successful facilitation requires more than being aware of the cognitive understanding individual students have about the particular topic being studied. It also involves having an insight into the way students feel about the topic, how they view learning, science, other students and the teacher, and how all these elements combine in unique fashion for each student. Appreciation of the uniqueness of personal learning contexts helps to explain why some students learn successfully, while others of apparently equal ability do not, even in apparently very similar circumstances. It helps to explain why particular students may learn on some occasions, but not on others, despite circumstances that to others may seem identical.

Note

1 It is also the case that the necessity to learn science in a second language (usually English, for many students in developing countries) brings with it considerable 'cultural baggage' that interferes with good learning.

• • • 8

Science education as enculturation

In Chapter 7, I argued that the learner cannot be separated from the socio-cultural milieu in which learning occurs. While the cognitive nature of the learning task and the scientific context in which it is located are both crucial factors influencing learning, they are bound together by an acting person who is uniquely located both socially and historically. Moreover, in most school learning situations, that 'acting person' is engaged in social interactions with others who are also uniquely located, and these interactions are themselves part of the construction of the learner's social identity. Consequently, the nature of the group changes as a consequence of the interactions within it. In short, learning is a complex, uncertain and socioculturally located activity. Its complexity can only be appreciated, and appropriate steps taken to facilitate better learning for all, by adopting a model of teaching and learning that recognizes the uniqueness of individual learners, includes the sociocultural contexts in which the individual is located and takes account of the complex nature of the interactions between the individual and the other elements in the learning context (the teacher, other students, learning materials etc.). Building such a model involves 'raiding' other areas of research and scholarship for appropriate intellectual and theoretical resources. The most promising area in which to commence this 'raiding' is the sociocultural theorizing of Lev Vygotsky.

Vygotsky's work was rooted in his concern to understand the social context of cognitive development and, in particular, the role of language in the development of higher cognitive functions. These functions, says Vygotsky, originate in social activity and, as they develop, are inextricably linked with language, which is itself a social construct. It is through social interactions – initially with parents or other care givers, family members and peers, later via teachers and other knowledgeable adults – that children learn the cognitive and communicative tools and skills of their culture.

> From the very first days of the child's development his activities acquire a meaning of their own in a system of social behavior and, being directed

towards a definite purpose, are refracted through the prism of the child's environment. The path from object to child and from child to object passes through another person. This complex human structure is the product of a developmental process deeply rooted in the links between individual and social history.

(Vygotsky 1978: 30)

Thus, in order to explain the psychological, says Vygotsky, we must look not only at the individual and his or her interaction with the external physical world (as constructivists argue), but also at the immediate social world in which the child is located and at the nature of the interactions that take place within it.

Every function in the child's cultural development appears twice: first, on the social level, and later, on the individual level; first, *between* people (*interpsychological*), and then *inside* the child (*intrapsychological*) ... All the higher [cognitive] functions originate as actual relations between human individuals.

(Vygotsky 1978: 57)

The path from external social plane to internal psychological plane comprises four steps: first, other people act on the child, then the child enters into interactions with those around him or her; third, the child begins to act on others and, finally, to act on himself or herself. Vygotsky's term for the process by which the social becomes the psychological is *internalization*. It is a process in which language plays a key role. As a tool, language creates the possibility of thought, organizes the thinking processes and both reflects and shapes the human society in which it is used. The relationships among Vygotsky's ideas, the notion of a personal framework of understanding and the theory dependence of science (Chapter 2) should be apparent in the following commentary.

Like tool systems, sign systems (language, writing, number systems) are created by societies over the course of human history and change with the form of society and the level of its cultural development ... The internalization of culturally produced sign systems brings about behavioral transformations and forms the bridge between early and later forms of individual development.

(Cole and Scribner 1978: 6)

Among Vygotsky's greatest insights is recognition of the ways in which children come to use language as a tool for problem-solving: 'children solve practical tasks with the help of their speech, as well as their eyes and hands', he states (Vygotsky 1978: 26). In fact, the more complex the problem, Vygotsky argued, the greater is the importance of speech. This is in stark contrast to the Piagetian view that action is primary, with language and other ways of using symbols following from the development of more general, underlying cognitive structures. Vygotsky's position is that speech and thought are initially independent of each other: there is a pre-intellectual phase in speech development and a pre-verbal phase in the development of thought. During early childhood, speech and thought processes begin to penetrate each other: children first use telegraphic or egocentric speech to accompany problem-solving, describing verbally what they are doing as they are doing it. Next, they use speech to plan problem-solving strategies, again verbalizing as they proceed with the task in hand in an apparent attempt to guide their own behaviour. In the early stages of language development, children act as though they believe that if speech is to direct behaviour it must be spoken. Eventually, as the child grows older and gains experience, speech goes 'underground', transforming into a kind of internal speech, an inner dialogue for the construction and reconstruction of meaning. What had started out as an external socially constructed artefact is transformed by the child, first into an external aid to help organize problem-solving, later into the very constructive core of thought itself. The construction of meaning through language goes on throughout our lives, building up an ever more complex view of reality, largely through linguistic exchanges with other people – either directly or indirectly, via books, movies etc. In summary, the development of complex mental functions involves two unique yet connected processes: mastery of the external means of thinking, such as speech, writing and mathematical notation; and learning to use those symbols to master, regulate and develop one's thinking.

Scaffolding and the zone of proximal development

Vygotsky was highly critical of the Piagetian view that learning must necessarily lag behind development – that is, the view that learning cannot occur until and unless the appropriate cognitive structures are in place to enable experience to be appropriately represented and acted upon. Vygotsky's counter suggestion is that, in general, children do function according to norms of development, as Piaget alleges, but it is incorrect to say that they function *only* at a particular level. With appropriate assistance, he says, 8-year-old children can solve problems at the level of a 9-year-old, or even a 12-year-old.

> This difference between twelve and eight, or between nine and eight, is what we call the zone of proximal development. It is the distance between the actual developmental level as determined by independent problem solving and the level of potential development as determined through problem solving under adult guidance or in collaboration with more capable peers.
>
> (Vygotsky 1978: 86)

In Vygotsky's view, teachers should concentrate their efforts in the zone of proximal development. Instruction should lead development, providing opportunities for students to engage in and acquire competence in intellectual functions that are on the verge of development. The problem with learning geared only to the child's level of independent problem-solving is that it lags permanently behind the child's developing mental processes. 'The only good learning', says Vygotsky (1978: 89), 'is that which is in advance of development', because it 'awakens and rouses to life functions which are in a stage of maturing'.

It is in the zone of proximal development that *scaffolding*, a term first used by Wood *et al.* (1976), plays a crucial role, enabling teachers to present ideas 'in advance of development' and to create opportunities for students to use and take control of them.

> If the child is enabled to advance by being under the tutelage of an adult or a more competent peer, then the tutor or the aiding peer serves the learner as a vicarious form of consciousness until such a time as the learner is able to master his own action through his own consciousness and control. When the child achieves that conscious control over a new function or conceptual system, it is then that he is able to use it as a tool. Up to that point, the tutor in effect performs the critical function of 'scaffolding' the learning task to make it possible for the child, in Vygotsky's word, to internalize external knowledge and convert it into a tool for conscious control.
>
> (Bruner 1985: 24–5)

Scaffolding doesn't alter the nature of the task for the learner. Rather, it holds the task constant while adjusting the level of the learner's participation through graduated assistance. By providing support, it extends the intellectual range of the student and permits the accomplishment of tasks not otherwise possible. In that sense it differs crucially from the behaviourist notion of 'shaping'. It is important, of course, that students don't remain forever dependent on the scaffold of adult assistance. There has to be a hand-over of control. Planning a smooth and effective hand-over, by changing the nature of scaffolding in response to the learner's development, is a critical aspect of building a curriculum for intellectual independence. Judging when learners are ready, and when they need more responsibility, requires sensitivity on the part of the teacher to each learner's current framework of understanding. Bruner sums up this gradual removal of scaffolds with the rallying call: 'Where before there was a spectator, let there now be a participant'. 'One sets the game, provides a scaffold to ensure that the child's ineptitudes can be rescued by appropriate intervention, and then removes the scaffold part by part as the reciprocal structure can stand on its own' (Bruner 1983: 60).

Education as enculturation

Building on Vygotsky's work, Leont'ev introduced the notion of *appropriation* as the sociocultural alternative to Piaget's notion of assimilation. Knowledge, skills, practices and language constitute a form of collective memory built up over many years. By acquiring elements of this collective memory, and learning how and when to use them, individuals are inducted into the cultural resources of society – in effect, being admitted into the community of practitioners and empowered to employ its resources as their own. Thus, individual development is shaped as much by cultural as by biological factors, as much by social factors as by individual effort. 'Humans' mental processes acquire a structure necessarily tied to the sociohistorically formed means and methods transmitted to them by others in the process of collaborative labor and social interaction' (Leont'ev 1981: 56).

In saying that learners appropriate understanding through social encounters, the point is being made that knowledge, skills and language have a social history and carry with them a cargo of sociocultural meaning and political significance. More expert others – teachers, family members, other adults and, sometimes, peers – play an essential role in the individual's ability to appropriate the cultural resources of the group. Not only do they provide a model of proper behaviour, they are also able to assist and guide the novice to go beyond what he or she can accomplish unaided. Here, again, language plays a key role. As Bruner (1971: 20) stated, some quarter-century ago, 'one of the most crucial ways in which a culture provides aid in intellectual growth is through a dialogue between the more experienced and the less experienced.'

Unlike Piagetian theory, in which teachers seem to be reduced to a largely peripheral role as the provider and manager of a suitable environment in which learning subsequently occurs, Vygotskian theory gives teachers a central role: leading children and students to new levels of conceptual understanding through social interaction. For Vygotsky, teaching comprises the activities associated with enabling the learner to participate effectively in the activities of the more expert, and learning is seen as *enculturation* via guided participation and modelled practice. Expert performance is modelled and learners are instructed and supported in their efforts to replicate it. Initially, considerable responsibility lies with the expert (the teacher), while the novices (students) perform only those aspects of the various tasks of which they are currently capable. Extensive guidance and support are provided for those aspects which are just beyond the students' current unaided capability. Over time, through assisted performance, the novices master all the component parts and gradually become capable of full and autonomous participation. As Vygotsky himself put it, what the child can do today, with help, she or he will manage alone tomorrow. Responsibility is gradually transferred from expert to (the former) novice until such time as the student is intellectually independent and no longer needs the teacher.

Translating these general ideas about enculturation into effective classroom practice requires more careful consideration of two key questions.

1 What do students need to know in order to be regarded as successfully enculturated? In other words, what is involved in moving from a commonsense understanding to a scientific understanding of natural phenomena and events?

2 How does enculturation occur? In other words, what is an appropriate pedagogy for effecting the shift from common sense to scientific understanding?

From common sense to science

As discussed in Chapters 3 and 4, it seems that students come to school science lessons with some well established ideas and views about natural phenomena and events that differ in a number of respects from accepted scientific descriptions and explanations. Claxton (1993) distinguishes between what he calls 'gut science', acquired through direct physical experiences, and 'lay science', acquired through social interaction and mass media experiences. He draws this distinction on the grounds that understanding leading to verbal explanations of phenomena and events is often different from that which informs and guides our non-verbal dealings with them (see also Gazzaniga 1988). Consequently, he says, when researchers ask students to express their ideas they may not be gaining insight into students' working knowledge of phenomena and events as much as being given the rationalizations that students 'cobble together when they are put on the spot' (Claxton 1993: 114).[1] For the purpose of discussion in this chapter, the term 'everyday understanding' will be used as a catch-all label to denote both of Claxton's categories, together with elements of traditional knowledge, 'street science' and the kind of media-influenced 'science talk' that is part science, part pseudoscience and part fantasy (Lucas 1991). Within the overall body of 'everyday science', each of these 'sciences' has its own place and its own function.

Among the characteristics of most kinds of everyday understanding (including 'everyday science') are the absence of clear definitions, the tolerance of ambiguity and inconsistency and the high level of context specificity. Because everyday knowledge is largely experiential, action-oriented and tailored to specific contexts, there is little need for establishing conceptual relationships across and between contexts. Everyday knowledge, therefore, tends to comprise a piecemeal or *ad hoc* collection of descriptive and explanatory items rather than a consistent and coherent set of theories. Its rational basis is not the rigorous consideration and criticism of 'hard evidence', but mutual understanding of common experiences through social interaction. Its role is to permit easy communication and, provided this function is adequately met, most inconsistencies and contradictions are tolerated. Indeed, because its use is often highly context-specific, inconsistencies will often go unrecognized or, if they are recognized, they will go unremarked. By contrast, concepts in science are located within conceptual structures that have particular relationships to other such structures. While scientific terms are often carefully and unambiguously defined, their real meaning is located in the role they play within conceptual structures (theories and models), a role that may be different in different theories. In Vygotsky's (1962: 93) words: 'the relationship [of a scientific concept] to an object is mediated from the start by some other concept . . . the very notion of a scientific concept implies a certain position in relation to other concepts, i.e., a place within a system of concepts.'

While the standards of validity for everyday understanding are easily met by context-specific meaning located in practical action, science seeks more universal meaning through abstraction. Science isn't just about 'making (personal) sense of the world', it is about producing objective knowledge of the world that others can use.[2] As Matthews (1993a) points out, there is an important distinction to be drawn between the theoretical objects of science (concepts, principles and theories) and the real objects, materials, events and phenomena that scientists study and are able to study more closely and more productively because of the abstract and mathematical nature of scientific thought and the community-based rationality of scientific methods of inquiry.

Some characteristics of scientific knowledge

The following piece of scientific knowledge is typical of the kind of knowledge students are expected to acquire at the upper levels of a school chemistry course. It has a number of features that can be taken as characteristic of scientific knowledge in general.

> The temperature falls when ammonium chloride dissolves in water because the combined enthalpies of hydration of the ammonium and chloride ions is less than the lattice energy of ammonium chloride.

First, it is expressed in very specialized language. The language of science includes words purpose-built for particular contexts, sometimes using Latin and Greek roots. In general, these words present few difficulties for students because teachers introduce them carefully and pay particular attention to clarifying their meaning. Much more problematic are dozens of common words (like contract, efficient and abundant) that are either not understood or understood as having the opposite meaning: about 50 per cent of 12–14-year-olds take *contract* to mean 'get bigger' and *abundant* to mean 'scarce', while *efficient* is often taken to mean 'sufficient' (Cassels and Johnstone 1985). Science also makes use of common everyday words, but uses them in a restricted or very specialized way. Words like *force, energy* and *work* spring to mind. Often, it is these words that cause learning problems because students think that they understand them, but do not always appreciate the particular specialized scientific meaning, and when its use is appropriate or necessary. As if all this wasn't confusing enough for students, scientists in different disciplines sometimes use the same word to mean entirely different things: consider, for example, *cell, nucleus* and *molar* as used by biologists and chemists.

Second, proper use of the language of science necessitates a considerable measure of conceptual understanding. As argued in Chapter 2, the language of science is theory-impregnated. Understanding the statement about ammonium chloride requires an understanding of solubility, ionic bonding, hydration and so on. Third, scientific knowledge is abstract knowledge. Indeed, it becomes increasingly abstract as learners progress. We may initially engage children in interaction with familiar real objects, through laboratory activities and so on, but our intention is to ascend a hierarchy of abstraction. According to Ausubel (1968), concepts with high levels of abstraction are more stable (that is, more resistant to forgetting) and more useful in dealing with new situations than are concepts with lower levels of abstraction. Consequently, their acquisition should be a major goal of teaching and learning science. The development of increasing abstraction and the search for relationships between these abstractions (scientific theory building) is also, of course, a major goal of science itself, and it is the high level of abstraction that gives scientific knowledge its particular explanatory power. It is the abstract concepts of a theoretical system that enable natural events and phenomena to become susceptible to scientific study. Theory does not create the objects being studied, nor does it derive from the naive observation of them. Rather, it is an enabling device by means of which we idealize, model and interpret. It is this recognition that is central to understanding the distinctive nature of scientific knowledge, and a vital part of learning about science. 'The concepts and techniques of a theoretical system enable natural events to become *scientific* events . . . It is as a scientific event that they are stripped of their everyday guises and become data or evidence in theoretical debate' (Matthews 1994: 130).

In scientific theory building, the complexity and diversity of the world is reduced and made more manageable, understandable and susceptible to control. Through idealization and abstraction, phenomena and events can be subjected to more systematic study via experimental inquiry and a search for correlations. The power of concepts to provide understanding is located in their connections with other concepts via interconnected conceptual systems, in which, of course, meaning may shift somewhat from context to context, or problem to problem. The problem for teachers is how to make the crucial move from a commonsense, empirically based set of descriptions of phenomena and events to the abstract, idealized (and sometimes mathematical) descriptions characteristic of theoretical science.

Together with its sometimes counter-intuitive nature, the high level of abstraction of scientific knowledge is one of the factors that makes science so difficult to learn. Unfortunately, teachers sometimes compound the problem by providing visually rich concrete experiences (laboratory work), yet demanding that descriptions and explanations for the phenomena or events observed are expressed in abstract theoretical terms that are often strange and unfamiliar to students. Even greater problems can be created by too early an insistence on representing observational data in symbol form – that is, as chemical or algebraic equations. When students think in terms of concrete experiences and teachers think in terms of abstract theoretical concepts, they are, in effect, 'speaking different languages'. As a consequence, much of the laboratory work in school science does little to help to build students' understanding (Hodson 1993c). Similar problems may arise from the use of analogies, similes, metaphors and over-simplified versions of a theoretical model by teachers to 'get the point across' more easily and more quickly.

Osborne (1996) has argued that Harre's notion of three 'levels' of theory might be helpful in assisting students to ascend the level of abstraction towards sophisticated theoretical understanding. Level 1 theories are concerned with describing and classifying tangible, directly observable entities. Level 2 theories concern entities that are only accessible to our senses through instrumentation or are, in principle, observable. Level 3 theories deal with theoretical entities for which there is no direct evidence. Osborne's suggestion is not for an invariable teaching progression in which students are first introduced to a simple conceptual language to describe events and phenomena, proceed to theoretical structures that relate these observations in cause and effect relationships and finally learn to use abstract systems. Rather, he is emphasizing the need to impress on students that the sophisticated theories of science ultimately rest on directly and indirectly observable events, and he is making a case for a much more overt teaching about science and its epistemology.

Learning about science

Although it is quite common to assert that education in science is concerned with the progressive disembedding of thought and the promotion of context-free generalized understanding, it is important to point out that what distinguishes scientific thought from everyday thought is not context-disembeddedness in the sense of being unrelated to contexts, but in the sense of *transcending* contexts. It is the high level of abstraction and idealization that renders scientific concepts applicable to many particular problems and contexts (Matthews 1994). Scientific knowledge is also characterized by its coherence and interrelatedness. Much everyday knowledge is found wanting when subjected to the scientific demands for such characteristics as coherence, consistency, precision, robustness, parsimony and predictive capability.

Next, as discussed earlier, scientific knowledge is that which has been subjected to, and has survived, critical scrutiny by members of the community of scientists, using whatever methods and criteria have been deemed appropriate to ensure the necessary degree of validity and reliability. In other words, it is both personally and socially constructed: personally constructed in the sense that individual scientists devise theoretical constructs and impose them on physical entities in order to study and explain them; socially constructed in the sense that once these constructs have been agreed by the community as constituting valid knowledge, they are taken for granted until there are good grounds for doubting them. It is the demand for consensus within the community of scientists, and the struggle of individual scientists to meet the community-based criteria of validity and reliability, that invests scientific knowledge with its particular kind of authority. Unlike everyday knowledge, which needs little beyond simple consensus or the personal authority of the knower for its justification, scientific knowledge has to survive rigorous critical scrutiny by members of the scientific community, who achieve consensus by employing well characterized methods and clearly stated criteria of judgement.

Longino (1994) identifies four conditions that a community of practitioners must meet if consensus is to count as *knowledge* rather than mere opinion.

• There must be publicly recognized forums for criticism.
• There must be uptake of criticism – the community needs to do more than merely tolerate dissent; it must act on it.
• There must be publicly recognized standards for evaluation of theory and practice.
• There must be equality of intellectual authority – what is included or excluded must result from critical dialogue rather than the exercise of political or economic power.

If it survives critical scrutiny by the community, using these public methods of evaluation and judgement, the knowledge item (model, theory, experimental procedure, instrumental technique or whatever) becomes part of the written record of the scientific community and is made available to others. Thus, scientific knowledge is cumulative, it builds on the knowledge of previous scientists. In other words, science has a history, and even though an idea may subsequently be displaced by another, it retains its historically located validity. Furthermore, by becoming a member of the scientific community, individuals become committed – sometimes explicitly, more often implicitly – to a set of underlying values. They are familiar to science teachers as 'scientific attitudes' (Gauld and Hukins 1980) and as 'ideological pivots' (Smolicz and Nunan 1975). There is, of course, much debate about what these values are, what they should be, whether science education reflects or distorts them and so on – a debate that is outside the scope of this book.

There is no doubt that the inculcation of 'scientific attitudes' has a high priority in the rhetoric of science curriculum development (Schibeci 1984; Bhaskara Rao 1992). It is commonly asserted that particular personal characteristics and attitudes are essential for the successful pursuit of science and that scientists themselves all possess a particular cluster of attitudes and attributes, including superior intelligence, objectivity, rationality, open-mindedness, willingness to suspend judgement, intellectual integrity and communality. It is alleged that it is these scientific attitudes that ensure that: (a) all knowledge claims are treated sceptically until their validity can be judged according to the weight of evidence; (b) all evidence is carefully considered before decisions are made; and (c) the idiosyncratic prejudices of individual scientists do not intrude into decision making about validity. Of course, evidence is always taken to be empirical evidence, agreement with the observed facts. Thus, a genuinely scientific person is regarded as someone who makes decisions solely in terms of a dispassionate weighing of the empirical evidence (the facts). The extent to which this reflects real scientific practice is a matter of some controversy; the extent to which this image of science should be projected through the curriculum is also a matter of debate.

A further matter for debate is whether Smolicz and Nunan (1975) are correct in their characterization of science and science education as being predicated on four ideological pivots:

- The anthropocentric view – man (their word) as conqueror and controller of nature.
- The principle of quantification and demystification – science as a rational process for obtaining illuminative information about the world through precise measurement.
- Positivistic faith – faith in the continued advance of technology through the application of an infallible scientific method based on observation and experiment.
- The analytic ideal – the assumption that the whole is best understood by a study of its component parts.

Argument about whether these are the ideals that underpin both science and science education, whether they should be and whether other ideals should be promoted instead continues to occupy many science educators around the world, but space precludes further discussion here (however, see Chapter 11 for a related discussion).

In summary, enculturation into science involves more than just changing specific conceptions from the commonsense to the scientifically approved views. It involves recognition of the need for coherent universal meanings, precision, parsimony and consistency with other theories and explanations. It entails a change in 'explanatory preferences': away from surface features and readily observable characteristics towards abstraction; away from local, context-bound meaning towards universal, context-transcendent meaning. Or, if not a change in 'explanatory preferences', an understanding of why scientists have these preferences and an awareness of when and how to employ them for oneself. It involves an understanding of the rationality of science – the role and status of scientific knowledge, the nature of scientific inquiry (especially the relationships of observation, theory and experiment) and the criteria of scientific validity. It involves an appreciation of the history of the scientific endeavour and major scientific ideas. It includes a commitment to a set of values and an ability to use appropriately a specialized mode of communication.

Munby (1980) sums up these capabilities in his notion of *intellectual independence*: the capacity of an individual to judge the truth of a knowledge claim independently of other people, and to exercise similar independent judgement with respect to views about science and scientific practice. Kuhn (1989) expresses similar views when she describes those encultured into science as capable of: consciously articulating the theories they hold; knowing what evidence supports them or would refute them; justifying why they hold those views rather than some other views that might also explain the evidence. In a sense, the scientific expertise that enculturation bestows is rooted in metacognitive awareness of epistemological issues: 'thinking about theories, rather than merely with them, and thinking about evidence, rather than merely being influenced by it' (Kuhn 1989: 688).[3]

Interestingly, Hammer (1994) has observed that the ways in which students use conceptual knowledge in problem-solving reflects the views they express in interviews about the role of conceptual knowledge. Similarly, Strike and Posner (1992) found that students' epistemological views and attitudes affect and are affected by their learning of science. In particular, 'students who did well in physics were more inclined to be realists about physics, to demand consistency in their beliefs, to be empiricists in their views of scientific method, and to reject cultural relativism' (Strike and Posner 1992: 165). They also found that confidence in one's ability to learn physics, approaching learning as a task of understanding rather than just remembering and valuing learning for its own sake facilitate and are facilitated by growth in physics competence. Of course, it begs the question of what counts as 'doing well in physics', and leaves unanswered the question of what 'physics competence' means. What kinds of attainment tests were used in this research? Would success in other kinds of attainment tests be associated with different epistemological views? And so on. Nevertheless, it does point to the importance of studies in the history, philosophy and sociology of science for bringing about better learning of scientific content and attitudes more favourable to successful learning in science. It also follows that evolution of a student's personal framework of meaning towards the kind of conceptual coherence found among scientists may require more explicit teaching about the role and status of scientific knowledge; in other words, a more overt concern with teaching and learning about science.

Effecting the change from common sense to science

If education in and about science is largely a matter of enculturation into the conceptual structures of science, its procedures, standards, values, criteria of judgement and mode of discourse, students need the support and guidance of someone already enculturated. It is here that the notion of *apprenticeship* is useful. As Lave (1988: 2) says: 'Apprentices learn to think, argue, act, and interact in increasingly knowledgeable ways with people who do something well, by doing it with them as legitimate, peripheral participants.' For Lave, apprenticeship is not just a process of internalizing knowledge and skills, it is the process of becoming a member of a community of practice. Developing an identity as a member of the community and becoming more knowledgeable and skilful are part of the same process, with the former motivating, shaping and giving meaning to the latter. 'Newcomers become oldtimers through a social process of increasingly centripetal participation, which depends on legitimate access to ongoing community practice' (Lave 1991: 68).

When they are given opportunities to participate peripherally in the activities of the community, newcomers pick up the relevant social language, imitate the behaviour of skilled and knowledgeable members and gradually start to act in accordance with community norms. However, for Lave, there is no formal didactic role for the experts or skilled practitioners. By contrast, Rogoff (1990) proposes a more formal, instruction-oriented apprenticeship model, in which novices are systematically coached, guided and supported by expert practitioners. 'Guided participation', as she calls it, depends on communication and negotiation between teacher and learner about what new knowledge or skill is needed and how it can be made compatible with existing understanding and capability.

> Children and their social partners build bridges from children's current understanding to reach new understanding through processes inherent in communication. They structure problem solving in a way that provides children with a level of support and challenge that comfortably stretches their skills . . . Guided participation involves transfer of responsibility for handling more complex features of a problem as children develop skill and is, hence, a dynamic process of structuring and supporting development.
>
> (Rogoff 1991: 351)

This approach, and the several other variations on cognitive apprenticeship that are rooted in Vygotskian theory (see Tharp and Gallimore 1988; Brown *et al.* 1989; Newman *et al.* 1989), involve teachers in providing guidance and coaching through the careful arrangement of appropriate curriculum materials and learning tasks (scaffolding), through modelling and demonstrating good practice, and through both tacit and explicit instruction as they participate in joint learning activities and problem-solving with apprentices/students. Teachers' greater knowledge and skills enable them to assist students in applying familiar knowledge in unfamiliar contexts and employing unfamiliar knowledge in familiar contexts. In addition, teachers' expertise with the established discourse (of science) enables them to support students in their attempts to master it.

Scaffolding strategies

The most appropriate form of scaffolding depends, of course, on the nature of the task, the learners and the situation. It also changes with time, as learners gain experience with the task. Early scaffolding steps are largely a matter of task induction or 'learner recruitment': finding connections between what is to be learned and what students already know and have experienced, establishing a context that is meaningful and relevant to the students, gaining their interest and commitment, identifying similarities and differences between the new situation and the old and ensuring that terminology is properly understood. Much of this can be achieved by teachers posing relevant and well structured questions, by reminding students of previous work, or by showing a video or presenting a demonstration.

Second phase scaffolding is basically a matter of ensuring an appropriate level of cognitive demand – that is, locating learning tasks within the zone of proximal development and reducing the number of steps in the learning task to a manageable number (decreasing the 'degrees of freedom', as Bruner calls it). Once complex tasks have been broken down into more manageable chunks, the teacher might carry out some of them and the student carry out some, while the remainder are shared. During this phase, the teacher highlights and directs attention to important features to be learned, emphasizes key vocabulary and introduces new terminology, functions as a kind of 'external memory' by providing appropriate information as it is required, assists the learner in analysing tasks, provides guidance and advice on strategies (possibly utilizing cue cards and 'think sheets'), models and demonstrates critical steps in procedures and furnishes evaluative feedback on student performance. Other aspects of scaffolding include reducing linguistic complexity, eliminating sources of distraction and reducing the level of 'noise' associated with hands-on work.

Throughout, the teacher is concerned with the affective and social dimensions of learning – with creating a supportive and emotionally safe learning environment and attending to the motivational aspects of good pedagogy. Wood *et al.* (1976) talk about 'frustration control', 'stress reduction' and 'face saving', when students make mistakes, as scaffolding activities. Following their lead, the definition of scaffolding could be extended to include all strategies for effecting a shift from a performance orientation to a learning or mastery orientation, and promoting an awareness of good learning strategies. Inculcation of self-sufficiency beliefs and improved self-esteem may widen the zone of proximal development by providing students with the confidence they need to sustain their effort and persistence during more difficult tasks, as well as stimulating a willingness to engage in them in the first place! Hatano and Inagaki (1992: 128) suggest that being 'free from urgent external need (e.g. material rewards, positive evaluations or correct answers)' is an essential condition for adoption of a learning orientation. Thus, meeting this condition could also be regarded as scaffolding.

The first step in phase 3 scaffolding – ceding responsibility to the learner – begins when students are encouraged to elicit the help that they feel is needed for task clarification or completion. Instead of learners simply receiving teacher guidance as and when the teacher determines, there is a negotiation of the nature and extent of teacher participation. The learner assumes increasing control, with the teacher acting as support as and when required, and what was formerly guided by the teacher is now guided and directed by the student. Through increasingly skilful questioning (something else that has to be taught to students, of course), students assume responsibility for structuring the task and allocating specific sub-tasks. In other words, students assist the teacher to assist. To put it another way, teachers and students co-construct both the learning activity and the knowledge that is developed through engagement in it. Knowing what kind of teacher assistance is required, and when it is required, is an important part of learning and is the basis of self-knowledge and metacognitive awareness. Teachers themselves should be aware that providing assistance at too high a level can sometimes be counterproductive, and that assistance given without request may be perceived by some students as interference. Hand-over is complete when students no longer need teacher assistance and are capable of self-direction.

Of course, being able to carry out a task without teacher assistance does not mean that performance is fully developed and securely acquired. First, there is a stage of conscious self-guidance, in which learners ask themselves questions: 'Where am I at?' 'What do I do next?' 'What do I need to know?' Knowing where to seek additional information, new techniques and so on is also part of learning and enculturation. Moreover, it is something that has to be fostered in students, if not directly taught to them by teachers. When this internal monitoring is no longer necessary, the student has achieved a level of performance that approaches that of the expert or connoisseur. So much has become internalized and removed from conscious control that performance is tacit and virtually automatic. There is no longer any need to think about it. While this is the desired goal of enculturation, there is an attendant danger that practice can become 'fossilized' and no longer subject to critical scrutiny, modification and development (Vygotsky 1978).

The importance of group work

Basing teaching and learning on an enculturation model is one way of solving one of the major dilemmas of science education: how to provide opportunities for students to construct and reconstruct their own personal framework of understanding, while ensuring that they incorporate the particular understandings listed in the curriculum plan. However, this style of teaching is time-consuming and expensive, and if it is to function effectively, it requires a small class size. One partial solution is to adopt group-based approaches, possibly involving peer tutoring and reciprocal teaching (Palincsar and Brown 1984).

In reciprocal teaching, the early period of teacher modelling, guidance and scaffolding gives way to a phase in which students assume the role of teacher towards other students. How often have we heard teachers say that they didn't really understand something until they began to teach it? Reciprocal teaching is based on such 'folk wisdom', and provides each student, in turn, with the opportunity to lead discussions on the meaning of text extracts, for example, using techniques of questioning, clarifying, summarizing and predicting. Advocates of such approaches report that reciprocal teaching results in better learning, improved self-esteem and enhanced metacognitive awareness (Hodson 1996).

Group work not only makes more likely the expression of alternative views about phenomena and events; it also creates a forum for challenge, debate and the construction of meaning. Groups are, in themselves, learning communities that, with skilful teacher guidance and support, can replicate essential features of the scientific community. When working well, learning groups can: (a) help students to identify and correct misconceptions, inappropriate inquiry strategies and poor learning methods; (b) stimulate the generation of new insights and new problem-solving strategies; (c) contribute substantially to self-esteem and personal motivation by providing an emotionally secure social environment in which students can see others having difficulties and overcoming them.

Of course, an enculturation model requires that teachers themselves have been successfully enculturated into science. In this approach, teachers are more than facilitators, organizers, managers and discussion leaders, they also have to be skilled practitioners of science. In order to introduce students to the cultural tools and conventions of the community of scientists, devise learning experiences that are scientifically significant as well as meaningful and interesting for students, guide, criticize and advise students and ask and answer critical questions, teachers must have a deep understanding of both scientific knowledge and scientific methods. Moreover, they must have a thorough knowledge of the historical development of science, its social, economic and environmental impact and the social, moral and ethical issues it raises for individuals and for society. This is a pretty daunting set of specifications, but one that holds out the prospect of a much more professional role for science teachers than some other models of teaching and learning. And it points to clear targets for pre-service teacher education programmes and for the provision of in-service professional development courses.

Notes

1 These comments also highlight the need to be careful with the context in which teachers set examination and test questions. Locating a question in a real world context when the topic was taught in an abstract, decontextualized way may result in students failing to recognize what knowledge is being sought.

2 'Objective' is used here in the sense employed by Karl Popper (1972) to describe knowledge that, once created, has an independent existence, and may have properties and consequences of which the originator of that knowledge is unaware.

3 Metacognition has been noted several times as a key element in learning science; it will be addressed further in Chapter 11.

• • • 9

Problems of assimilation and exclusion

As discussed in Chapter 7, all individuals are members of a number of social groupings, some of which are long-term associations, others of which are merely temporary. Effective participation in these social groups is, of course, dependent on possession of the appropriate cultural knowledge – that is, the shared understandings, beliefs and language, codes of behaviour, values and expectations of the group. Thus, each person's profile of cultural knowledge is unique, reflecting her or his particular constellation of group memberships. For school-age students, the major groupings of the family, the peer group and the school create distinctive 'social worlds' which may or may not have common cultural knowledge. Phelan *et al.* (1991) suggest that points of similarity and difference between these three social worlds lead to four types of transition into the culture of the school, a transition that is crucial to students' prospects of using the education system to further their life chances and career prospects. Their conclusions are that:

- congruent worlds facilitate smooth transitions;
- different worlds require transitions to be managed;
- diverse worlds lead to hazardous transitions;
- highly discordant worlds result in transitions being resisted or proving impossible.

In the first case, the sociocultural characteristics of the groups are not identical, but there is sufficient common ground to make transitions relatively unproblematic. In the second case, there are some differences that require students to make adjustments and reorientations as they move between groups. 'Border crossings' (to use Henry Giroux's 1992 term) can be made, but they are not always easy and may, in Phelan *et al.*'s (1991: 232) words, have significant 'personal and psychic costs'. In the third situation, the real or perceived differences are such that transitions require more extensive adjustment and reorientation. Successful entry into the culture of the school may even require rejection of the values and aspirations of the other two worlds. It is in this kind of situation, the authors say, that we find adolescents teetering between school success and failure, involvement and disengagement, commitment and apathy. In the final scenario, the values, beliefs and expectations of the three social worlds are so discordant that border crossing is usually resisted. For those few who try, the emotional stress is such that they quickly give up. It is here that Bourdieu's notions of *habitus* (all the sociocultural experiences and influences that shape us as human beings) and *cultural capital* are useful. According to Bourdieu, some habitus are recognized as cultural capital by the school and are reinforced through academic success, while others are not (May 1994). For students who do not have cultural capital, whose family group places little value on academic success or whose peer group may even promote anti-school behaviour, it is crucial that the classroom cultivates a sense of belonging and self-worth and assists them in managing these hazardous border crossings. In many schools, however, and especially in science lessons, the pervading climate is impersonal, even cold and hostile. Little wonder that many decide that science is not for them.

Early school science experiences

The sociocultural dimensions of learning science are never more sharply in focus for students than when they transfer to secondary school and have their first experiences of the science laboratory. It is during these early stages that teachers seek to establish the culture of school science and to create the special code of school science laboratory behaviour. According to Delamont *et al.* (1988), entry into the world of school science is presented by teachers as a *rite de passage* in which the major themes are:

- Danger and the need for constant vigilance – sometimes the sole content of the very first secondary school science lesson.
- Artefacts of special status – especially the Bunsen burner, which the authors refer to as 'the sacred flame of science'.
- Measurement and the need for precision – a constant focus in both hands-on activities and teacher exposition.

Another prominent aspect of this culture of school science education is the demand for mastery of abstract, academic knowledge, which only later, if at all, will be revealed as capable of application to real world matters. Often, students' intuitions about the real world are discredited or ignored, driving a wedge between school science and everyday understanding. The fairly clear message is that what children know about the physical world is neither valued nor valid. While learning outside school is located in authentic contexts, that inside is often decontextualized. While everyday learning is directed towards tangible achievable goals, that in school is promoted as being valuable for its own sake. While learning outside school is a fusion of the cognitive, affective and social, that inside is often presented as culturally neutral, value-free and emotionally detached, despite arguments such as that presented in Chapter 2 for a more humanized and realistic view of science. These messages are underpinned by the use of a specialized, impersonal style of communication. It is here, perhaps most of all, where it is impressed on youngsters that previous everyday experience is of little use. For the most part, this image of science is presented without explanation or justification, as self-evidently the way science is. In many school curricula there is little attempt to show the ways in which science resembles and differs from other ways of knowing, other ways of inquiring and other ways of solving problems. Little, that is, in the way of a critical approach to learning about science.

Regardless of the style of learning experience employed on any particular occasion, language plays a key role. First, enculturation into science is, in large part, a matter of acquiring familiarity with the specialized language of science and an ability to use it appropriately, in both its spoken and written forms, for a variety of purposes and in a variety of contexts. Second, teachers organize learning experiences and manage the activities of the classroom through linguistic exchanges with students. Third, teachers assist students to understand, guide and support their efforts, monitor their progress and provide feedback on their learning progress through dialogue. Thus, talk is one of the principal means by which students move from everyday com- monsense understanding, and the personal language of everyday discussion in which it is usually expressed, to scientific understanding and the formal technical language in which it is expressed. And it is teacher talk, in particu- lar, that scaffolds this transition. Teacher talk can also serve to maintain and reinforce certain myths and stereotypes and, for some students, can contribute to the problems of border crossing into the subculture of science.

The power asymmetry between teacher and students is never more in evidence than in the ways in which language is used in the classroom. Teachers can (and usually do) decide what will and will not be talked about, who has the right to speak and for how long, what is the 'correct' way to speak and to behave while speaking and listening, and what counts as legitimate knowledge, satisfactory evidence and proper argument. By choos- ing the language of expression, teachers decide in favour of a particular way of thinking and, therefore, in favour of the interests and values that under- pin it. They also decide what is an acceptable way of expressing those thoughts. Because teachers set and enforce the rules of classroom discourse, and are not required to explain or justify them to students (though some, of course, do so), there is a danger of distortion and bias. Of course, teachers are not entirely free agents; there are constraints on their freedom imposed by curriculum guidelines or directives issued by the Ministry of Education, local education authority or school board, and there are constraints imposed by the need to adopt the language of the community of scientists. Each of these influences projects a further set of explicit and implicit messages that privilege some views, interests and values, and discount or reject others. Taken together, the rules about the conduct of lessons, the conventions con- cerning who can speak and what can be spoken about (including what can be challenged) and the particular form of school talk and science talk impose a set of conventions and restrictions that can be so formidable that many children are prevented from gaining access to science education.

> It is not surprising that those who succeed in science tend to be like those who define the 'appropriate' way to talk science: male rather than female, white rather than black, middle- and upper-middle class, native English-speakers, standard dialect speakers, committed to the values of North-European middle-class culture (emotional control, orderliness, rationalism, achievement, punctuality, social hierarchy, etc.).
>
> (Lemke 1990: 138)

Many students do not share these values and do not possess the approved forms of language. They already believe that school is a waste of time: it confines them against their will in physically unattractive surroundings, imposes on them a code of conduct that is unfamiliar and unwelcome and often denies them any measure of choice and self-determination about what and how they study. To compound matters, these already disenchanted students are presented with a science curriculum that is remote from real life and couched in an alien language. Even if they make the effort to learn science, they are presented almost daily with unappealing messages about the nature of science and scientific practice. Science is presented as complex and difficult, and so only accessible to 'experts' who have subjected themselves to a long and arduous training. Scientists are portrayed as dispassionate and disinterested experimenters, who painstakingly reveal the truth about the world. Scientific knowledge is delivered as established and certain knowledge that is not to be challenged or doubted by students. The language of science is depersonalized through excessive nominalization (replacement of active verbs by abstract nouns) and an almost exclusive reliance on the passive voice. Many students do not see themselves, or their experiences, interests, aspirations, values and attitudes, reflected in the science presented to them, or in the ways in which it is presented. It is little wonder they decide that science is not for them.

Groisman *et al.* (1991) describe some other features of science classrooms – the size and arrangement of the teacher's and the students' desks and benches, use of time constraints, emphasis on individual written work as the (only) basis for student assessment and so on – that contribute further dimensions to the culture of the science classroom and to the establishment of its language, values, expectations and code of behaviour. For most students, this is a startling change from what they were used to in primary school, and for many it may constitute a formidable barrier to entry into science.

Exclusion from science

Two questions should be asked at this point.

- Is the culture of the science classroom conducive to good learning?
- Is it conducive to effective border crossing by all students, regardless of gender, ethnicity, social class and sexual orientation?

Some would argue that it is precisely because school science excludes most everyday knowledge, practical skills and commonsense understandings that it remains, for many children, peripheral to their needs and interests and irrelevant to the way they see their lives. It is important to recognize, however, that the decontextualizing of knowledge may have a more detrimental impact on working-class children than on those from middle-class homes (Domingos 1989). It should also be remembered that media images can play a significant role in determining students' enthusiasm (or lack of it) for science and science education. In Western society, television, newspapers, comics and movies provide fragments of knowledge (some valid, some fanciful, some entirely fictional) and, perhaps more importantly, convey attitudinal and emotional messages about science and technology – about use of animals, hazards to human health, environmental degradation, for example. Science is presented by the media in ways that are strikingly different from school science's impersonal and orderly presentation of abstract notions. Furthermore, it isn't just 'everyday science' in the sense of everyday conceptual understanding (what we might call 'commonsense science') that the media promote, it is 'everyday science' in the sense of an everyday *image* of what science is, what scientists do and how science impacts, for good and bad, on people and on the environment. The media also play a part in building students' perceptions of who has a place in science. When members of a particular group don't see themselves included in media representations of science and science education, they are dissuaded from seeking admission.

To say that science is widely perceived as masculine is, perhaps, no longer considered controversial.

> There are at least four distinct senses in which it can be argued that science is masculine. The most obvious is in terms of numbers – who studies science at school, who teaches it, who is recognized as a scientist. Secondly, there is the packaging of science, the way it is presented, the examples and applications that are stressed. Thirdly, there are the classroom behaviours and interactions whereby elements of masculinity and femininity developed in out-of-school contexts are transformed in such a way as to establish science as a male preserve. And finally there is the suggestion that the type of thinking commonly labelled scientific embodies an intrinsically masculine world view.
>
> (Kelly 1987: 66)

Arguments parallel to those used to criticize science and science education for their androcentrism have been used to criticize them for Eurocentrism and classism. In other words, the culture of science and the culture of science education are incompatible with the knowledge, values, aspirations and experiences of many children from ethnic minority cultures and from low SES communities (Hodson 1993a, 1998; Stanley and Brickhouse 1994).

Costa (1995) has utilized Phelan *et al.*'s (1991) work to describe the ways in which different students effect (or not) the transition into the culture of school science. She describes the various patterns in the relationships between students' social worlds and their success in school science in terms of five broad categories of student. These five student 'types' experience the same science curriculum in very different ways. Their experiences are positive or negative to the extent that the values, beliefs and expectations of their family and peer groups are consistent with those of the science classroom. When there are major discrepancies between communities in terms of concepts, theories, methods, language, values and behaviours, border crossings become difficult, if not impossible. Costa's student types are:

- *Potential scientists* – where the worlds of family and friends are congruent with the worlds of school and science, and the transition into the culture of school science is smooth and unproblematic. These students have educational aspirations and career plans in which science has a prominent role.
- *Other smart kids* – where the worlds of family and friends are congruent with school, but not with science. These students can manage the transition into the culture of school science without too much difficulty. While science is not personally interesting to them, they can make instrumental use of it in pursuit of educational purposes.
- *'I don't know' students* – where the worlds of family and friends are inconsistent with both school and science. Transition into the culture of school science is hazardous, though possible at some personal cost. Often, these students find a way of meeting the demands of the system and obtaining reasonable grades without ever really understanding the material.[1]
- *Outsiders* – where the worlds of family and friends are discordant with both school and science. These students tend to be disillusioned with or alienated from school, in general, so that transition into the culture of school science is virtually impossible. They neither know about nor care about science.
- *Inside outsiders* – where the worlds of family and friends are irreconcilable with the world of school but potentially compatible with the world of science. Although these students have a natural interest in the physical world, and the intellectual ability to cope with science, transition into the culture of school science is prevented through lack of support both inside and outside school, and by their distrust of schools and teachers.

As teachers struggle to provide a science curriculum suitable for an increasingly diverse school population, it is important to know how some students negotiate boundaries successfully while others are impeded by them. It is likely that students of different ethnic groups will perceive boundaries differently and use different adaptation strategies as they move or attempt to move between social settings (Aikenhead 1996, 1997). Similarly, girls may perceive boundaries differently from the way boys perceive them and, therefore, may adopt different strategies for effecting transition. Moreover, for any one individual, patterns are not necessarily stable over time, and may be profoundly affected by changes in classroom or school climate, family circumstances and peer group friendships. In Costa's California-based study, all students in the 'inside outsider' category were African-Americans. Just as significant is the observation that most of those for whom transition into the world of school science is smooth and unproblematic were from white middle-class family groups. It is also the case that transitions were generally smoother for boys than for girls.

The dangers of assimilation

The apprenticeship model of teaching and learning, intended to overcome the relativist charges against constructivist pedagogy and provide a more personalized form of enculturation into science, can sometimes increase resistance to science in the ways just described. Paradoxically, it can also become a stultifying assimilation. Because they are advocates for the established scientific view and for the scientific way of building knowledge, teachers seek to create an environment in which this knowledge is presented as reasonable, useful and worthy of incorporation into a personal framework of understanding. This entails helping students to go beyond the evidence normally available to them through the provision of contrived experiences that (a) contradict or weaken an everyday view, or (b) support the scientific view. Teachers also construct 'a good case' for the scientific way of building theory through experiment, correlational studies, literature-based research and theoretical argument, and may even model what counts as a good explanation or good inquiry in science. The danger inherent in this approach is that, because of the asymmetry of the teacher–student relationship, students will come to accept science as a superior way of knowing simply on the authority of the teacher or the textbook.

The relationship between teachers and students is asymmetric in the sense that teachers urge students to include scientific views in their personal frameworks of understanding, sometimes even urging them to accept such views as *true* accounts of the world (Nadeau and Desautels 1984). It is asymmetric in the sense that teachers know more than students and have more experience of science, so that they are seen by students as a source of authoritative, reliable and valid knowledge. It is asymmetric in terms of feelings, in that teachers are usually confident in their knowledge (of science), while students may be anxious and may be experiencing 'culture shock' as they begin to recognize the inadequacies of their everyday knowledge for coping with the tasks that the teacher sets them. Above all, it is asymmetric in terms of power and control. Invariably, it is the teacher who sets the agenda and establishes the nature of the discourse. The asymmetry of teacher and learner is, of course, essential to learning within the zone of proximal development. So, too, is retention of control by the more expert of the nature of the activities, at least in the early stages. However, in many school learning situations, this asymmetry can be such that it interferes with, and even inhibits, good learning.

Paradoxically, a major part of the problem is that, on the one hand, school life is surrounded by too many rules and too rigid a code of behaviour and, on the other hand, the purpose of the learning enterprise is often unstated and remains, for many children, a mystery. Learning in the contrived settings of school is different from learning in the natural settings of home, community and work. There are significantly different 'ground rules', which create different demands on all parties involved. What may seem on the surface to be similar learning tasks are, in practice, approached very differently because they are embedded in different rules of conduct, interpretation and communication. One of the tasks facing students in school is to come to terms with the distinctive remoteness of much of school learning from everyday reality and its tendency to present problems and ideas in a highly abstract and formal way. Students have to relearn not only what counts as a problem or as an answer to a question in this new social setting, but also how to express them in an approved form.

The 'mystery' for students is that they are frequently asked to do things for no better reason, seemingly, than because the teacher 'says so', and they are required to accept a particular view for no better reason than because 'it's in the book' or 'it's on the syllabus'. Because of time pressure and the ever-present need to get through an overloaded curriculum, class sizes that are too high and curriculum resources and facilities that are less than ideal, many teachers adopt a highly directive role through which students are socialized into a 'right answer orientation'. The hand-over of control of learning from teacher to learner is often incomplete. As a consequence, many students remain at a level where they are dependent on algorithms and on what Edwards and Mercer (1987) call 'ritualized learning': they know what to say and do, but are unable to work from basic principles or to tackle novel problems with any real confidence of achieving a successful solution.

Questioning questioning strategies

It becomes clear to most students, very early in their school careers, that teachers know the answers to the questions they ask. As a result, students feel that question–answer interactions are more a test of their knowledge than an invitation to speculate or to engage in a rational appraisal of evidence. The implicit message is that teachers know all the answers and it is the students' task simply to find them. This is reinforced by an excessive use of closed questions – 'closed' in the sense that they have a single right answer or a very narrow range of possible right answers. It is also the case that most questions are pitched at too low a level of cognitive demand to form the basis for useful discussion. Even when the question is phrased in such a way that significant student–teacher interaction might occur, teachers often leave insufficient time for students to formulate a response before they ask a different student, ask an alternative question or supply the answer. However, silences don't always indicate incomprehension or lack of understanding.

They may be 'thinking times' that students need in order to assemble a satisfactory answer. Therefore, impatient teachers, keen to move the lesson along at a brisk pace, may be denying students sufficient opportunity to think. When teachers extend this 'wait time' (say from one to three seconds), the frequency and quality of student responses usually increase (Rowe 1974; Swift and Gooding 1983). Moreover, there is much greater elaboration of answers, increased frequency of student-initiated questions and comments and more critical responses to the utterances of other students.

Wood (1991) states that the more questions teachers ask, the less children will say. Conversely, the less frequent the questions, the more likely it is that students will provide an elaborated response. Moreover, the less frequently teachers interrogate children, the more likely those children are to listen, make unsolicited contributions and ask questions of their own – both of the teacher and of other students. He concludes that it is more productive for teachers to talk about their own views and ideas (and, presumably, why they hold them) than constantly to ask questions. When teachers speculate, express opinions and make clear their reasoning processes, he says, students are likely to respond similarly.

> Where teachers, in one sense, answer their own putative questions to provide possible answers, opinions and so on, children as young as four years of age reciprocate by adopting a similar cognitive-linguistic stance and remain relatively active and forthcoming at the same time.
>
> (Wood 1991: 116)

Just as teacher questions are often badly deployed, and so contribute to a 'right answer orientation', so teacher talk is often poorly utilized. Quite properly, teacher talk is used to hold and direct students' attention, highlight significant points, provide a common vocabulary, give insight into procedures, establish the context of meaning and so on. It is also improperly and, perhaps, unconsciously used to privilege particular views, interests and values and to marginalize others, and to include some students and exclude others.

Language issues

Bakhtin (1981, 1986) points out that not only do we have a national language (in this case, English), but we also communicate regularly in a range of social languages and employ a variety of speech genres that are the characteristic modes of expression of particular sub-groups in society. Speech genres include everyday greetings, dinner table conversations, verbal exchanges concerned with buying and selling goods and services, cross-examination of witnesses by courtroom lawyers, intimate talk between close friends or lovers, military commands, urgent communications between colleagues engaged in a specialized task, mother–infant talk and so on. They are not formalized languages, but they are distinctive and have clear purposes and socially agreed meanings. Each of us uses speech embedded in these social languages and speech genres to convey meaning quickly and reliably. Moreover, because speech is socioculturally constituted, each genre carries with it the common assumptions, interpretations and values of the group whose genre or social language it is.

School classrooms can be regarded as distinctive speech communities in which language is selectively used by teachers and systematically acquired by or imposed on students. Moje (1995) shows how some teachers utilize a language of belonging ('*You* are a scientist', '*We* believe that . . .' etc.) to foster student participation and cooperation and to establish and maintain the culture of school science: the laboratory as a 'special place', with specialized apparatus and ever-present danger; the need for accuracy and precision; the priority of observation; the disinterestedness of scientific inquiry; and so on. Building solidarity through language enables teachers, thereafter, to exercise considerable influence over students' views and their underlying values. It seems, however, that this influence is frequently too rigid, assertive and controlling. When teachers ask questions, for example, they do so in a particular way and expect answers to be presented in a particular way (the 'right' way). By responding to this (often unstated) directive, students confirm the superior status of the teacher's language and frame of reference. Perhaps unconsciously, teachers shift students into their preferred mode of discourse.

> When they engage students in conversation, (teachers) constantly structure the dialogue so as to shift students away from their own experiential frames of reference toward thinking about issues and events in the abstract, decontextualized, technical-rational discourse that is the usual speech genre of middle-class teachers . . . although conversational exchanges occur, it is not true dialogue, because the teacher's authoritative voice is privileged at the expense of the student's voice.
>
> (O'Loughlin 1992: 815)

Language serves as a means of identification and solidarity; its adoption signals membership of the community, in this case the community of school science students. But language is also used to signal the authority of the teacher and her or his right to control the curriculum, in terms of both classroom management and curriculum content. Of course, teachers have it in mind that students will arrive at particular understanding – that specified in the curriculum plan. It is this understanding that constitutes enculturation into science. Consequently, teachers define and control classroom discourse in order to achieve it: they ask specific questions, direct attention to x, y and z rather than to a, b and c, introduce easy ways of arriving at preferred solutions and acceptable views and so on. By these means, teachers not only set the agenda and define the topic for discussion, they also establish the criteria of relevance and appropriateness of student contributions, thereby ensuring that particular views are introduced, validated and utilized, while others are seen to be disapproved, discouraged or ignored. It is here that difficulties can arise. Often, they privilege certain views and marginalize others, claiming that to do otherwise would take too long and be too uncertain. As Edwards and Mercer (1987) say, the supposed freedom of students in contemporary classrooms to express their own views is largely illusory. In many cases, teachers retain too strict a control over what is said and done, and over the conclusions and interpretations arrived at, though they may sometimes do so unconsciously.

Reinforcing the culture of certainty and compliance

One of the most powerful ways of imposing meaning is by presumption and presupposition, simply *assuming* a particular interpretation. Many aspects of learning science and learning about science are simply taken for granted; they are rarely, if ever, questioned by teachers or students. This is part of the 'illusion of certainty' (Bencze and Hodson 1998) that permeates the culture of school science and serves to silence some students and foster a rigid conformity in others. It is this climate of authority and conformity that inclines students towards a 'right answer orientation' rather than an explanations-oriented approach rooted in an understanding of fundamental principles. In the language of Chapter 6, it promotes a performance orientation rather than a mastery or learning orientation. In simple terms, when students perceive that the social climate of the classroom is such that the teacher's knowledge and style of discourse is highly valued and their own is not, they become reluctant to proffer alternative views, however sensible they may be, and are content with repeating verbatim what the teacher says.

Some students come to see their task as memorizing a series of definitions and reproducing them on demand, mastering a set of algorithms for solving standard problems and carrying out the teacher's instructions for (pseudo) experimental inquiries in order to obtain a predetermined set of results. They do not see their role as being to think or to question the source, relevance, validity and reliability of what they are given; nor to design, conduct and interpret scientific inquiries for themselves and by themselves. These students succeed in the sense of being able to say and do the 'right things', and to gain the marks that are made available for such conformity, but they fail in the sense of gaining a robust and usable set of meanings to incorporate into a personal framework of understanding. What they learn is how to do classroom tasks, how to be neat, how to finish on time, how to look busy and to fill up the available time, how to avoid attracting the teacher's attention and, if it is practical work, how to tidy away and write things up in the approved form. They may also develop passive-resistance techniques, such as 'silence, accommodation, ingratiation, evasiveness, and manipulation' (Atwater 1996: 823). What they do not learn is how to employ their knowledge in novel situations and how to use it to develop a deeper and richer understanding. Such students have not been enculturated into science; rather, they have been acculturated and assimilated into school. They have learned their own version of Fatima's rules!

Note

1 In a particularly insightful study, Larson (1995) describes a student (Fatima) who consistently and successfully 'plays the game of school' according to a set of invented rules and conventions (e.g. 'Don't read the textbook, just memorize the bold-faced words and phrases'). Although they may not understand the material they reproduce in tests, students like Fatima achieve acceptable grades and can make instrumental use of science education in pursuit of other goals.

• • • 10

Authenticity in science and learning

The case built over the course of the preceding chapters is that science education should be seen as a matter of enculturation into the knowledge, practices, language and values of the community of scientists, a process that necessitates close contact with a more knowledgeable member of that community, who acts as guide, mentor and support. It has also been argued that each student possesses a unique personal framework of understanding, in which experience, emotions, values, sense of self and social identity play a crucial mediating role, determining what is regarded as significant and when/how it is utilized. These frameworks of meaning are, of course, in constant flux, development and interaction. Moreover, as circumstances change, especially social circumstances, different elements of understanding are accessed. Of course, teachers have a personal framework of understanding too, and it is important for them to be mindful not to operate all the time within the 'scientific aspects' of it, especially if these are not fully shared with and understood by the students. Teachers' use of aspects of their personal framework of understanding that are radically different from those of the students can be responsible for learning difficulties and, at the more extreme level, for impeding students in crossing the border into the subculture of science.

Eventually, as an individual's framework of personal understanding develops, areas of coherence emerge and, as they grow, relationships are established among them. Points of mismatch and conflict may be recognized, and either resolved or tolerated. It is also likely that many remain undetected and unrecognized. At the same time, elements that constitute one's sense of personal identity – values, commitments, social aspirations, elements relating to gender, ethnicity, social class, sexual orientation and peer group membership, for example – exert an increasing influence on what is attended to and what further understanding is incorporated. In Aikenhead's (1996: 14) words, 'learning science is influenced as much by diverse subcultures within a student's life-world as it is by a student's prior knowledge and the "taught" curriculum.' Who we are, or who we believe ourselves to be or aspire to be, determines what we pay attention to and what we seek to learn. It is also the case that who we are is determined by what we already know and have experienced. Whatever knowledge is successfully incorporated into a student's personal framework of understanding is used as a 'tool': it acts to change, modify or reinforce underlying beliefs and commitments; it makes acquisition of further knowledge possible; it orients learning in particular directions; and so on.

Given the uniqueness of each individual's personal framework of understanding, it is to be expected that a class of students will respond in a variety of ways to a particular set of learning experiences. During the teaching of a particular topic, different 'learning histories' will be evident within the class and, for a particular student, there will be qualitatively different learning histories on different topics. Demastes *et al.* (1996) describe four distinctive patterns of conceptual change that might contribute to such learning histories.

- *Cascade of changes* – a change of one key conception precipitates a sequence of related changes over a relatively short timescale.
- *Wholesale changes* – an existing conception is completely replaced by a new idea as a consequence of the rational appraisal of evidence and argument.
- *Incremental changes* – gradual, piecemeal change, characterized by early use of a new term (possibly in rote recall fashion) within an otherwise unchanged framework, followed by a gradual shift to appropriate and more extensive use.
- *Dual constructions* – utilization of logically incompatible conceptual frameworks.

Whether the authors are correct in their fourfold characterization is less important than the overarching point that learning science is far more complex and idiosyncratic, and far less rational and predictable, than much of the conceptual change literature would have us believe. Indeed, Demastes *et al.* (1996) suggest that Posner *et al.*'s (1982) view of conceptual change, with its essential conditions, should be confined to explaining the first two categories in their typology – that is, those changes in personal understanding that resemble a Kuhnian scientific revolution. The category of 'incremental changes' is best reserved for the kind of changes and modifications to personal understanding that resemble Kuhnian normal science. These changes are described by Rumelhart and Norman (1981) as *accretion* (the gradual accumulation of factual data that can be successfully interpreted) and *tuning* (the extension and development of the interpretive framework).[1]

It is the fourth category in the typology (dual constructions), and the finding that this characteristic is not restricted to young children, but is equally common among older students (and, presumably, among adults), that is explored further in this chapter. Despite areas of coherence and consistency, it seems that the personal framework of understanding of most individuals remains essentially fragmented into context-related 'chunks'. Even conflicting ideas can remain within the individual's personal framework of understanding, to be accessed and used in different contexts. Over time, as the individual's personal history unfolds, their relative significance and usefulness may change.

The case I intend to argue is that this should not be regarded as problematic, provided that students recognize that this is the case, gain some good understanding of their own knowledge and how it is organized, learn how to recognize the circumstances in which different chunks are appropriate and can use them properly and access them quickly and reliably as the need arises.

Context-dependent learning

Scribner (1984) has shown both the situation-specificity of complex problem-solving algorithms used by a range of blue-collar workers and the separateness of these strategies from mathematical knowledge taught in school. Many similar findings (Lave 1988; Schliemann and Carraher 1992) point to the highly specific task-related nature of much everyday knowledge. Indeed, Lave (1988) argues that cognition and learning should be regarded as 'practices' – activities inherently part of routine, everyday experience – rather than activities occurring solely in an individual's mind. In other words, thinking, knowing and learning are encounters between 'cognitive agents' and specific situations, and are best studied in their embedded, routinized, everyday context. Consequently, highly personal methods of solving problems are often developed and used successfully in practical situations by those who seem unable to solve logically similar problems in a formal mathematics test. In Scribner's (1984: 39) words, 'skilled practical thinking is goal-directed and varies adaptively with changing properties of problems and the changing conditions in the task environment.' It has little to do with the kinds of knowledge and skills generally taught in school. Indeed, research by Carraher *et al.* (1985, 1987) and Saxe (1991) in a wide variety of work and domestic situations shows that two distinct systems of arithmetic procedures and practices (one symbol/rule-based, the other meaning-based) function largely independently of each other. George (1995) has identified similar differences between the universalistic meanings and formal reasoning of school science and the particularistic meanings and goal-oriented reasoning of what she calls the 'street science' of everyday life, and Layton *et al.* (1993) have shown that the kind of scientific knowledge and the kind of reasoning used in real world situations, even by those educated in science, are very different from what is taught in school science. Even within school, styles of reasoning and the kinds of explanations proffered by students may vary with context. In addressing topics in an STS-oriented programme, for example, students tend to use either a scientific mode of reasoning or a social and moral-ethical one, depending on how they perceive the question (Fleming 1986). In chemistry, many students seem unable to transfer understanding and problem-solving skills between the atomic/molecular level of theoretical understanding and the macroscopic level of real materials (Staver and Lumpe 1995).

The notion that coherence and consistency among ideas is related to particular contexts, rather than extending across the whole of personal knowledge, can, to an extent, be used to describe science itself. There are some very striking differences between, for example, the ways in which biologists and physicists conceptualize and conduct investigations. Even within biology, there are major differences between functional biology, with its concern for 'proximate causation', and evolutionary biology, with its concern for 'ultimate causation' (Mayer 1988). As discussed earlier, scientific method really has precise meaning only within the context of particular investigations. What is appropriate depends on the unique circumstances of the particular inquiry. Most practising scientists focus on fairly narrowly defined problems, so that expertise in science commonly means having detailed personal knowledge of a very restricted aspect of science and how to investigate it. By working in relatively circumscribed contexts, scientists develop conceptual and procedural knowledge that is tailor-made for, and distinctive to, those contexts. Coherence and consistency at more general levels is not usually a concern.

In practice, scientists do not acquire complete all-embracing theories and all-powerful methods; rather, they build up their expertise piecemeal, by becoming familiar with largely separate concrete problem-solutions (fragments of theory, experimental procedures, instrumental techniques and so on), each of which is useful in a particular context (Kuhn 1977). Over time, these fragments constitute a unique framework of understanding, within which many important relationships are established, but within which there are still isolated and seemingly mutually incompatible elements. This should not be interpreted as an attempt to deny the existence of certain interdisciplinary themes (such as randomness, reductionism/holism, concern with the nature of time and so on) that transcend subject boundaries and serve, periodically, to unify the work of scientists in seemingly disparate fields. According to Holton (1986), for example, it is scientists' commitment to what he calls *themata* – many of which occur as diadic or triadic choices (synthesis versus analysis; constancy versus evolution versus catastrophic change) – that guides research, permits bold and inventive leaps of imagination and enables scientists to 'suspend their disbelief' when things are not going well. Nor is it an attempt to deny that some scientists are committed to the search for unifying theories, and from time to time produce them – the Newtonian and Einsteinian revolutions, for example. Rather, it is to state that the preoccupying concerns and the scope of expertise of most scientists and technicians are usually somewhat more modest and restricted.

Of course, everyday practices and professional practices are also 'social practices', in that tasks are embedded not only in a specific problem-context but also in a specific social setting. Thus, knowledge is intimately related to the specific social situations, interactions and communities that have generated, validated, maintained and used it. Within these communities, knowledge, and the practices it informs, is co-constructed and expressed through a particular community-approved style of discourse. It follows that knowledge cannot be considered as generalizable either over contexts or over individuals. Nor can its acquisition or use. Cognitive development should, therefore, be seen as the successive mastery of a series of context-specific knowledges and modes of discourse, where 'context' is writ both large and small – large in the sense that it means a community context, small in the sense that it means a particular problem situation.[2] Students build up a repertoire of context-specific knowledges through social interaction, negotiation and co-construction of meaning, with different social contexts providing different inputs into the individual's construction of a personal framework of understanding. Within this model of learning, the kinds of age-related universals considered by Piaget are less important than the context-specific contributions of different social groups. Learning is regarded as an active, continuous and changing series of negotiations between the individual and the social environments in which she or he moves. In addition, because of the interactive nature of social encounters, the social context is both the product of interaction and the impetus and guide for development.

The social context not only facilitates and structures learning and the development of understanding, it also motivates the learner because it provides the authentic contexts within which apprentices gain a sense of self, feelings of increasing competence and recognition and a sense of ownership. In a sense, these are the sociocultural equivalents of the fruitfulness cited by Posner *et al.* (1982) as the key to cognitive restructuring. However, while it is the contextualized nature of learning that leads to a sense of ownership, it may be recognition of more universalistic and generalized meanings that effects the transition from novice to expert status, and eventually to scientific connoisseurship.

Recognition of the highly context-specific nature of much of everyday knowledge and practice does not entail the view that cognitive activities are absolutely specific to the context in which they were originally learned. To function satisfactorily in a complex world, we must be able to generalize some aspects of knowledge and skills to new situations. The interesting questions centre on what is generalizable and transferable. Perkins and Salomon (1989) argue that there are general cognitive skills, but they function in contextualized ways. When experts are faced with atypical problems that don't yield to straightforward approaches, they apply general strategies – such as reasoning by analogy with systems they understand better, searching for counter examples and misanalogies, exploring 'extreme case' scenarios, employing visualization techniques and thought experiments and solving simpler parallel problems – all of which function in a contextualized way to access and deploy a rich database of conceptual and experiential knowledge.[3] Another effective approach is to use a generalized level of control or problem management rooted in metacognitive awareness, asking such questions as 'What am I doing now?', 'Is it getting me anywhere?', 'What else might I try?'

In general terms, it seems that experts not only know more than novices, but have more accessible and usable knowledge because it is differently (better) organized. While novice problem-solvers access concepts, procedures and equations one by one, experts access related clusters of relevant knowledge, and while novices tend to address superficial features of a problem, experts are able to use more powerful overarching principles (Larkin 1983).

While novices use means–end analysis and attempt to employ previously learned formulae and algorithms, experts are more holistic and attempt to work from first principles, drawing on their stock of experiential knowledge for exemplars (Carey 1986). In other words, experts function at a more general level than novices. Indeed, some have argued that educationally assisted development is the process by which thought becomes increasingly disembedded from situational contexts, the process by which students are 'distanced' from everyday thinking. Two points should be made in response.

- School itself is a 'context' and, within it, school science is a particular specialized context, making special demands and requiring special codes of behaviour and language use, as earlier discussion illustrates. Thus, learning in school is as much situated (in this case, situated in school, with its distinctive sociocultural features) as any other kind of learning.
- Science is a 'context' and should be considered as a community practice, with complex rules and procedures, rather than as just a body of knowledge or method of inquiry.

The key to developing academic competence is not to disregard context-based knowledge, or to attempt to solve problems without it, but to recognize when to invoke and how to apply contextual knowledge and to recognize how generalized strategies and localized knowledge interact. In the case of science education, this also means exploring the ways in which conceptual and procedural knowledge develop together.

Learning science, learning about science, doing science

Fundamental to the enculturation model of learning is the argument that we understand something to the extent that we use it appropriately for the purpose for which it was designed, and that we come to understand it *as* we use it appropriately, or as our attempts to use it correctly are monitored and supported by others more expert than ourselves. In other words, we do not understand and then use, we understand *as we use*, and we use (properly) as we come to understand. This line of argument raises the issue of *context of use* and whether that should be a major issue in curriculum design. Sadly, as stated several times previously, school science often attempts to decontextualize the teaching of scientific concepts, possibly in an attempt to emphasize their context-transcendence. It seeks to separate knowing from doing, treating knowledge as 'an integral, self-sufficient substance, theoretically independent of the situations in which it is learned and used' (Brown *et al.* 1989: 32). The outcome is to render concepts 'empty' or inert, to produce the kind of learning that Edwards and Mercer (1987) describe as ritualized knowledge. It is a state in which students know some definitions, routines and algorithms, which they can apply successfully in the precise context in which they were acquired, but cannot deploy in novel situations or use to generate new insights and understanding. By contrast, advocates of approaches based on theories of situated cognition claim that understanding is developed (only) through continued, situated use. In other words, learning is successful when embedded in authentic and meaningful activity. Authentic activities are the ordinary day-to-day actions of the community of practitioners. Thus, to learn science is to engage in the activities of the community of science, alongside a skilled practitioner who acts as guide, mentor and support (the notion of apprenticeship discussed previously).

Two questions should be asked at this point.

- What is it that scientists do?
- Can all that students need to learn in school science courses be learnt by doing science?

Providing an answer to the first question involves detailed considerations in the history, philosophy and sociology of science that are outside the scope of this book, although some of the relevant issues were raised, very briefly, in Chapter 2. Providing an answer to the second question involves a critical inquiry into the distinctions and relationships among *learning science, learning about science* and *doing science*. While they are in some senses separate, and can best be achieved by different teaching and learning strategies, they are also closely related.

While there is a strong case for regarding as nonsense the notion that the processes and methods of science are knowledge-free and that scientific processes can be taught independently of content (Hodson 1992), it would be equally absurd to regard scientific knowledge as independent of the methods that generated and validated it. Scientific knowledge and scientific method develop together, with theory building and experimentation proceeding hand-in-hand (Hodson 1988). Authentic problems involve scientists using and developing their procedural knowledge and conceptual understanding *as* problems are tackled – though, of course, they also learn in other ways. So it is with learning science in school: content knowledge and process knowledge are utilized together and develop together.

Concepts and theories can be regarded as tools, to be used for the purposes for which they were designed, and able to be explored and developed by attempting to widen and extend their use. Those purposes include, for example, description, explanation, prediction and control. They are also employed in designing, interpreting and communicating the findings of scientific inquiries, for which scientists also need procedural knowledge – knowledge of the methods and techniques of scientific inquiry. By engaging in these activities, scientists intend to extend, develop and change both their conceptual and procedural knowledge. If learning experiences in school are to be authentic, they should be designed to provide opportunities for students to test the robustness of their conceptual understanding in these contexts of use and to engage in activities focusing on describing, explaining, predicting, inquiring and controlling as a way of developing that understanding.

Because processes and concepts are interdependent, it is reasonable to suppose that engaging in the processes of science changes one's conceptual understanding. In other words, process skills play a crucial role in the development of understanding. Just as the possession of conceptual knowledge determines the ways in which students use the various processes of science, so the processes students engage in will profoundly influence the development of their conceptual knowledge. Through engagement in scientific activity (making scientific observations, scientific classifications and so on), conceptual knowledge is manipulated, tested, evaluated and, thereby, modified. Put another way, conceptual development in individuals is stimulated and assisted by scientific activity. There is a synergic relationship between conceptual knowledge and procedural knowledge: they proceed hand-in-hand, they develop hand-in-hand. Therefore, encouraging students to deploy the processes of science (in conducting investigations and solving problems) is a way of developing their conceptual understanding. What is crucially different between this suggestion and the process approach is that here the various sub-processes of science are regarded as the pedagogic means to the goals of learning science and learning about science, not as ends or goals in themselves.

It also follows that students will understand procedural knowledge to the extent that they can use it themselves and evaluate whether it has been used appropriately and skilfully by others. And it follows that they will acquire a deeper understanding of the overall nature of scientific inquiry by conducting scientific inquiries. However, students will no more discover the methods of scientific inquiry for themselves than they will discover the ways in which conceptual knowledge in science is organized. These things have to be taught. Gott and Duggan (1995, 1996) focus on some of the features of experimental inquiry that can be systematically taught, identifying what they term the 'concepts of evidence' essential to an appraisal of the reliability and validity of experimentally gathered data. Those associated with experimental design include variable identification, fair test, sample and variable types; those associated with measurement include relative scale, range and interval, choice of instrument, repeatability and accuracy; those associated with data handling include tables, graph types, patterns and multivariate data. Two points should be made: (a) not all scientific inquiry is experimental, and (b) scientific inquiry is idiosyncratic.

Many fields of scientific endeavour deal with events that are remote and inaccessible in time and space, and so make little or no use of experiments. In some fields, experimentation may be possible in principle but is ruled inadmissible for ethical reasons, or is too difficult, dangerous or expensive. It is here that correlational studies play a crucial role. In a sense, studies seeking correlations among variables are more faithful than experimental inquiry to the supposed open-mindedness of science, because they make fewer assumptions about the nature of the interactions. They also provide opportunities to study phenomena and events in natural settings rather than the contrived situation of the laboratory. It is the case that many field settings are simply unsuitable for experimental inquiry because they are too complex or too fragile and uncertain. Making science experiences in school more authentic necessitates a shift away from the current preoccupation with experimentation and the 'illusion of certainty' that accompanies it. Bencze (1996) provides a detailed argument for the adoption of correlational studies in science education and a critical discussion of their distinctive features, including systematic inquiry via statistical control.

Authenticity also involves recognizing that, in the real world of scientific practice, success in the creative enterprise of doing science comes to those who can choose a course of action that is well suited to the situation. There are no rules for making these kinds of choices; there is no algorithm that can be applied. All decisions are local – determined by the particular circumstances of individual investigations – and, therefore, idiosyncratic. As in games playing, success comes to those who can improvise and exploit opportunities, rather than to those who slavishly seek to follow strict guidelines. As Albert Einstein is reputed to have said, to be a successful scientist it is necessary to be an unscrupulous opportunist!

Pedagogical issues related to learning about the scope of scientific investigation and acquiring (some of) the tacit knowledge necessary for successful inquiry are addressed in Chapter 12. So, too, is the second question posed above: 'Can all that students need to learn in school science courses be learnt by doing science?'

In search of a pedagogy

What guidance can be drawn from this and earlier chapters to assist the design of effective teaching and learning activities? First, they should be of interest and significance to the learner: *prioritizing the affective* was quite deliberately chosen as the title for Chapter 6 to indicate the necessity for engaging students in activities they perceive as meaningful and important. Without a sense of ownership and commitment there is unlikely to be significant learning. Bettencourt (1992: 83, my italics) makes the point that 'understanding starts with a question, not any question but a *real* question. A question that because it is real does not remain detached from us . . . Said in another way a real question expresses a desire to know. This desire is what moves the questioner to pursue the question until an adequate answer has been found.' Real questions may be raised or generated by students or teachers; they may arise directly from lesson activities or be prompted by concerns in the wider community. This latter point speaks directly to the matter of politicization and the design of science curricula around matters of social, economic and environmental significance. It should also be noted that part of enculturation is learning, with appropriate teacher guidance and support, how to put questions in a form that is susceptible to rigorous and critical inquiry.

Previous chapters have emphasized the need to acknowledge and build on the knowledge and experiences that students already possess, but also to test and challenge existing understanding in a careful and sensitive way that encourages and promotes the inclusion of formal scientific knowledge into students' personal frameworks of understanding, but does not necessarily require them to discard commonsense meanings that may have other uses. In addition, it has been argued that students' attempts to construct further understanding within the zone of proximal development must be supported by well designed and appropriate scaffolding that leads novice members of the community of scientists closer to the ways of thinking and acting that constitute authentic science. Herein lies one of the major dilemmas for the science teacher: how to provide opportunities for self-directed, active learning that also has the characteristics of authentic scientific activity, while ensuring that students arrive at the particular understanding designated by the curriculum plan; and, moreover, to achieve all this within a classroom that may encompass enormous cultural and social diversity.

In my view, the most effective form of learning is likely to be inquiry-oriented, personalized and collaborative, and conducted in accordance with the norms and values of the community of scientists, under the guidance of a skilled practitioner. Learning by inquiry allows for classroom activities to be teacher-led (and modelled), negotiated and shared between teacher and students or student-led, with varying amounts of teacher guidance and support. Although it has previously been argued that inquiry is both fluid and idiosyncratic, it is useful for present purposes to regard it as comprising five phases:

- initiation;
- design and planning;
- performance;
- interpretation;
- reporting and communicating.

Initiation is a matter of generating interest and commitment, and finding a focus for the inquiry. Interesting questions may be asked by students or teachers; they may arise naturally in the course of lessons or be triggered by concerns outside school. In many cases, it may be necessary for teachers to stimulate interest, curiosity and questioning by displaying objects or photographs, conducting demonstrations, showing a video or movie, reading a poem or story, focusing attention on a newspaper cutting or item from a news bulletin, looking at some examples of advertising or product labelling, taking students on a field trip, giving them some exploratory investigative work to carry out or engaging them in a reading, writing or discussion task.

The remaining phases are, perhaps, self-explanatory: students work individually or in groups, and alongside the teacher, to gather information that will address the issues and questions raised in the initiation phase. In broad terms, inquiries can be regarded as either literature/media-based or field experience/laboratory-based, so decisions have to be made about the objects, phenomena and events to be studied, the sources of information to be consulted, the kinds of experiments to be conducted and so on. These decisions, made in negotiation with the teacher, will lead into a performance phase that will sometimes draw on knowledge and capabilities students already possess and will sometimes require the acquisition and development of new ways of thinking and acting. Literature and media-based inquiries may require library and archive skills, computer skills or other specialized knowledge and techniques that students do not already possess. Similarly, laboratory-based investigations may require certain bench skills for manipulating materials or the ability to use a range of laboratory instruments to collect accurate data. Again, students may or may not already have these capabilities. Inquiries may also require additional mathematical skills for manipulating data. The point being made here is that inquiry-based learning provides a stimulus for the acquisition and development of a wide range of new skills, not merely the opportunity to utilize those already perfected.

The reporting and communication phase may involve oral and/or written reports, use of diagrams, drawings, charts and graphs, and may involve students in constructing models, taking photographs and making videos. It is in this phase that students learn about the distinctive styles of communication adopted in laboratory and field reports, academic scientific papers, newspaper articles and textbooks, and can contrast them with diaries, logbooks and interactive journals. Each has a different function, and the form and style of communication reflects both the function and the nature of the anticipated audience.

At each major stage of an inquiry there should be sub-phases in which students plan what to do, do it and review the results – sometimes in collaboration with the teacher, sometimes independently. It is this repeating cycle of planning, acting, reflecting and reviewing that gives inquiry-based methods both their personalized character and their potential for fostering self-directed learning. Because teachers participate extensively and supportively in the inquiry activities and in the various kinds of talking that attend them, they provide a powerful model of good inquiry. However, students acquire and develop their own skills of inquiry through involvement in inquiry activities: by trying to use them; experiencing success, making mistakes and reflecting on them; gaining feedback, advice and support from the teacher, and perhaps from other students; reformulating their plans; trying again. Through these activities, students refine and develop their existing understanding, learn new skills and acquire new conceptual and procedural knowledge. Of course, language plays a key role throughout these activities – in the negotiation, coordination and management of the group's activities and in deliberation on conceptual and procedural issues arising at each phase of the inquiry.

Within groups, language is used for such things as: asking leading questions and making them operational; observing, measuring and deciding how to record data; hypothesizing; identifying trends in data; reasoning, making inferences and drawing conclusions; deciding how to present the report. Students become familiar with what these processes are by using them; they become familiar with what language is appropriate by talking about them – planning, conducting, monitoring and reflecting on them. They also learn about the processes of planning, managing, monitoring and reflecting! Through collaborative experiences, individual students internalize what is involved in the phases and sub-phases of inquiry. In other words, social acts become internal processes; the inter-mental dialogue of social interaction becomes the intra-mental dialogue of inner speech. It is in teacher–student talk occurring in the context of collaborative inquiry that learning groups and individuals are kept 'on track' and crucial elements of meaning and understanding are passed on. Through 'collaborative talk' (Wells and Chang-Wells 1992), teachers focus attention in the zone of proximal development and enable each learner to appropriate key aspects of the teacher's more expert knowledge, skills and understanding and, having internalized them, to use them independently or in group-directed activities. In this way, conceptual knowledge and procedural knowledge that is first encountered, discussed and mastered in social interaction with peers and teachers becomes part of the student's personal framework of understanding. For example, students learn about control and systematic manipulation of variables in experimental investigations by talking about the procedures with the teacher and with group members, trying them out and reflecting on the outcome of their efforts.

An important distinction that should be drawn is that between inquiry in a general sense ('Let's find out about x, y and z') and inquiry in the more specific sense of scientific investigation through experiment or correlational study. In the first case, inquiry may have much in common with inquiry-based learning in other areas of the curriculum, such as history, where students use books and other archive materials, interview people, watch videos and so on, in order to gain new knowledge or test and develop existing knowledge. In the second case, the learning activities are based directly on the distinctive characteristics of scientific inquiry. This distinction is elaborated in Chapter 12.

Learning the language of science

The Vygotskian perspectives discussed in earlier chapters have established that language shapes our thinking. Not only does it enable us to understand how and why things are, or are perceived to be by various social groups, it also enables us to see how they might be. The language we possess determines both how we see the world and how we *can* see the world. It is also the means by which the conceptual and procedural knowledge, frames of reference, historical traditions and values of the community of scientists are encoded. Enculturation into science, therefore, entails not just being an 'investigative apprentice', but also being a 'semiotic apprentice' – acquiring familiarity with the language and symbol systems employed by the community of practitioners.

Learning the language of science is not just a matter of acquiring a few specialist terms and purpose-built vocabulary items. It involves introduction to, and gaining familiarity with, what Lemke (1990) calls the 'thematic patterns' of science – the ways in which concepts and ideas are related within a much broader network of interdependent meanings. It also entails getting used to some of the other distinctive features of scientific language: the tendency to utilize universal rather than particularistic meanings; the use of technical terms and symbols in preference to colloquial terms; and the use of familiar everyday words in restricted and specialized ways. Scientific reporting is distinctive in being expository, analytical and impersonal, and making little or no use of metaphoric or figurative language. Enculturation entails being able to use this language appropriately and being able to present ideas and findings in the distinctive genres of science, particularly the scientific paper and the laboratory or fieldwork report. Lemke (1990: 22) argues at some length that many science teachers seem to expect all this to occur unaided:

> Students are not taught how to talk science: how to put together workable science sentences and paragraphs, how to combine terms and meanings, how to speak, argue, analyze, or write science. It seems to be taken for granted that they will just 'catch on' to how to do so ... When they don't catch on, we conclude that they weren't bright enough or didn't try hard enough. But we don't directly teach them how to.

The notion of apprenticeship implies that students will learn the language of science by interaction with someone who is already an expert, and by using it themselves in carrying out authentic tasks. Thus, teachers should model appropriate language use, make explicit reference to its distinctive features, provide language-based activities that focus on them, create opportunities for students to act as autonomous users of the language and provide critical feedback on their success in doing so. There also needs to be much more *metatalk* (talk about talk), with teachers explaining why they are adopting a particular linguistic form. Students need to know that while everyday language will suffice on some occasions, a specialized language of science is necessary on others. They need to know the circumstances in which different codes are applicable and they need lots of practice in switching between them.

As an aside, it is worth noting Lemke's (1990) observation that students pay much more attention to what is being said when teachers shift from the formal language of science to the colloquialisms of everyday speech, adopt more humanized ways of talking about science and lace their explanations with humour and references to personal experience. This should not be interpreted as a case for abandoning scientific language in class in favour of the colloquial. It is a case, however, for a more thoughtful use of familiar language to assist learning, and it is a case for helping students to recognize how the language of science is used, consciously and unconsciously, to disadvantage, exclude, alienate and disempower. It is also a case for students to acquire a self-conscious and critical understanding of the language of science and the ability to use it in pursuit of their own and the local community's interests.

Given the earlier discussion concerning the sociocultural location of language, and its accompanying sociopolitical cargo of meaning, important questions of authority, culture and power are raised. Whose view of reality is being promoted? Whose voices are heard? And why? In most classrooms there is a conscious or unconscious reflection of middle-class values and aspirations that serves to promote opportunity for middle-class children and to exclude children of ethnic minorities and low SES, who quickly learn that their voices and cultures are not valued. When the speech genres and interpretive frameworks of some children are disregarded or specifically rejected as inferior, school science becomes implicated in a continuing suppression of opportunity and perpetuation of privilege. As O'Loughlin (1992: 816) says:

> To the extent that schooling negates the subjective, socioculturally constituted voices that students develop from their lived experience, therefore, and the extent that teachers insist that dialogue can only occur on their terms, schooling becomes an instrument of power that serves to perpetuate the social class and racial inequalities that are already inherent in society.

To ignore these matters, and to act as if power relationships do not impregnate classroom events, is to ensure the perpetuation of the political status quo and the continued exclusion of significant numbers of students from a satisfactory science education. To recognize the sociopolitical context of the classroom and to acknowledge the ways in which values and culturally determined meanings permeate all aspects of the language used in classrooms is to take a major step in facilitating border crossings and rebuilding society along more socially just lines. The notion of a personal framework of understanding can now be expanded to include knowledge of, and ability to use properly, a range of social languages and speech genres. It is important that students recognize the sociocultural location of different speech genres and modes of discourse, including their own familiar everyday social language. Equally important is that they learn how and when to use other modes of discourse, and not to be intimidated or manipulated by the power inherent in those with which they have, as yet, little familiarity. This is a crucial aspect of the politicization of science education, the ultimate goal of which is to ensure that students are enabled to use a range of powerful discourses, especially the discourse of science and technology, to effect social change.

Notes

1 Carey's (1986) distinction between strong restructuring (changes in core concepts and their interrelations) and weak restructuring (establishment of new relationships and addition of new concepts) also parallels the Kuhnian distinction between revolutionary and normal science.

2 It is surprising how often 'context' is left undefined. Frequently, readers are left to judge for themselves whether the writer is referring to the physical context, the immediate social context, the wider cultural context or the specific cognitive context of the problem. Each of these meanings has been employed somewhere in this book, and many of them are used in this chapter. My hope is that definition has been made apparent by the context in which it has been used!

3 It follows that the wider the range of contexts experienced, the more likely it is that contextually relevant items can be accessed – a conclusion with some important curriculum implications.

• • • 11

Walking the line: enculturation without assimilation

Perhaps the major problem in science education is not that students sometimes have conceptions of phenomena and events that are incompatible with scientific views. Nor is it that these alternative conceptions are resistant to change. Rather, the problem is that students have not recognized that they are able to incorporate different aspects of meaning, additional connotations and new relationships into their personal framework of understanding, in order to extend the usefulness and range of applicability of their knowledge, without necessarily giving up their previous, trusted understanding. Not only do we need to ensure that students develop the ability to add to their understanding, we also need to ensure that they acquire the second order understanding that includes: (a) recognizing that alternative conceptions and explanations exist (and alternative methods, too); (b) appreciating that the appropriateness and usefulness of knowledge are determined by context; (c) knowing what knowledge to access and how to use it in a variety of problem situations and social contexts.

The fundamental point is that one's way of thinking is relative to context and, sometimes, even unique to context – where 'context' includes the physical context, the immediate social context and the wider cultural context, as well as the specific problem context. Since we all move between and among a multiplicity of contexts, we are all capable of holding multiple perspectives (meanings) of our world. These different perspectives create, for each individual, a complex web of understanding around any given phenomenon or event, which I have called a *personal framework of understanding*,[1] and within which students can hold a multitude of diverse and sometimes contradictory views – among them, of course, some entirely erroneous views. Moreover, these personal frameworks of understanding include substantial elements of personal experience, feelings, emotions, attitudes and socioculturally determined knowledge, beliefs, values and customs. One of the goals of teaching is to assist students in building a deeper, broader, richer and more robust personal framework of understanding and, in the context of science education, this means helping them to incorporate 'official' scientific meanings. A further goal is assisting them in recognizing the boundaries for applicability of different ways of knowing, and then learning how to effect successful border crossings, how to move freely between different ways of knowing and different kinds of discourse. Just as much emphasis is needed, therefore, on enhancing students' ability to recognize when to use a particular aspect of their existing understanding as on building new understanding. In other words, emphasis should also focus on being able to appreciate the *functional appropriateness* of different aspects of one's personal framework of understanding. There are two major aspects to this understanding:

- knowing when to use science, rather than some other way of knowing;
- knowing when to use a particular chunk of scientific knowledge (a particular model, theory, technique or procedure), rather than some other.

Science and everyday knowledge

As stated earlier, my notion of a personal framework of understanding is such that taking on new meaning doesn't necessarily entail relinquishing the old. New and old meanings can exist side-by-side. Scientific understanding that cucumbers and tomatoes are fruit, for example, does not preclude the commonsense understanding that they are located in the vegetable section of the grocery store, together with plant roots, tubers and leaves. What is important is recognizing when particular meanings are appropriate and being able to use them properly in the appropriate discourse. There are situations in which the scientific approach has very obvious utility; for certain types of question it can provide a well tested and powerful answer. In other situations, everyday knowledge is far more useful and appropriate. A central goal of science education is to show students when their own needs and purposes are best served by scientific knowledge and scientific ways of proceeding, and when they are better served by other ways of knowing and acting. It should be noted, however, that some students may be resistant to the notion that there are different ways of perceiving things and to the view that concepts used in science are more fluid than textbooks sometimes claim and public understanding usually declares. They may want to know the proper or true version! Overcoming this problem is part of the learning about science component of the curriculum.

Perhaps Black and Lucas (1993) put their finger on the essence of this notion when they use the term 'children's informal ideas' in science. All of us have informal ideas, including scientists. It is OK to have them. What is important is that we know when their use is acceptable and when it is important to use the more formal understanding established by the scientific community. When scientific meanings are added to a learner's personal framework of understanding, they may replace an existing idea, cause it to be modified or exist alongside it. Admixture of formal scientific knowledge may not always bring about a change at a more intuitive level, because academic and everyday knowledge (formal and informal) may be encoded and stored differently. Formal and informal can exist alongside and largely separate from each other precisely because they are used on different occasions and for different purposes. Different elements in an individual's personal framework of understanding have different status and different roles in pursuit of different purposes. Moreover, our theoretical structures are reflexive. We use our knowledge to interact with the world and, thereby, our knowledge and understanding become changed. Our personal frameworks of understanding are subject to continual modification and development as we attempt to make connections among: (a) our current understanding; (b) objects, phenomena and events in the real world; (c) the world of scientific ideas. The important question is how to develop the necessary scientific understandings without sacrificing the personal, and all the while retain a measure of learner autonomy.

Learning about scientific knowledge

Crossing the border from everyday understanding to scientific understanding (and back again) can be assisted by developing an appreciation of how these two knowledge stores compare and differ: for example, recognizing that the concepts in everyday knowledge – 'spontaneous concepts', as Vygotsky (1962) calls them – are constructed from the 'bottom up', and while they are rich in personal meaning, they remain local and, for the most part, unrelated to and isolated from other concepts. By contrast, scientific concepts are constructed from the 'top down', as abstract and idealized notions linked with others into generalized systems of interrelated understandings. However, the plausibility and intelligibility of scientific concepts depend, to an extent, on everyday understanding. In Vygotsky's (1987: 177) words, they can 'arise in the child's head only on the foundation provided by the lower and more elementary forms of generalization which previously exist.' Moreover, as scientific concepts are developed, they 'grow downward into the domain of the concrete, into the domain of personal experience' (*ibid.*: 220). As they do so, they interact further with everyday concepts, sometimes precipitating change in them, and sometimes not.

According to Kozulin (1990), Vygotsky first used the term zone of proximal development to refer to the interaction between scientific concepts and everyday understanding. Because the notion of science education as enculturation is firmly rooted in Vygotskian ideas, it follows that this point of interaction should be a major focus of attention for teachers. In Chapter 12, it is argued that laboratory and fieldwork experience assist the development of scientific concepts 'downwards' by providing concrete manifestations of scientific abstractions, and assist the development of everyday knowledge 'upwards' by building up each student's stock of episodic knowledge (White 1991, 1996). In other words, laboratory work itself, if thoughtfully employed, is located in the zone of proximal development and so can be considered a major Vygotskian strategy. In a sense, by simplifying, selecting and idealizing real experience, the contrived experiences of well designed laboratory work and fieldwork constitute a kind of scaffolding.

When moving from commonsense understanding to scientific understanding, we don't just change the content of our understanding, we significantly change its character, towards one that is systematic, coherent, analytical and mathematical. Rowe (1973: 7) has observed that 'while inconsistencies in results among ideas may not disturb the beginner, they become intolerable to the more advanced learner, who begins to be governed by an accumulated set of relationships which he [*sic*] expects to hold true.' In part, this is because 'more advanced' learners have begun to recognize that science is more than a collection of context-specific explanations. Rather, it is a set of interrelated concepts and conceptual structures that aims to produce generalizable and universalist knowledge (Matthews 1994). But achieving that awareness is sometimes a long and difficult process. Children may sometimes use quite different ideas about an entity to explain its behaviour in different contexts – for example, different views about wood in the context of plant growth and the context of fuel (Barker and Carr 1989). They may switch from one sort of explanation to another for the same phenomenon – for example, using explanations based on weight, size, surface area, texture, the presence or absence of holes and so on, for floating and sinking. As Driver *et al.* (1985: 3) comment:

> The need for coherence, and the criteria for coherence, as perceived by a student are not the same as those of the scientist: the student does not possess any unique model unifying a range of phenomena that the scientist considers as equivalent. Nor does the student necessarily see the need for a coherent view, since *ad hoc* interpretations and predictions about natural events may appear to work quite well in practice.

Nor will children be able to differentiate between theory and evidence, unless they are taught. Failure to appreciate the proper relationship between theory and evidence, says Kuhn (1989), can lead to excessive theory-dependence, a state in which no discrepant events can be recognized as more than merely 'rogue data'. Paradoxically, it can also lead to acute data-dependence, a state in which students are unable to make the critical judgements necessary to interpret and rationalize data because they are unwilling to rely on any theory at all.

Students who have not learned that scientific theory is coherent and consistent, and who do not understand the relationship between hypothesis and evidence, and among theory, observation and experiment, are rooted in a 'methodology of superficiality' (Gil-Perez and Carrascosa-Alis 1985) that cannot lead beyond commonsense knowledge. What is needed to effect the transition to more sophisticated conceptual understanding is more sophisticated understanding of the nature of science – in particular, understanding of theories as complex structures rather than simple statements, experiments as central to both theory testing and theory building, the ways in which the community of scientists generates and validates new knowledge, the role and status of that knowledge and, crucially, when its use is appropriate and inappropriate. But students will not come to know about and understand these philosophical issues unaided. They must be taught. Therefore, teaching located in the history, philosophy and sociology of science is essential to science education based on an enculturation model. Science conceptions are more abstract and often more difficult to understand than everyday views. They may, therefore, only be recognized as more fruitful by those familiar with and committed to a more scientific way of viewing things.

Developing an epistemological profile

It is important not to over-emphasize the overall coherence of scientific knowledge: first, because it is not an entirely true portrayal; second, because it would contribute to problems of border crossing. As individuals learn more science and more of other things, too, their personal frameworks of understanding become more complex by addition of concepts and ideas (what Hewson (1981) calls 'conceptual capture') and by reorganization and restructuring (what Ausubel et al. (1978) call 'progressive differentiation'). These concepts and ideas can be arranged in a number of different ways, rather like a series of maps can be organized to represent rainfall, population or geographical features. Not only do these 'maps' differ from person to person, but each of us has a number of different 'maps' available to us, which together constitute our personal framework of understanding. Scientists differ among themselves in the ways in which they organize and use their knowledge (Chapter 2); they choose (consciously or unconsciously) from the 'maps' available to them and according to the situation in which they find themselves. Knowing which 'map' to use in particular circumstances is a key part of scientific connoisseurship. For students, knowing which 'map' to choose is the passport to smoother border crossings.

Hammer (1994) describes students' epistemological beliefs as located on two continua:

- from science as a collection of separate bits of information to science as a coherent system of interrelated concepts (though I would prefer 'coherent systems');
- from science as a set of formulae for gaining correct solutions to problems to science as conceptual knowledge capable of giving insight into phenomena and events.

The location of student beliefs on these two continua relates to how they view learning and how they use scientific knowledge in problem situations. Those who see science as a coherent and consistent conceptual structure that can be used to explain, argue and reason are likely to use it as such in addressing problems, while those who expect only occasional associations between conceptual knowledge and class tasks are likely to try to apply algorithms in order to solve problems. In short, those with some understanding of the structure of scientific knowledge view learning as applying and modifying personal understanding, while those who don't have this understanding view learning as the storing of knowledge provided by an authority (the teacher or the textbook). In other words, learning more about science contributes very substantially to increasing scientific expertise and intellectual independence.

Mortimer (1995) has developed the notion of an 'epistemological profile' for concepts in physics, in which the earliest form of the concept is the *realist* level, corresponding to our everyday notions and strongly rooted in commonsense understanding. Then comes the *empiricist* level: understanding located in careful observation and precise measurement. Next comes the *rational classic* level: formal abstract knowledge located within a Newtonian framework. Finally, with an appreciation of relativity theory, the concept reaches the *rational modern* level. For any particular concept, epistemological profiles will differ between individuals in direct relation to their education and experience; and for any one individual, profiles will differ from concept to concept, with some concepts understood at high levels, others at relatively lower levels and some at the lowest level of all. Teaching and learning science has two goals: first, to lead students through this profile of development at an appropriate pace; second, to ensure that students become self-consciously aware of the existence of such a profile. In other words, students should know that concepts may have this history of development, and they should know, for any particular concept, where their own understanding is located. Such self-conscious understanding might also provide students with some guidance on how best to proceed in directing their own learning and in determining what further knowledge and/or experience to seek. This could be interpreted as self-consciousness playing a role in shifting students from a performance orientation to a mastery orientation.

It is worth noting, once more, that development of understanding of a concept at a new, higher level does not necessarily entail its usefulness at a lower level being at an end. As discussed previously, a superseded theory can still be employed as a model by scientists seeking to gain a measure of control and predictive capability. Similar opportunities are available to all: each of us is entitled to pitch the level of sophistication of an explanation in relation to the task in hand. Understanding the nature of epistemological profiles includes understanding how to select the level appropriate to the context. Thus, in addition to learning which concepts to employ, depending on the task in hand, students need to learn which epistemological level of that concept is appropriate. This decision is influenced by the matter being addressed and by the levels of understanding of those with whom the student wishes to communicate. In other words, it depends on the social context as well as on the problem context.

Two further points are worth making. First, in Vygotskian terms, the transitions between levels in the profile constitute zones of proximal development within which scaffolding may be necessary. Second, the ability to work at different levels within an epistemological profile may be one of the keys to achieving smooth border crossings. It is also related to an evaluation of the intelligibility, plausibility and fruitfulness of a particular idea. In making a similar point, White and Gunstone (1989) argue that Posner *et al.*'s (1982) condition of intelligibility is usually reasonably well served by conventional teaching methods (question–answer methods, practical exercises, working through standard problems etc.) and that teacher authority reinforced by a good demonstration is often sufficient to ensure that students see a new idea as plausible. However, convincing students that they should be dissatisfied with their existing ideas, and that the new ideas being described are likely to be more fruitful, is more difficult, and requires them to pay attention to the matters under discussion here. Gaining this kind of understanding and commitment, therefore, is central to science education.

Learning about learning

Also crucial is the capacity to *reflect* on one's own understanding of these matters and to understand and control one's own learning. Achieving the potential to change one's own personal framework of understanding is not only a spur to further learning, but also the key to creative thinking. It is critical reflection on one's own understanding and processes of learning that is the base for continued development towards connoisseurship. However, the capacity to engage in critical reflection, and the attitudinal commitment that drives it, also have to be taught.

Novak (1989, 1990) provides much useful advice on the ways in which concept maps and Vee diagrams can be used to help students acquire the habit of reflecting on epistemological issues. These strategies also help to give students insight into their own thought processes and their own learning histories, and can play a part in developing more productive learning strategies. Much more emphasis in science classrooms needs to be placed on these and other methods that give students a generalized knowledge of the processes of thinking and learning and a much deeper understanding of, and control of, their own learning. Learning how to learn more successfully is one important key to feelings of control and competence. As discussed in Chapter 6, feelings of being in control of one's learning are essential to good motivation. They are also, of course, at the heart of intellectual independence.

Students can construct, or co-construct with teacher support, an understanding of their own learning processes, just as they construct and co-construct their own views of the world and their views about themselves. Those who understand and know how to monitor and regulate their learning are far more effective and successful learners than those who do not; those who learn to reason about their own knowledge, to question how and why it fits in with other ideas are, in general, more successful in learning. This understanding also influences how students perceive errors in their work – as evidence of failure or as a source of useful information for modifying future actions. By 'learning how to learn' I do not mean the various memory tricks, 'superlearning' techniques and test-taking strategies that claim to raise performance test scores (important though these may be for some students in the short term), nor the generalized study skills tips that promote techniques for improving concentration levels and for managing time more efficiently, though these too are of value for many students. Rather, I am concerned with learner behaviours that promote deeper processing and reflection on ideas and their deployment. Teachers in the PEEL project identified a number of student behaviours that militate against good learning, such as rarely contributing to discussions, not reading instructions and test questions carefully, regarding assessment tasks as subsequent to learning (rather than part of it) and not relating lesson material to existing knowledge and previous experience (Mitchell and Mitchell 1992). They also identified some productive learning behaviours, including: willingness to communicate promptly with the teacher when they don't understand or perceive that they have insufficient information; checking their work (and the teacher's work) for errors; actively searching for links to existing knowledge and previous experiences; willingness to proffer their own views and experiences, and to challenge and criticize the views of others, including the teacher's. Over 70 procedures to foster good learning behaviours and inhibit poor ones have been developed (Baird and Northfield 1992). For example, working in groups to formulate suitable sub-headings for insertion in text encourages more careful reading; deleting unnecessary data from instructions for laboratory tasks encourages a more minds-on approach to practical work; and contributing items for inclusion in the end-of-topic test or end-of-year examination encourages students to take greater responsibility for their learning. However, as mentioned in Chapter 4, a wide variety of metacognitive activities should be employed, because students quickly routinize any task and may fake good learning behaviour in order to win teacher approval (White and Mitchell 1994).

Understanding and believing

Despite their fragmentary and localized character, personal frameworks of understanding exhibit some interesting overarching interpretive structures (Bloom 1992, 1995), though these also change over time and may vary quite substantially from individual to individual, according to sociocultural environment. Anthropocentrism, anthropomorphism and zoomorphism are often dominant viewpoints for young students, guiding much of their thinking and contributing very substantially to their personal understanding. More sophisticated scientific knowledge doesn't necessarily displace these ways of thinking, though it may help students to view them more objectively. In parallel with Toulmin's (1972) identification of an individual's epistemological and metaphysical beliefs as a central aspect of conceptual ecology that gives personal understanding its stability and coherence, Cobern (1993) argues that different cultural environments produce different worldviews (sets of beliefs, held consciously or unconsciously, about the nature of reality and how one gains knowledge about it) that predispose people to feel, think and act in particular ways. As a consequence, there are likely to be very significant cross-cultural differences in the way people (including, of course, students and teachers) conceptualize and interact with the natural world (Ogunniyi *et al.* 1995). This raises some important issues for teaching science in non-Western societies and in multi-ethnic communities.

According to Cobern (1991, 1996), a worldview includes seven logico-structural categories – self, non-self or other, classification, relationships, causality, time, space – which collectively comprise presuppositions about what the world is really like and, therefore, what counts as important and valid knowledge about it. Because a worldview includes fundamental beliefs about causality and about humanity's place in the world, it is relatively easy to see how it could be incompatible with the fundamental metaphysical underpinnings of science, thus creating hazardous or impossible border crossings into the subculture of science for some students. These points raise all kinds of questions about the relationships among belief, knowledge and understanding that are outside the scope of this book. Suffice it to say that for the purposes of further discussion:

- Development of a personal framework of understanding is taken as the principal goal of learning science.
- Learning about science is assumed to include a critical consideration of the role and status of scientific knowledge.
- Informal personal beliefs and beliefs located in other 'ways of knowing' (including religion and philosophy) are recognized as having a profound influence on learning.
- The promotion of particular beliefs is not seen as one of the purposes of science education. Rather, the principal purpose is the pursuit of understanding.

Worldview theory can be particularly helpful in distinguishing between thinking and knowing, understanding and believing. By thinking, one builds an epistemological case for particular understanding (the goal of the learning about science emphasis discussed earlier). But believing is a metaphysical process by which one comes to accept as true that which one comprehends. Worldview theory helps us to unpack the metaphysical aspects of science (what it knows and assumes about the nature of being and existence) and to recognize when these features may be in conflict with a student's fundamental presuppositions about such matters. Aikenhead (1997: 220) describes how the interests of First Nations people in survival, coexistence and celebration of mystery are not in sympathy with the drive of Western science to achieve mastery of nature through objective knowledge based on mechanistic explanations. Nor are the holistic perspectives of Aboriginal knowledge, with its 'gentle, accommodating, intuitive, and spiritual wisdom' in sympathy with reductionist Western science and its 'aggressive, manipulative, mechanistic, and analytical explanations'. Border crossing is inhibited not so much by the cognitive demand of the learning task as by the discomfort caused by some of the distinctive features of science, features that are often exaggerated and distorted by school curricula into a scientistic cocktail of naive realism, blissful empiricism, credulous experimentation, excessive rationalism and blind idealism (Nadeau and Desautels 1984).

Clearly, those with a pre-existing worldview that is in harmony with the scientific perspective will find it easier to learn science because it 'makes sense' to them in terms of fundamental assumptions and underlying values. Science teaching will support and enhance their pre-existing worldview. Those whose worldview differs substantially may experience difficulties in learning science. As Cobern (1995: 289) says, 'One scientist trying to convince a colleague, or even a scientist from another field, is not the same as trying to convince those outside the scientific community.' When there is a clash of worldviews the situation is, he says, like Charles Darwin presenting his *Origin of Species* to a public with very different, religion-based views of origins. Speaker and audience don't share the same fundamental ideas about the world and so may 'talk past each other'. Mutual incomprehension is, indeed, a poor basis for effective teacher–student relationships!

Problems of this kind have been identified by Kawasaki (1996) and Jegede (1998), but are not restricted to the Japanese and African students these authors describe. They exist for Europeans and Americans, too, especially if they have strong religious or aesthetic conceptions of the natural world (Cobern 1996; Roth and Alexander 1997). The problems run considerably deeper than cognitive or epistemological concerns. Science teaching may threaten, disrupt, overpower, marginalize and eventually replace longstanding beliefs and values that underpin some students' sense of personal and cultural identity – in other words, students become assimilated. Alternatively, students may simply resist this perceived attempt at displacing their worldview and decide that science is not for them. Interestingly, strongly held beliefs do not always prevent students from understanding and being able to use scientific knowledge that contradicts them. For example, Demastes *et al.* (1995) show that students can construct a perfectly adequate scientific understanding of evolution despite a clear rejection of its truthfulness that is rooted in strong religious beliefs. Both knowledge structures (evolution and creationism) can be part of an individual's personal framework of understanding, because they are used for different purposes. In some ways, this reflects the distinction between scientific theories, taken as 'true' descriptions and explanations in the sense discussed by Hodson (1982), and scientific models, used for their predictive capability but not regarded as true. Moreover, as Ogunniyi *et al.* (1995: 822) observe, 'the Japanese never lost their cultural identity when introducing Western science and technology, because they introduced only the practical products of Western science and technology, never its epistemology or worldviews'.

Jegede (1995) has developed the notion of *collateral learning* to describe how individuals can hold and develop Western scientific thinking alongside traditional African knowledge and understanding. Regarding each individual as being in possession of a unique personal framework of understanding, and regarding each educational encounter as creating a unique learning context, allows for Jegede's description of four categories of collateral learning (parallel, simultaneous, dependent and secured), located on a continuum, to be extended to all students in all classrooms.

Assisting border crossings

As Krugly-Smolska (1996) points out, all science classrooms, whatever their ethnic composition, can be regarded as *multicultural*, in that gender culture, adolescent or child culture, the culture of the local community (including, of course, religious views), 'pop' culture, school culture and the culture of science are all represented. For each class of students, this complex of subcultures will be different, and will forge a unique sociocultural context for learning that individual students will experience in some ways that are common and others that are unique to them. It is conflicts between and among these various subcultures that give rise to problems of access. Unfortunately, the borders between subcultures are often unrecognized and can seem invisible to teachers, and even to students. To assist students in effecting smooth border crossings between subcultures, enabling them to cross freely backwards and forwards as social circumstances dictate, teachers need to know much more than they sometimes do about science and about the subcultures other than their own that are represented in the class. Clearly, too, science teachers need to be more cognizant of the ways in which transition into the culture of school science can be eased for those students who currently experience difficulties, or who quit in the face of excessive emotional stress. Phelan *et al.* (1991) describe some of the strategies that students might be encouraged to adopt, many of which involve fostering new interests and new friendships; Pomeroy (1994) emphasizes changes that science teachers can effect, including provision of career support, adoption of culturally sensitive pedagogy, promotion of science language skills and epistemological studies.

It is of paramount importance to make clear that gaining access to science does not require students to give up or suppress important features of their lives outside the science classroom. This entails the creation of a school culture that values differences, ensures that all students feel a sense of belonging and self-worth, centralizes the ideal of social justice and places a high value on teachers who can, themselves, move freely and comfortably between different social settings. It also requires a curriculum that shows students how science impacts on the lives of *all* students, on the lives of their friends and families and on the environment, both locally and globally. A politicized, issues-based curriculum (see Chapter 2) is more likely to foster the notion that science is a culturally embedded activity, and to direct attention to the conflicts of interests and values that exist within and between societies, than the more usual academic, abstract, theoretical approach. By confronting scientific and technological problems located in different sociocultural contexts, and dealing with controversial issues, students recognize 'multiple realities' within the classroom and across other cultural boundaries.

What I am moving towards is the notion that border crossings are eased by helping students to become more conscious of what is involved in border crossing – yet another aspect of metacognitive awareness, advocated several times previously as a key element in bringing about better learning in science. What I am seeking is a kind of 'cultural awareness' that involves students understanding the social location of beliefs and practices, acknowledging the context-dependence of most of what they think and do and recognizing the existence of different modes of discourse, each having a distinctive sociocultural origin. Part of this cultural awareness entails recognizing that science itself is a subculture, with its own distinctive knowledge, language, methods, rationality, criteria of validity and reliability, and values; part entails students reflecting on their personal frameworks of understanding and considering carefully the circumstances in which they came to hold particular views and develop particular skills.

As with constructivist pedagogy (Chapter 4), the first step is for teachers to gain insight into the unique structure of each student's personal framework of understanding. Bloom (1995) shows how sensitive use of a form of concept mapping he calls 'context mapping' can begin to provide teachers with this information. However, it should be noted that:

- total insight is not possible, even if it were desirable;[2]
- techniques of research and assessment/evaluation can provide only limited insight;
- students may wish to conceal some aspects of their understanding;
- the act of inquiring may precipitate change in students' understanding;
- personal frameworks of understanding are in constant flux and change;
- other events, of which the teacher may be entirely unaware, may 'colour' the particular selection from their personal framework of understanding that students make available at any one time.

These considerations account for some of the problems encountered by researchers into children's conceptual understanding in science. Testing is a novel social and cognitive experience that demands a particular kind of intellectual manoeuvre and response. Children unfamiliar with this situation will often be unable to respond properly or will simply provide an answer (any answer) they believe will satisfy the questioner, rather than struggle to understand a style of question that seems incomprehensible to them. This concern is highlighted by Hughes and Grieve's (1983) work showing that young children will readily provide adults with answers to the most bizarre questions (such as 'Which is heavier: yellow or red?'). Of course, children don't have views on these matters, but they are willing to provide an answer (any answer) rather than disappoint the questioner. They are merely anxious to please. Social circumstances, rather than understanding, have determined the response.

Johnson and Gott (1996) refer to a 'translation interface' between the different frames of reference of child and researcher that casts doubt on whether they can understand each other and establish meaningful communication. The situation is, they say, rather like that of a twentieth-century scientist trying to gain insight into the thinking of a seventeenth-century scientist. Their solution is threefold: find 'neutral tasks' (not located in either frame of reference, but accessible to both); interpret 'on neutral grounds'; triangulate (employ related tasks to sample different aspects of understanding). More simply, Millar (1989) urges researchers to ask students *why* they give a particular response, and Cobern (1996) suggests constructing concept maps from transcripts of such interviews. In this way, teachers might gain some insight into the complexity of individual understanding. Then they might probe further, and enquire into what other understanding and problem-solving strategies children have in this subject area, and in what circumstances they regard them as being appropriate. I am suggesting this as a useful teaching strategy and as an aid to 'cultural awareness', as well as a research strategy.

Science teacher as anthropologist

The literature of teacher education is replete with metaphors: teacher as broadcaster, teacher as gardener, teacher as tour guide and so on. Perhaps there is room for another: *teacher as anthropologist*. It is part of the teacher's job to help students to gain an understanding of what, for many, are alien cultures (the subcultures of science, school and school science, each with its language, beliefs, theories, values, attitudes and code of conduct) and to assist them in moving freely and painlessly within and between them (Pomeroy 1994; Aikenhead 1996); and, of course, to leave unharmed after their sojourn. My argument is that students can only understand science properly (that is, at a personal level) if they understand 'where it is coming from' (i.e. what its fundamental beliefs and assumptions are). Teaching for personal understanding isn't just a matter of providing discrepant events and a clear argument for the validity of a new idea. While these are important, and comprise a useful framework for another useful metaphor – 'student as novice researcher' (Gil-Perez 1996) – they are insufficient for enculturation without assimilation. Students also need to understand the fundamental metaphysical considerations and value positions that underpin scientific knowledge and scientific inquiry.

Tyson et al. (1997) suggest something similar when they make a case for conceptual change to be viewed through three lenses: an ontological lens (the student is looking out at the world), an epistemological lens (the student is looking in at their own knowledge) and a social/affective lens. As

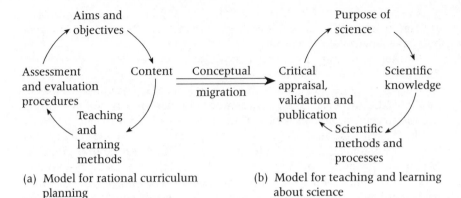

Figure 11.1 Adapting a model from curriculum theory.
Source: Hodson 1993d.

they say, and as I have argued throughout this book, all three aspects impact on learning and can impede or facilitate border crossings. However, their model is too static and too 'logical' for my purposes. Above all, it is too impatient of culturally determined differences in worldview: 'students have to *stop* thinking of concepts like heat, light, force, and current as material substances' (Tyson *et al.* 1997: 400, my emphasis). The approach I am seeking does not equate understanding with belief, nor does it seek to displace other worldviews with the 'approved' scientific view. Rather, it seeks to equip students with the knowledge, self-knowledge and confidence to move freely between them. Aikenhead (1996: 41) expresses this view particularly well.

> Border crossings may be facilitated in classrooms by studying the sub-cultures of students' life-worlds and by contrasting them with a critical analysis of the subculture of science (its norms, values, beliefs, expectations, and conventional actions), *consciously* moving back and forth between life-worlds and the science-world, switching language conventions explicitly, switching conceptualizations explicitly, switching values explicitly, switching epistemologies explicitly.

Some years ago, in making a similar case for a more explicit consideration of the nature of science, I suggested that teachers might find it interesting, helpful and amusing to 'borrow' the familiar model of 'rational curriculum planning' and adapt it to the task of describing the scientific enterprise in terms of purpose, knowledge store, methods of inquiry and procedures for evaluation (Figure 11.1).

I am now inclined to believe that this doesn't go 'far enough' or 'deep enough', and that students' interests might be better served by deploying the more socially oriented approach of King and Brownell (1966), who describe the disciplines (including science) in terms of eight characteristics.

- As a community – a corps of competent people with a common intellectual commitment to building understanding.
- As a particular expression of human imagination – an idea that has much in common with Gardner's (1984) notion of multiple intelligences.
- As a domain – each discipline defines and develops its particular sphere of concern and interest.
- As a tradition – it has a history and is built on the activities and discourse of its forebears.
- As a syntactical structure – a distinctive mode of inquiry and collection of methods for generating and validating new knowledge.
- As a substantive structure – an array of concepts, 'laws', models and theories.
- As a specialized language – a form of 'intellectual shorthand' for conveying meaning quickly and accurately, as well as a distinctive form of argument.
- As a valuative and affective stance – fundamental beliefs about the nature of being and a complex of emotional dynamism and (scientific) aesthetics.

Studying these matters and making them explicit to students involves confronting and dispelling the many distortions and falsehoods about science that are commonly projected by school science curricula. Prominent in this distortion of science are the following ten myths.[3]

1 Observation provides direct and reliable access to secure knowledge.
2 Science starts with observation.
3 Science proceeds via induction.
4 Experiments are decisive.
5 Science comprises discrete, generic processes.
6 Scientific inquiry is a simple, algorithmic procedure.
7 Science is a value-free activity.
8 Science is an exclusively Western, post-Renaissance activity.
9 The so-called 'scientific attitudes' are essential to the effective practice of science.
10 All scientists possess these attitudes.

It is, of course, female students and members of ethnic minority groups who often experience the greatest barriers to successful border crossing into the community of science. Consequently, demythologizing science should pay particular attention to dispelling the notion that science is an exclusively European or North American (i.e. white ethnocentred) and masculine practice, and should address questions about the rationality of science and its correspondence (or not) with other ways of knowing and other 'sciences' (African science, feminist science etc.) (Hodson 1998). The explicit comparison of science with other ways of knowing (philosophy, religion etc.), including everyday knowing and indigenous science (what Ogawa (1995) calls 'multisciences teaching') is, perhaps, the principal means of achieving Jegede's (1995) goal of *secured* collateral learning, in which students can pass freely and confidently between different knowledge structures and worldviews, as the need arises. Roberts (1998) provides a particularly graphic example of 'multisciences teaching' in her comparison of the indigenous knowledge of the Pacific Islands peoples with Western science, in terms of its empirical database, theory building and predictive capability, testability, cause and effect, context specificity and so on.

As a tailpiece to this chapter, it is worth noting the frequency with which metacognition, other forms of self-knowledge and the notion of reconstructing understanding under the watchful and supportive eye of an expert have arisen as key elements in the personalization of learning. Reconstructing and extending one's personal framework of understanding with respect to an identified set of chosen roles, developing better learning strategies, reflecting on the nature of science and scientific inquiry, achieving knowledge of self as student and as sociocultural being and knowing how to reconstruct it have all been discussed. Similar matters arise at least twice more, in Chapters 12 and 13, in the guise of reflection on and reconstruction of learners' views of themselves as effective inquirers and, in particular, as scientific investigators.

Notes

1 A number of writers, including Strike and Posner (1985, 1992), Hewson and Thorley (1989) and Demastes *et al.* (1995), have used Toulmin's (1972) metaphor of a *conceptual ecology* (a complex of ideas, analogies, metaphors and beliefs) to describe personal understanding.
2 This reference to desirability is in respect of ethical issues that could be raised by probing too deeply into students' personal frameworks of understanding.
3 I am not claiming that all ten myths are promoted by all science curricula. Rather, most curricula promote one or more of them and, across the range of curricular provision, all ten are in evidence.

• • • 12

Exploring and developing personal understanding through practical work

Ever since the 'curriculum revolution' of the 1960s, science educators have extolled the virtues of practical work as an enjoyable and effective form of learning. Indeed, as Nersessian (1989: 179) says, 'the predominant ideology among science educators is that hands-on experience is at the heart of science learning'. It has to be admitted, however, that the case for extensive practical work has often been made on the grounds of 'strong professional feelings', rather than on the basis of empirical research evidence attesting to its effectiveness in bringing about learning. If anything, research evidence suggests that laboratory work, at least as currently practised, is largely un-productive.[1] For many students, what goes on in the laboratory contributes little to their learning *of* science or to their learning *about* science. Nor does it engage them in *doing* science, in any meaningful sense. It would be more productive of good learning to be conscious of the distinctions among these three elements of science education (and, of course, the interactions among them) and to plan separately for them, at least for some of the time.

In activities focused on learning science, the teacher often has it in mind that students will reach particular knowledge and understanding, and chooses to approach this learning via hands-on activities for reasons of motivation, interest, clarity and so on. In activities focused on learning about science, the major concern is with acquiring knowledge and understanding of the processes and sub-processes (strategies and tactics) of scientific inquiry and with understanding the role and status of evidence in scientific knowledge building. In doing science, students are practising and developing their own abilities to design, conduct, interpret and report scientific investigations. What may be a well designed activity from the perspective of one of these orientations may not be so from another. Too often, it has been assumed that these significantly different goals can be achieved simultaneously, through a common experience. Moreover, it has been assumed that practical work necessarily means benchwork and that benchwork necessarily means experi-ments. In my view, these are serious misunderstandings of the relationship between science and science education, and serve to weaken the pedagogical power of hands-on activities (Hodson 1993c).

The importance of the distinctions among learning science, learning about science and doing science is evident in the responses of teachers when practicals 'go wrong'. Nott and Smith (1995) suggest that there are three common responses: 'talking your way out of it', 'rigging it' and 'conjuring it'. The first involves the teacher encouraging the students to engage in critical evaluation of the experiment in order to 'assign blame' – faulty apparatus, inadequate bench skills, errors in instructions, 'hard luck' and so on. Rigging is where the teacher uses her or his expertise to manipulate the variables in such a way that 'good results' are obtained. Conjuring involves the fraudulent production of 'good results' by secret manipulation of the apparatus, contamination of the materials or other forms of sleight of hand. Clearly, conjuring is counter-normative behaviour from the perspective of scientific inquiry. Indeed, it is widely deplored by the scientific community. However, it appears to be widespread in science teaching. Those who engage in it justify their actions in terms of the learning benefits that accrue to students: it improves understanding, avoids confusion, gets the point across, aids motivation and so on. It is also justified by the need to get through an overcrowded syllabus, conform to the demands of the departmental workscheme and meet the demands of examinations. It does, however, raise some interesting and important questions concerning the nature of evidence and the role of inquiry.

Conjuring is most necessary when practical work is concerned with learning science, when particular outcomes are essential to good understanding. Rigging can be seen as deployment of craft knowledge and tacit understanding to ensure good technique. In that sense, *tweaking*, as a less pejorative term than 'rigging', may be seen as an integral part of learning about science, from both the teacher's and the students' perspectives. Indeed, students need to learn how to do it for themselves; it is part of scientific connoisseurship. 'Talking your way out of it' may be appropriate to the doing science phase, when things going wrong is to be expected and is a key part of the learning experience. Perhaps 'talking your way *through* it' and learning how to do so, and how to replan or reorient the inquiry, is a more apt expression (see Nott and Wellington 1996).

Of course, questions of control also relate to motivation. Often, teachers allow young children to engage in fairly unstructured personal investigations, while requiring older students to carry out practical *exercises*, according to a set of explicit directions, at the very time in their lives when they are struggling to establish their individuality. Little wonder that their interest and enthusiasm decline. What students of all ages appear to value is cognitive challenge, though work must not be so difficult that it cannot be understood and (relatively) easily carried out, doing a 'proper experiment' (one that has a clear purpose and one that 'works') and having a sufficient measure of personal control and independence (see Chapter 6). To put this in Vygotskian terms, laboratory tasks need to be located in the student's zone of proximal development and to provide many more opportunities for a hand-over of control from teacher to learner. However, for the reasons given above, the need for control is closely related to whether the activity focuses on learning science, learning about science or doing science. The nature of that control, and whether it is apparent to the learner, is elaborated a little below.

Learning science

It could be argued that the very concreteness of laboratory experiences contributes substantially to the problems of much conventional practical work, and serves to distract the learner from the important conceptual issues, thereby hindering rather than promoting concept acquisition and development. Although students in laboratory classes spend a great deal of time handling real materials (magnesium and sulphur, magnets and iron filings, geraniums and gerbils), they are required to discuss and interpret their findings and to provide explanations of observed behaviour in terms of abstract concepts (electrons, chemical bonds, magnetic fields, chromosomes and the like). In most contemporary curricula, it is familiarity with these abstractions that constitutes the real learning goal. While laboratory work is lengthy in the sense that it occupies a lot of time, it is often fleeting in the amount of contact time it provides with the conceptual core of the learning. Moreover, there are many occasions where the underlying abstract concepts we seek are very difficult to tease out from the observable effects: Brownian motion as evidence for the random motion of molecules, colour changes during the progressive dilution of potassium permanganate solution as evidence for a particulate theory of matter, the behaviour of iron filings on a card placed over a magnet as evidence for magnetic lines of force and so on. So, although students perceive the laboratory as a place where they are active (in the sense of 'doing something'), many fail to see the connection between what they are doing and what they are learning, in terms of both conceptual knowledge and procedural knowledge. It is here that teacher scaffolding is crucial.

One form of scaffolding is the reduction of *noise*. Frequently, students are put into the position where they have to understand the nature of the problem and the experimental procedure (neither of which they have been consulted about), assemble the relevant theoretical perspective (with only minimum assistance from the teacher), read, comprehend and follow the experimental directions, handle the apparatus, collect the data, recognize the difference between results obtained and results that 'should have been obtained', interpret those results, write an account of the experiment (often in a curiously obscure and impersonal language) and all the time ensure that they get along reasonably well with their partners. In short, practical work, as presently practised, has too many unnecessary barriers to learning, too much noise.

In many cases, experiments can be made simpler by cutting out some of the less crucial steps and by using simpler apparatus and simpler techniques. There is much to be said for pre-assembly of apparatus. Many students struggle to set up complex apparatus, and feel that they have done enough before the conceptually significant part of the activity has got under way. A similar case can be made for the pre-weighing and pre-dispensing of materials, and for the recalibration of apparatus, to reduce the number of chunks of information that have to be processed or the number of measurements that have to be made (Johnstone and Wham 1982). An extension of this idea is, of course, the use of programmable calculators and computers to convert raw data into final results, thereby reducing what we might call mathematical noise. Even more powerful in this respect is the use of computers for data capture, processing and presentation, and for monitoring and controlling experiments, thereby enabling more complex and lengthy experiments to be undertaken.

Laboratory work is often seen by teachers as a means of obtaining factual information and data from which conclusions will later be drawn. It has usually been assumed that these data are 'pure' and unaffected by students' existing ideas and, therefore, students have not usually been involved in the designing and planning of experimental investigations. More often than not, the conceptual framework is provided by the teacher, leaving little room for the construction of personal meaning. Problem identification, hypothesis formation, experimental design, methods for manipulating and interpreting observational data are all under teacher control and, as Zilbersztain and Gilbert (1981) state, 'interaction with the teacher is an occasion for the presentation of the *teacher's* knowledge' (emphasis added). Because students often have a different framework of understanding, failure to engage them in the thinking that precedes an experimental investigation renders much of the ensuing laboratory work pedagogically useless.

One of the roles of laboratory work is to provide the direct experiences that give real concrete meaning to abstract conceptualizations. Often, however, instruction stops when students can recall and use an idea correctly in a single context – the one in which it was presented to them. The proper understanding that constitutes enculturation into science involves much more: it involves using and attempting to use the particular model or theory in a range of different contexts in order to ascertain its limitations and inadequacies, as well as its capacity for explanation and prediction. 'Not-examples' are just as important as examples in facilitating thorough understanding of a concept or theory (Fensham 1998). The goal of these activities is to find out in what circumstances a concept or theory can and should be used, in what circumstances its use is inappropriate and in what circumstances an alternative model or theory must be sought, or the current theory suitably adapted. Hands-on work generates essential data on which to base such judgements. However, it is through talk among students and between students and the teacher that conceptual understanding is fully explored and developed. As Driver (1983: 49) reminds us, 'Activity by itself is not enough. It is the sense that is made of it that matters.' Sense is made of practical work through talk occurring before, during and after actual performance. Through talk, the laboratory tasks become 'minds-on' as well as hands-on. Explaining, arguing, constructing analogies and metaphors, giving counter examples and so on are all ways of exploring ideas and testing their rational justification. It isn't always necessary to 'discover' for oneself; critiquing someone else's discoveries and theories, especially through discussion with others, can often be more productive than hands-on work.

There is much to be said for alternative approaches to laboratory work, such as the predict–observe–explain tasks developed by Gunstone *et al.* (1988) (see Chapter 4) and the collection of strategies Tunnicliffe (1989) calls 'challenge-based science'. Even more control of outcomes is possible with computer-based activities. There are many experiments that are too difficult, too expensive, too time consuming or too dangerous to carry out in any other way. Moreover, the use of computer simulations, as opposed to real experiments, enables the teacher to tailor the learning experience precisely to the teaching/learning goals, instead of the more usual situation of having to fit the learning goals to the complexities of reality. One can decrease or increase the level of complexity, include or exclude certain features, adopt idealized conditions and generally create an experimental situation that enables learners to concentrate on the central concepts without the distractions, difficulties and boredom that are so much a feature of experiments with real things. By eliminating the noise of concrete experiences, and providing instant feedback on the appropriateness of speculations and predictions, computer simulations and databases enable learners to spend considerably more time manipulating ideas as a way of building understanding than is possible in conventional laboratory work (Kirschner and Huisman 1998).

Because they enable students to explore their theoretical understanding and to conduct investigations they consider relevant to that understanding quickly, reliably and safely, computer-based activities may often be superior to conventional bench work at bringing about concept development. Interactive video and the technology of virtual reality offer even more exciting possibilities. Often, these more controlled learning experiences can be used to assist students towards the kind of conceptual understanding specified in the curriculum. Subsequently, laboratory work and field experiences of various kinds can be used to provide opportunities for students to test out their new understanding on the real world.

Before these kinds of activities can take place, however, it is important for students to acquire a rich background of what White (1991) calls 'episodes' or 'recollections of events'. There are two senses in which these early experiences are crucial. First, it is important for students to have direct experience of the phenomena and events that science addresses. It isn't enough to read about forces of magnetic attraction and repulsion, magnesium burning with a brilliant white flame and light bending as it passes through a prism. Students need to see these things at first hand, to handle objects and organisms for themselves and to experience phenomena directly, in order to build up a stock of personal experience. Because many science concepts depend on experiences not encountered in ordinary day-to-day life, students need lots of opportunities for 'messing about'. Furthermore, concepts for which students have only one contextual referent are less likely to be remembered or to be used than those for which they have a rich and varied array of referents and associations. This is the aspect of practical work that Woolnough and Allsop (1985) describe as 'getting a feel for phenomena'. Second, students need direct experience of laboratory apparatus (they need to read meters, use microscopes and connect circuits, for example) in order to develop both the capacity and the confidence to use equipment appropriately and skilfully. This is not an argument for an intensive bench skills training programme. Rather, it is a suggestion that, on occasions, the adoption of some kind of familiarization programme may be a necessary precursor to successful scientific inquiry or a productive laboratory exercise.

Elsewhere, I have argued that the acquisition of laboratory skills has little, if any, value in itself (Hodson 1990). Rather, these skills are a means to an end – that end being further learning. To attempt to justify practical work in school in terms of skill development is to be guilty of putting the cart before the horse. It is not that practical work is necessary in order to provide students with particular laboratory skills; rather, it is that particular skills are necessary if students are to engage successfully in practical work. Two points follow: we should teach only those skills that are of value in the pursuit of other learning and, when such is the case, we should ensure that those skills are developed to a satisfactory level of competence. My own view is that when successful engagement in an experiment requires a skill that students will not need again, or levels of competence that they cannot quickly attain, alternative procedures should be found, such as pre-assembly of apparatus, teacher demonstration or computer simulation.

Learning about science and doing science

Allowing students to undertake their own investigations contributes substantially to their understanding of the nature of science, provided that a sufficient range of scientific inquiries is considered. As argued previously, not all inquiries are experimental; it is important that students are provided with opportunities to undertake correlational studies and to engage in technological problem-solving. Both provide substantial scope for exploring, challenging and extending both conceptual and procedural knowledge. It should also be recognized that many worthwhile scientific inquiries can be conducted outdoors – in the school grounds, field centres, forests, beaches and mountains – and in museums, zoos and botanic gardens. These venues also provide some invaluable opportunities for students to work with scientists and to engage in worthwhile community work and politicized environmental action (Eisenhart *et al.* 1996; Helms 1998).

There is also much to be gained from encouraging students to reflect on their own, and the group's, personal learning progress. For example, when students reconsider and reinterpret laboratory activities conducted earlier in the course, they are able to draw meaningful parallels between the development of their personal understanding and the growth of scientific knowledge.

However, 'getting a feel for scientific practice' involves more than an awareness of the nature of observation and experimentation; it includes an understanding of the ways in which scientific research is negotiated, reported and appraised. Achieving that level of understanding requires that we utilize a wide range of other active learning experiences – among them, the use of historical case studies, simulations and dramatic reconstructions, role playing and debating, computer-based activities and thought experiments.

The use of computer simulations is a particularly powerful technique for enabling students to engage in the more creative aspects of science that provide an understanding of the nature of scientific practice. In most laboratory-based lessons, students do not have opportunities to engage in hypothesis generation and experimental design because teachers are unwilling to provide the time, meet the cost or run the risk of students adopting inappropriate, inefficient or potentially hazardous experimental strategies. Consequently, teachers tend to design all the experiments, usually in advance of the lesson, and students merely follow their instructions. With a computer simulation, poor designs can go ahead and any problems can be discovered by the students and modified, or eliminated, quickly and safely. In this way, students learn from their mistakes and are led to investigate more thoroughly and more thoughtfully. More importantly, they learn that designing experiments is not a specialized and difficult business carried out by white-coated experts in sophisticated laboratories. Anyone can do it, including them. Too often, experiments in class are presented as the only way of proceeding; computer simulations enable different groups of students to come up with different procedures, some of which will work well, some less well, some not at all. This is more like real science. There are at least three learning goals embedded in such experiences. First, students learn much more about the phenomena under investigation and the concepts that can be used in accounting for them, because they have more time and opportunity to manipulate those concepts. Second, they acquire some of the thinking and strategic planning skills of the creative scientist. Third, they learn that science is about people thinking, guessing and trying things that sometimes work and sometimes fail. Through such experiences science can be demythologized and made accessible to everyone.

Modelling and the transition to autonomy

The enculturation by apprenticeship model asserts that the most effective way to learn to do science is by doing science, alongside a skilled and experienced practitioner who can provide on-the-job support, criticism and advice, and is able to model the processes involved and invite criticism from the learner. As Ravetz (1971: 177) has commented, learning to do science occurs 'almost entirely within the interpersonal channel, requiring personal contact and a measure of personal sympathy between the parties. What is transmitted will be partly explicit, but partly tacit; principle, precept, and example are all mixed together.' Clear and skilful demonstration of expert practice (modelling) and the provision of opportunities for critical questioning, interspersed with opportunities for guided participation by the 'novice', provided they are informed by critical feedback from the 'expert', comprise the stock-in-trade of the apprenticeship approach to the teaching and learning of complex tasks in real life practical situations (Lave and Wenger 1991). For the more formal situation of school-based learning, the following three-phase approach may be relatively easily implemented.

- *modelling*, where the teacher exhibits the desired behaviour;
- *guided practice*, where students perform with help from the teacher;
- *application*, where students perform independently of the teacher.

Teacher modelling is, of course, predicated on the assumption that observation of skilled performers facilitates learning. Thus, teacher modelling of authentic inquiry (both laboratory/fieldwork-based and literature/media-based) can play a crucial role in enculturation. First, it demonstrates a commitment to the value of inquiry as a means of learning: the teacher models the learning process by acting as a more expert learner. Second, it shows students how scientists plan, conduct, interpret and report scientific inquiries: the teacher models scientific investigation by acting as a more expert scientist.

When teachers model scientific inquiry it is important to choose an authentic question – that is, one for which they don't already know the answer. Too often, laboratory work in schools creates the impression that scientists spend their time confirming knowledge they already possess. Too often, also, it creates the impression that science is unrelated to everyday life. Hence, it is important, especially with young children, to investigate something in the immediate environment – something real! Moreover, in the early stages, especially in primary schools, it is important to ensure that the modelled investigations involve as many as possible of the individual sub-processes in which children are expected to develop proficiency, and that they might reasonably be expected to employ in their own investigations. Predicting, observing, measuring, identifying and manipulating variables, recognizing trends in data, using suitable scientific concepts to hypothesize and model, and describing, recording and reporting in appropriate scientific language can all be modelled by the teacher, with attention focused on their essential features. It is important, too, to explore the notion of a 'fair test' and to discuss the importance of both standardization of technique and accuracy of measurement in ensuring reproducibility of data. At all levels, attention should be directed towards the need to record procedures and data fully, clearly, carefully and accurately, using lists, charts, graphs and so on as appropriate. Criteria for good recording and reporting should, of course, be discussed with the students.

It is anticipated that students will become more expert in each of the five phases of inquiry (Chapter 10) by observation, practice and experience, through evaluative feedback provided by the teacher and via inter-group criticism and discussion, and through intra-group reflection on the activity, both as it progresses and on completion. Crucial to the notion of apprenticeship is continuing dialogue about the way the inquiry is progressing, including a frank discussion of problems encountered, lines of inquiry that prove fruitless and barriers to progress that prove insurmountable. Students' suggestions and advice should be sought, and some of them acted upon. When teachers accept students' ideas (and, of course, contribute ideas to students' own investigations), it encourages students to help each other, and assists in building a suitable climate for cooperative learning.

To achieve intellectual independence, of course, students must take responsibility for their own learning and for the planning, executing and reporting of their own inquiries. In other words, learning as assisted performance must enable students, eventually, to go beyond what they have learned and to use knowledge in creative ways – for solving novel problems and building new understanding. Consequently, alongside the modelled investigations, students should work through a carefully sequenced programme of (a) investigative exercises, during which the teacher acts as learning resource, facilitator, consultant and critic, and (b) simple holistic investigations conducted independently of the teacher. Investigative exercises provide opportunities for students to learn through a cycle of practice and reflection and, with the assistance of the teacher, to achieve a level of performance they could not achieve unaided. Eventually, students will be able to proceed autonomously: choosing their own topics and problems, and approaching them in their own way. By this stage, they are responsible for the whole process, from initial problem identification to final evaluation and communication to others. As a consequence, they experience both 'the excitement of successes and the agony that arises from inadequate planning or bad decisions' (Brusic 1992: 49).

By engaging in holistic scientific investigations, alongside a trusted and skilled critic, students increase both their understanding of what constitutes doing science and their capacity to do it successfully. There is much to be said for the use of an investigator's logbook in which students can reflect on the progress of their investigation: 'What have I learned?', 'What should I do next?', 'Do I need to rethink my goals, or replan my strategy?' Reflections like these, and the requirement to discuss them with the teacher, help to give students insight into the idiosyncratic and reflexive nature of scientific investigation – a major aspect of learning about science.

Paradoxically, it is the very idiosyncrasy and personalization of scientific investigation (doing science) that provides students with the stimulus for recognizing and understanding the interrelatedness of learning science, learning about science and doing science. It is also the reason why doing science cannot, in itself, meet all the goals of science education. In any scientific inquiry, students accomplish three kinds of learning. First is enhanced conceptual understanding of whatever is being studied or investigated. Second is enhanced procedural knowledge: learning more about experiments and correlational studies, and acquiring a more sophisticated understanding of observation, experiment and theory. Third is enhanced investigative expertise, which may eventually develop into scientific connoisseurship. Providing opportunities for students to report and debate their findings, and supporting them in reflecting critically on personal progress made during the inquiry, are key elements in achieving this integrative understanding. However, because of the idiosyncratic nature of scientific investigation, and the highly specialized but necessarily limited range of conceptual issues involved in any particular inquiry, doing science is insufficient in itself to bring about the breadth of conceptual development that a curriculum seeks. One cannot learn sufficient science by restricting activities to doing science.[2] It takes too long and is too uncertain. Moreover, not all topics lend themselves to a doing science approach. Nor can one learn enough about science by restricting activities to doing science. Learning about science involves more than an awareness of the nature of observation and experimentation: it includes an understanding of the ways in which scientific research is prioritized, conducted, reported and appraised; it includes some appreciation of the history, philosophy and sociology of science and scientific practice. In short, students need to appreciate that scientific practice is a complex, socially constructed activity. Such awareness cannot be achieved solely by conducting personal investigations on matters of interest to oneself.

It is also the case, as argued above, that restricting the curriculum to learning science and learning about science will guarantee that most students are unable to do science for themselves. Though necessary, conceptual knowledge and knowledge about procedures that scientists can adopt, and may have adopted in particular circumstances in the past, are insufficient in themselves to enable a student to engage successfully in scientific inquiry. That ability is only developed through hands-on experience of doing science in a critical and supportive learning environment. Moreover, conducting whole investigations and engaging in practical problem-solving in real contexts are valuable because the tension that arises when individuals confront obstacles that prevent them from achieving desired goals is a powerful incentive, forcing them to 'proceduralize' knowledge that might otherwise remain inert (Prawat 1993). Through such activity, procedural and propositional knowledge become fused into 'strategic knowledge' – knowledge that can be used in real contexts. It has long been a legitimate criticism of school science education that, although students may learn 'textbook knowledge' well, they are often unable to deploy it appropriately and successfully in real contexts.

Notes

1 Throughout this section, the terms 'laboratory work' (the expression commonly used in North America), 'practical work' (the more usual term in the UK, Australia and New Zealand) and 'experiments' are used virtually as synonyms. To a large extent, this reflects common usage. However, it is also a deliberate ploy on my part to illustrate the confusion that can arise in science curriculum debate as a consequence of the failure to acknowledge that not all practical work is conducted in a laboratory, and that not all laboratory work is experimental (Hodson 1988). In a more detailed consideration of these matters (Hodson 1993c), the distinctions between practical work (active learning methods) and laboratory work, and between different kinds of laboratory work, are used to reconceptualize active learning in science.
2 In Chapter 10, I posed the question 'Can all that students need to learn in school science courses be learnt by doing science? Finally, I have answered it!

• • • 13

Exploring and developing personal understanding through language

When psycholinguists refer to the heuristic function of language, they are arguing that the very act of using language contributes to learning. Struggling to convert partly formed ideas into articulated speech, or into coherent written language, helps to develop those ideas. Hence, language-based activities can be utilized to explore, develop, extend, enrich and reorganize a student's personal framework of understanding. If learning science is about constructing a complex web of concepts and conceptual relationships into which 'official' scientific knowledge is woven, if knowledge becomes meaningful once it is integrated with what is already known in ways that are personal to the learner and if understanding is extended and developed when learners reflect on the relationships between their existing understanding and new knowledge items in the light of current and previous experience, then language can play a clear and important role. What is at issue here is the shifting of emphasis from language as an instrument of teaching to language as a means of learning and a tool for thinking. This shift of emphasis entails a much more active use of talking, listening, reading and writing activities than has been usual in science teaching, especially at secondary school level.

The classic research of Ned Flanders (1970) indicates that, on average, two-thirds of each lesson comprises talk, and two-thirds of this is teacher talk. Thus, a 45-minute lesson provides for ten minutes of student talk and, in a classroom of 30 children, each student has about 20 seconds for an activity described above as a key element in building a rich and robust personal framework of understanding. Clearly, we need a shift of emphasis. It is also the case that, in question–answer sessions, sufficient time is rarely allowed for students to assemble a response before the teacher rephrases the question, asks a different question or asks a different student. More significantly, in the context of the current discussion, no time is allowed for students to elaborate their answers. Another paradox is that as the cognitive demand of the matter under consideration increases, teacher questions become longer and more complex, while student answers get shorter, frequently descending to the level of 'yes', 'no' and 'I don't know'. In other words, students are doing less talking and teachers are doing more in the very situation where student talk would be of most value. It seems that traditional question–answer sessions provide the teacher with an opportunity to use language to organize thought, but don't afford the same opportunity to students. It is noticeable that students working in groups allow each other much more time to formulate a response and to elaborate it. Moreover, they also create more opportunities for students to comment on each other's responses.

Major criticisms can also be levelled at the ways in which many science teachers use reading and writing activities (Glynn and Muth 1994; Rivard 1994). In general, it seems that secondary school science teachers do not place much value on reading, devoting no more than 10 per cent of class time to it, and often restricting it to short bursts of activity pitched at what the Bullock Report (Department of Education and Science 1975) calls the *literal* comprehension level. There are two issues to consider: first, texts are often too difficult for students; second, through unfamiliarity with language-based learning methods, teachers do not create enough opportunities for students to proceed to the higher levels of *inferential* comprehension (where readers can appreciate some of the subtleties of the text and can 'read between the lines' for implicit messages) and *evaluative* comprehension (where readers are able to judge for themselves the value and quality of the material). Many of the writing activities that teachers provide are similarly impoverished: students spend large amounts of time slavishly copying notes from the blackboard or from teacher dictation, transferring material verbatim from textbooks to notebooks and constructing reports of laboratory activities to a rigid specification that leaves no scope for the expression of personal understanding and feelings.

Text and talk

There are several ways in which spoken and written language can be contrasted. Written discourse is more abstract; often it is more complex and difficult, requiring greater intellectual effort to comprehend it. Because the author is not present, meaning cannot be supported by gesture or intonation; nor can the reader seek further information or ask for clarification. On the other hand, an absent author cannot be diverted from an argument in pursuit of red herrings, although readers can be so diverted. Written text has more permanence and so has an archival function, though audiotapes and video material containing spoken language are increasingly being used for such purposes. Further, because written material is produced over a longer time period than speech, there are more opportunities for reconsideration of key ideas, error detection and elimination, and other forms of editing that ensure a more detailed and considered product. A major difference to be noted in the context of the present discussion is the opportunity written material affords for supporting critical thinking. While spoken language is well suited to the negotiation of collaborative action, written language is more supportive of individual or group-based reflection. A dialogue can be established between the reader's thoughts and the writer's words. Text can be used as a 'thinking device' for exploring, testing, reinforcing and refining existing knowledge, as well as for developing new understanding. It should also be noted that writers frequently use their own text in this way – thoughts are often clarified and elaborated through writing activities. There is also a very significant difference, says Wells (1993), in the ways experience is represented. Oral language is a more dynamic mode, in which reality is expressed in terms of processes, actions and happenings; written language takes a synoptic perspective, with reality and experience being viewed in terms of objects, definitions and explanations. The former is a language of negotiation and action, the latter is a language of symbolic representations and relationships, which makes it an ideal medium for providing detailed instructions and information.

Given these differences, and the fact that spoken language is employed in situations involving more than one person, while text can be used by individuals working alone, text and talk are likely to be used differently by teachers. Talking is commonly used for negotiating, planning, monitoring and evaluating actions, while pre-prepared text is used for providing detailed information and instructions, and student writing is used for recording data and reporting experiences and results. However, the most valuable and productive learning may occur when talk and text are used to complement and enrich each other.

> For it is when participants move back and forth between text and talk, using each mode to contextualize the other, and both modes as tools to make sense of the activity in which they are engaged, that we see the most important form of complementarity between them. And it is here, in this interpenetration of talk, text and action in relation to particular activities, that, I want to suggest, students are best able to undertake what I have called the semiotic apprenticeship into the various ways of knowing.
>
> (Wells 1993: 10)

There are three points being argued here. First, students learn science (and learn about science) by talking, reading and writing. Second, talking about text is especially productive. Third, in the same way that students learn to do science by doing science alongside a skilled practitioner, students learn to read, write and talk science by doing so in the company of a more skilled practitioner, who models, guides, criticizes and supports.

Talking and listening

If talking is as productive of learning as I am claiming, science teachers have to control their natural inclination to organize, sequence and present knowledge. They have to allow children the space to talk, and refrain from correcting children's poorly formed views too early. If students are given time to talk, they may 'talk themselves into a better understanding'. However, productive talk doesn't just happen, it has to be planned. Furthermore, discussions can often lapse into the regular, informal social interaction mode unless teachers ensure that the form of discourse is a scientific one.

McClelland (1983) lists four conditions he regards as essential for good discussion.

* The topic under discussion needs to be problematic but within the scope of participants' current knowledge. (My own view is that much valuable discussion occurs when students have to seek knowledge just beyond their current understanding, locate appropriate sources and acquire additional skills – that is, when it is pitched in the zone of proximal development.)
* Talk should be between 'consenting peers' (friendship groups are preferred). Teacher involvement introduces a power asymmetry that can be counterproductive (but see later).
* Groups of three to six members are best. Small groups do not generate sufficient breadth of views, while large groups can fragment into active and passive members, or into separate discussion sub-groups.
* Students need to have the expectation that a worthwhile outcome will result.

A number of other conditions could be appended. First, students must be sufficiently interested to participate. Second, the teacher needs to have created a safe, trusting, non-threatening and supportive environment in which all students feel confident to contribute and allow each other 'space' in which to talk. It is important that any feelings of injustice or hurt are dealt with promptly and effectively. Above all, it must be *authentic* discussion, in which students express their views in their own way, diversity of views is encouraged and the strength of feelings is acknowledged by the teacher. However, it is crucial that teachers also provide guidance, point students in the direction of additional data or alternative ideas and introduce new ways of thinking and specialized language. For example, while students' use of familiar language may facilitate a willingness to explore ideas, its continued use can disguise a lack of understanding. It is important for teachers to introduce scientific language and to show students how to employ it properly. It is a crucial part of the enculturation process. This is not just an issue relating to purpose-made vocabulary – *photosynthesis*, for example. Students also need to learn the specialized ways in which scientists use everyday words and expressions and become familiar with the forms in which scientific reporting and argument are couched. However, there is also a danger that students may pick up the teacher's vocabulary and linguistic patterns and use them 'mechanically' to hide their lack of understanding. A useful tactic is to require at least two very different ways of expressing a viewpoint. As always, it is a matter of striking a balance between too much teacher direction and too little.

Barnes (1988) distinguishes two kinds of talk, located at opposite ends of a continuum: *exploratory* talk, through which students consider and organize their ideas; and *presentational* talk, through which they report to others on what they currently understand or have recently learned. Exploratory talk occurs during laboratory activities, in activities devised specifically to encourage talking (such as formulating definitions of key concepts, preparing a tape–slide sequence or shooting a video, devising a set of questions, selecting text and visual aids to illustrate an idea) and in preparing for group presentations. During inquiry-based activities, exploratory talk is also used to create a sense of group cohesion and purpose, and to manage and organize the work (see Chapter 7). It shapes the nature of the inquiry, enables consensus to be reached, establishes the limits of the group's current understanding and identifies those areas in which the teacher's help needs to be sought. Presentational talk can range from simple 'show and tell' activities, in which students describe an object or recount an investigation or event to other students, to elaborate multimedia group presentations to the rest of the class, other students (both within the school and outside), parents or invited members of the local community.

There are two major points to be made. First, learning to speak clearly and concisely in order to convey information, ideas and opinions to others in a comprehensible way is an important aspect of enculturation into science and a key component of education for responsible citizenship. Second, all kinds of productive talking are involved in preparing group presentations, especially if audio-recorders are used to edit, rework and refine presentation. Post-presentation evaluation can be a productive time for reflection and consolidation of learning. By reviewing each presentation from the listener's perspective, teachers and students can co-construct an evaluation checklist of points to keep in mind during the preparation of oral presentations. These kinds of activities are invaluable in providing teachers with insight into the personal frameworks of understanding of individual students.

There are many ways in which presentational talk can be made to mimic the seminars, debates and conferences of the scientific community, thus playing a significant role in teaching students about science and the ways in which scientific knowledge is negotiated by practitioners. The immediacy of such activities can be a major stimulus to thought: feedback is immediate, critical questions are asked, leads and ideas from others can be utilized at once as the basis for a change or modification of views. When students have to explain, defend their views and answer questions, they develop a deeper understanding and are led to explore and develop their personal framework of understanding. When students have to convince others of the intelligibility, plausibility and fruitfulness of their ideas, they necessarily evaluate, elaborate and synthesize aspects of their understanding, make explicit what otherwise might remain implicit, examine critically their own thinking, identify discrepancies, contradictions, gaps in understanding, inconsistencies, vagueness and so on. They have to paraphrase and find alternative forms of expression, making more extensive use of everyday language; they can't just use the jargon phrases of the textbook. They have to locate some easily recognized examples, perhaps use similes, analogies and metaphors, and find some connotations to help other students to make sense of what they are hearing.

A mode intermediate between spoken and written language is the lecture or teacher exposition, an extended oral presentation of pre-prepared material. Although it has been fashionable in recent years to be dismissive of teacher presentation, it does enable the language of science to be modelled. It is an occasion for 'talking science', as Lemke (1990) says. Teacher exposition can be a powerful scaffolding tool in the enculturation processes, introducing students to the specialized terminology of science and its distinctive mode of representing experience, and using formal aspects of the language of science alongside more familiar everyday language. By shifting backwards and forwards between scientific language and everyday language, and by using everyday exemplars, similes and analogies, graphic metaphors, personal reminiscences, stories, anecdotes and jokes, teachers can make science more meaningful, exciting, humanized and accessible. Teacher talk is a way of introducing new ideas and new terminology carefully, systematically and sensitively. Skilful teacher talk helps to focus attention, picks out and emphasizes key ideas, clarifies meaning, points out similarities and differences and so assists students to sort out their own ideas in relation to their various other views.

Reading activities

There are three major categories of learning goals deriving from reading activities: first, students acquire and develop conceptual and procedural understanding; second, they learn about scientific communication (and, by implication, about other forms of communication); third, they gain insight into their own understanding and how and when it can be deployed. It is with respect to the second point that it is important for students to be given the opportunity to work with a broad range of text types: textbooks, magazines and newspapers, academic papers and reports, biographical and historical material, works of fiction and so on. Comprehension at the inferential and evaluative levels necessitates an understanding of the ways in which changes in the writer's purpose and intended audience lead to the adoption of different writing styles and the use of different structural conventions. Critical scientific literacy includes the ability to move freely between these different modes, as both reader and writer. Indeed, it could be argued that being able to read and listen with understanding, evaluate the nature and quality of an argument and express one's views clearly and persuasively is among the most important aspects of science education, regardless of whether one sees science education as primarily concerned with preparation for responsible citizenship or with the acquisition and development of investigative skills and theory building capability. Moreover, acquiring the ability to read effectively for further learning is essential to the development of intellectual independence and lays the necessary base for lifelong learning.

Because texts in science are often very rich in information, make use of unfamiliar terminology, adopt an impersonal and abstract style, deal with matters that are remote from the everyday experience of most children and contain many counter-intuitive ideas, they are often more difficult to understand than texts used in other areas of the curriculum. Sutton (1992) makes the point that school science textbooks often give the impression that they are designed for teachers, rather than for students. Ironically, homework tasks are often based on commercially produced texts that are more difficult than the teacher-produced materials used in class – where the teacher's help is available! Presented with a text whose content and knowledge base is unfamiliar and, possibly, lacking in motivational appeal, students may: (a) ignore the text altogether and continue to rely on their existing knowledge; (b) use a 'surface processing' approach to extract key words and phrases; or (c) distort or misrepresent the text to make it compatible with their existing understanding (Roth and Anderson 1988). There are two ways of addressing these problems. One approach is to encourage students to learn and adopt one of the several generic reading strategies, such as SQ4R (Thomas and Robinson 1972) and MURDER (Danserau 1985); the other is to provide many more reading tasks that require students to interrogate the text. By engaging with the text in more active ways, students not only explore and develop understanding about the matter under consideration, they also develop the skills and supportive attitudes that enable them to use text more successfully in the future. In other words, when students are encouraged to regard text as a resource to support discussion, argument and the co-construction of understanding, they are more inclined to develop the habits of searching for more subtle levels of meaning in texts and evaluating texts more critically.

Expert readers are distinguished from novice readers by the extent to which they use existing knowledge to make sense of the text, monitor their comprehension as they proceed (through self-questioning), deal promptly with any failure to understand, identify key ideas and evaluate their significance as they encounter them, actively search for consistency, coherence and discrepancy, attend to misunderstandings and misconceptions as they become aware of them, reformulate and synthesize knowledge as they read and so on (Pearson *et al.* 1992). These attributes can be fostered by engaging students in more authentic, active reading: reading for specific purposes, made clear to the learner in advance, and requiring active engagement with the text. Davies and Greene (1984) urge teachers to replace the often rather vague and unhelpful instructions they give students in connection with reading tasks (e.g. 'read pages 45–55, there will be a test next week') with much more purposeful *directed activities related to text* (DARTs) that periodically require students to stop, reflect on what they have read so far and attempt to make sense of it. DARTs can be pitched at almost any level of conceptual sophistication but, at all levels, it is the specific nature of the instructions that is the key to ensuring active, reflective and purposeful reading. The simplest examples include: reading a section of text and discussing with others what is likely to follow it; completing sentences, tables and charts from which items have been omitted; identifying important vocabulary and significant points by underlining and highlighting; paraphrasing the key arguments; writing definitions; deciding on appropriate titles and sub-headings for lengthy extracts of text; reordering scrambled text; 'translating' text into diagrams, flow charts and concept maps; designing posters or logos to represent something described in the text.

It is important not to over-use DARTs; much of their impact lies in their novelty, and they can irritate and bore students if used too frequently. As quickly as possible, and wherever possible, teachers should engage students in *authentic* reading tasks that require close attention to text and make more extensive use of alternative text types. Material that is problem-oriented or issues-based, and deals with social, economic or environmental matters, is ideal for meeting the first requirement – see, for example, material produced by the SATIS Projects (Holman 1986; Hunt 1990).

At a more sophisticated level, students might work in groups to formulate a set of questions on a text for use by other students, or even read and criticize written material produced by other students. They might prepare a 'position statement' or a set of debating points, subject texts to a rigorous appraisal for evidence of sociopolitical bias, sexism and racism, assess text readability for other students or assemble an annotated bibliography for use by other students or parents. Following explicit teaching relating to text organization, voice, use of metaphor and techniques of argumentation, students might be asked to identify the structural features employed by various authors in pursuit of their purposes. Mallow (1991) provides some valuable insights into these matters and presents useful advice on how to read different text types. Such awareness underpins two crucial elements in the development of critical scientific literacy: the ability to communicate one's ideas concisely and effectively, and the ability to respond critically to the ideas of others. Many significant aspects of learning science and learning about science could be located in an activity in which students collect, criticize and display samples of writing on science from newspapers and popular magazines, textbooks of various styles, scientific magazines and academic journals, cartoons, advertisements and product labels. This activity might usefully be extended to include television programmes and advertisements, movies and works of fiction. As a brief aside, it should be noted that young children may find it easier to assimilate new ideas if they are presented in a narrative style. Thus, there is a strong case for utilizing a wide range of children's literature in primary school science courses.

Writing activities

Much of what has been said about the need for active reading can be developed as a case for active writing. Lunzer and Gardner (1979) found that, on average, an 11-year-old science student in a UK school spends about 11 per cent of class time engaged in writing, and a 15-year-old up to about 20 per cent. However, at least half of that time is devoted to copying from the blackboard or from dictated notes, and another sizable chunk is spent filling in blanks in worksheets. Sadly, in many schools, little has changed in the intervening two decades.

It is important not to confuse the physical activity involved in this kind of 'closed' writing with the worthwhile cognitive activity that underpins more 'open' writing tasks. Indeed, active writing in the sense being explored here does not have to entail very much physical writing at all. Concept mapping and the use of word burrs (Sutton 1992), false concept maps and 'instances and misconceptions tables' (Osborne 1997), for example, involve virtually no writing, yet they can be particularly powerful in stimulating reflective thinking, especially in group learning situations. Similarly, in 'free writing' and 'free association' activities (Juell 1985), students are able to set aside the usual concerns with spelling, grammar and structure in order to concentrate on brainstorming ideas with other students.

The traditional emphasis on grammar, spelling and other technical aspects of writing can be enormously inhibiting, and can divert students from the principal learning goals: acquiring and practising the distinctive forms of scientific discourse; exploring and developing conceptual and procedural knowledge; gaining insight into one's personal framework of understanding and learning how to select and utilize particular aspects of it in particular circumstances. Of course, scientific discourse has its required forms and approved conventions, and it is important for students to know what they are and how to employ them appropriately. However, too early and too rigorous a concern with these matters can be distracting, and even alienating. Students can become so concerned with the 'correct' way of saying something that they don't explore their own thoughts. In addition, without the kinds of reading activities discussed earlier, students can be so intimidated by the supposed authority of the textbook that they are reduced to copying extensive passages almost verbatim. As Flick (1995: 1068) remarks: 'when students research topics in the library, the result is a parody of the intended product through plagiarism and paraphrase.'

The Writing Across the Curriculum team (Martin 1976) identified three main kinds of writing used in schools: *transactional, expressive* and *poetic*. In transactional writing, the writer has to be logical and truthful, and is required to adopt certain codes and conventions. It is the language for presenting facts and for reporting, arguing and theorizing. Whereas transactional writing is generally impersonal, expressive writing assumes that the writer and her or his experiences and feelings are of interest to the reader. This kind of writing may have very little or no formal structure: it just follows the ebb and flow of the writer's thoughts and feelings, as in a diary or logbook. It is a style of writing that is often discouraged in science, especially in secondary school.

If science learning is to be personalized, it would make sense to personalize student writing tasks. If science learning is impacted by students' attitudes, feelings and emotions, it would make sense to create opportunities for students to express them. If personal frameworks of understanding are highly idiosyncratic and reflect the complexity of each student's network of sociocultural relationships, it would make sense to use a style of writing that permits their exploration and development. All these points create a case for much more extensive use of expressive and poetic writing in science. Expressive writing may be a much better vehicle than transactional writing for expressing doubts, asking questions and speculating about ideas. It may also have value in reducing some of the barriers that restrict access for girls and some ethnic minority groups. Expressive writing enables learners to explore a new idea or theory against and within a complex web of other ideas, memories and feelings, and to play around with new relationships and associations. Thus, it may be essential to the process of trying out and coming to terms with new ideas – to 'thinking on paper'. Learning logs and journals, especially team journals and journals that establish a dialogue between students and teacher, are particularly effective. When writing in their journals, students do not confine themselves to strictly scientific matters. They frequently incorporate other personal experiences, employ metaphor and analogy, make reference to books, movies and TV shows, and so on. This is the process by which they make personal sense of new scientific knowledge. Aikenhead's (1996, 1997) idea of maintaining a 'dichotomized notebook' – with 'my ideas' (or commonsense understanding) on one page and 'subculture of science' ideas on the facing page – may help to focus attention on the transcultural aspects of learning science. As Aikenhead (1996: 29) says, 'The task of border crossing is made concrete by identifying it as crossing a line on a notebook page.'

Bruner (1990) suggests that we acquire and grow in our ability to communicate and understand our experience through language by applying narrative structures, including emphasis on human action, sequential ordering of events, taking a narrator's perspective and seeking a resolution or conclusion. Narratives are part of children's language from their very first attempts at substantial communication. And, moreover, both science and science learning could be seen as narratives. In science, knowledge is accumulated by means of people systematically investigating objects, phenomena and events in the physical world. Thus, scientific discovery is a story. In science learning, new understanding reinforces, enriches or modifies a personal framework of understanding, enabling us to see and interact with the world and with other people in new ways. Personal development of any kind, and the insight and opportunities it brings, is also a story. It follows that storytelling should be afforded a much more prominent place in the science curriculum. By such means, we can encourage students to humanize science, express their own views, speculate, hypothesize and predict, and look for connections to other things that they know and have experienced, using a combination of familiar and authentic scientific language (Sutton 1996). Poetic writing may have a useful role in this context, too, as well as art work, music, drama and role playing. Narrative may be a particularly effective means of assisting border crossing by highlighting differences in worldview and other culturally determined knowledge, experience and values (Bajracharya and Brouwer 1997).

This is not to suggest that transactional writing has no place in science education. Quite the contrary: transactional writing promotes lucid and orderly handling of information and ideas; it permits ideas to be manipulated, juxtaposed, compared and contrasted. Further, students learn how to read this style of written material more critically by writing it themselves. In the form of short expository exercises – note making, summarizing, explaining, analysing, paraphrasing, comparing and contrasting, formulating questions and so on – transactional writing is an excellent way of focusing attention on discrete bits of knowledge; in the form of extended essays, it is a valuable way of synthesizing ideas. In short, all three styles of writing are important, for different purposes. What students need to know, and this constitutes a crucial part of enculturation, is when a particular style is appropriate.

Another major problem is that almost all writing in school science is produced for the same audience and for the same purpose: the audience is the teacher and the purpose is assessment. Invariably, it entails the writer telling the teacher what she or he already knows. Moreover, the student knows that the teacher already possesses this knowledge, and is aware that the only purpose of the exercise is to enable the teacher to assign a mark or grade. In other words, it is not genuine or authentic communication. Rather, it is part of the game of school: the game of 'getting the right answer'. By varying the audience, and by insisting that writing fulfils a genuinely communicative purpose, teachers can ensure that students are better motivated, clearer about expectations and enabled to practise and develop a wider range of writing skills.

The writing equivalent of DARTs include such things as rewriting and paraphrasing exercises, completing an unfinished text, writing text from diagrams, pictures and tables of data. Each of these activities can have a significant role in enhancing conceptual understanding. However, as with reading activities, it is important to begin as early as possible with *authentic* authoring tasks, in which students write for a real audience, with a real purpose in mind and in a style that suits both audience and purpose. Suitable audiences include: other students; parents or family members; an Uncle George figure, who invariably 'gets the wrong end of the stick' and has to be 'put right' (as in the Nuffield schemes); some section of the public; themselves. The purpose may be to inform, explain, persuade, argue a point of view, express emotions and feelings or encourage action. Authentic writing tasks may take the form of a technical report, diary entry, field trip notes, TV or film script, fictional story, letter, action or protest letter, brochure or newsletter, poster, newspaper article, guidelines and instructions, poetry, drama or role-play script.

Authentic authoring, especially when located in a group learning setting, provides rich opportunities for the co-construction of meaning. Not only are students learning how best to communicate with their audience, they are also exploring what they already know and what they need to know before they can prepare a coherent product. Hence, there are important learning experiences at all stages of the authoring process: planning, producing and evaluating. In planning, students have to assess what they already know, select what is relevant to the purpose, seek additional knowledge and understanding, organize their ideas, establish relationships among them, express them in appropriate form for the anticipated audience, ensure clarity of expression, attend to coherence and consistency of argument and so on. These matters are in constant review throughout the production stage and, of course, are at the forefront during the evaluation stage. Thus, cooperative writing encourages students constantly to question, challenge and seek alternative perspectives. It involves them in the exploration of ideas, problem-solving and decision making. In other words, it creates opportunities for what Bereiter and Scardamalia (1987) refer to as the 'knowledge-transforming' mode of writing, as distinct from the 'knowledge-telling' mode.

Too often, writing tasks (like most teaching and learning activities) are under strict teacher control, whereas the major learning benefits accrue when students have control and make their own decisions, in collaboration with others, about what to write and how to write. Of course, students also need guidance and support from the teacher and, crucially, continuing instruction concerning the techniques of writing and the ways in which they can be deployed for particular purposes. Without an adequate and developing background knowledge of such matters, effective choices cannot be made; without regular critical feedback, significant progress will not be made. Writing does not necessarily improve with practice unless that practice is accompanied by guidance, exemplification, criticism and support. Part of this continuing instruction should include opportunities to read and criticize both good and bad examples of text, preferably written for a variety of purposes and audiences.

In many ways, authentic writing is like authentic scientific inquiry. Not only do students learn to do it by doing it, alongside a skilled practitioner (the teacher) acting as guide, critic, facilitator and supporter; they also learn that writing is a dynamic and interactive process. It is an untidy and unpredictable activity: however detailed the plan, it seems that as soon as words are put to paper, they are subject to criticism and evaluation that may lead to new ways of expressing ideas, new ideas or even a reconsideration of the plan or the underlying purpose. Every writing move changes the situation in some way. This, of course, is where the word processor is of such inestimable value, enabling even extensive changes to be made quickly and painlessly, and radically changing students' perceptions about revising, redrafting and editing. Computer technology also opens up the possibility of engaging in cooperative writing ventures with students in other schools, possibly in other countries, perhaps in the form of a regular exchange of newsletters on scientific matters. The Science Across the World project (British Council 1997) provides just such an opportunity and one, moreover, that is focused on the kinds of issues and politicized approach discussed in Chapters 1 and 2.

Reading, writing, talking and doing science

While it has been useful for the purposes of the foregoing discussion to look separately at activities concerned with talking, listening, reading and writing, it is clear that they are mutually interactive. Thus, learning is enhanced when students talk and write about what they read, talk about what they write and read what their peers write. Significant learning also occurs at the intersection of language-based activities and hands-on inquiry, when students talk and write about their laboratory-based and fieldwork investigations. It is through this combination of talking, reading, writing and doing science, and their interaction, that students are stimulated to reflect on these processes, on their learning and its development and on the nature of science itself.

Enculturation into science also involves an adjustment to one's self-image to incorporate 'self as scientist'. This particularly difficult aspect of border crossing can be promoted through language-based learning experiences. It seems, for example, that students often read text as story, subconsciously regarding the author as the scientist behind the storyline (Abt-Perkins and Pagnucci 1993). With appropriate encouragement, students can begin to see themselves in that role, identifying personally with the actions and struggles of scientists and the contexts in which they work. Reinforcement comes, of course, through writing personal accounts of scientific investigations, both real and imagined. As argued earlier, it is personal stories rather than objective, third person accounts that provide the best opportunities for students to explore, develop and consolidate their new understanding, make sense of new experiences, reflect on their learning progress and explore their sense of belonging within the scientific community. 'It helps us to find out what we are currently thinking when we tell a new story, what we used to think when we tell an old one, and what we think of what we think when we hear what we ourselves have to say' (Schank 1990: 146).

Enculturation into science also involves learning to 'read and write' in other modes of symbolic representation. Effective use of equations, diagrams, charts and graphs is the most immediately relevant, and little more needs to be said about them, beyond expressing the well established view that students need extensive opportunities to work with and construct them. It is also increasingly important for students to be literate with respect to video technology and the techniques of advertisers. They might learn much about their personal framework of understanding by designing a logo, drawing a picture, assembling a collage, writing an advertising jingle or shooting a short video. What is crucial is that students learn to move freely between these different ways of representing knowledge, are sensitive to their strengths and weaknesses and acquire the skill and confidence to detect and evaluate whatever implicit messages they may project.

A wide range of reading and writing activities, and a more varied experience of these alternative ways of representing knowledge, can be achieved by using commercially available or teacher-produced 'Jackdaws' and other styles of multimedia package. These collections of print and non-print materials on particular topics, issues, persons or events may include textbook extracts, newspaper cuttings, photographs, biographical data, maps, computer programs and so on. When students compile their own Jackdaws, alone or in groups, teachers can require the inclusion of certain items, while leaving most of the decision making to students, thereby ensuring the practising of particular skills within a form that encourages personalization, idiosyncracy and creativity. With a requirement for a written or audiotaped rationale for why students made particular selections, a substantial measure of critical reflection can also be encouraged.

Jackdaws are particularly well suited to inquiry-oriented learning and can be used to support both language-based/media-based inquiries and laboratory/fieldwork investigations. They can form the basis for portfolio-based assessment schemes and can provide teachers with much deeper insight into students' personal frameworks of understanding than is possible by other means. They also provide a valuable resource for encouraging and supporting individual and group-based reflection on learning, personal understanding and science. It is this kind of reflection, and the attitudes associated with it, that facilitates smoother border crossing into the subculture of science.

• • • 14

Making it work: the role of the teacher

It was argued in Chapter 12 that for activities concerned with learning science (acquiring and developing conceptual understanding), teachers may need to retain some degree of control over the statement of the problem and the evaluation and interpretation of the results, while for activities concerned with learning about science, it is important for students to have some control over planning and strategy, and to engage in discussion about how the data that can be collected and the interpretations that can be made depend on experimental design. For activities designed to give students experience of doing science, it is important for control of most aspects of the inquiry to be ceded to the students. It was argued in Chapter 6 that the more control students exercise, the greater the sense of ownership and, therefore, the greater the motivational power of the activity is likely to be. There is also evidence that management problems are decreased and student learning is enhanced when students assume greater levels of control (Roth and Roychoudhury 1993).

The amount of student control that is desirable on any particular occasion is, of course, a matter of professional judgement. Teacher control and decision-making functions, in part, as scaffolding that enables the activity to be brought within each student's zone of proximal development. Schibeci (1987) describes a style of investigation in which responsibility is shared between teacher and students. Teacher demonstration raises a problem or issue, which is explored via teacher-led question–answer sessions and small group discussion. Each student group generates a hypothesis and then collaborates with the teacher in designing an experiment to test it. After conducting the experiment, the students draw whatever conclusions they can, and formulate a tentative explanation. Each group then presents its findings for scrutiny and criticism. Finally, the teacher provides a critical overview and summarizes the main findings. Jones and Kirk (1990) envisage teacher scaffolding (though they don't use that particular expression) operating within a five stage framework.

- *Focusing* – generating interest; directing attention to important features of an investigation; asking questions.
- *Exploring* – supporting students as they carry out investigations to answer their questions.
- *Reporting* – acting as critic and discussion leader as students report their findings to the class.
- *Consolidating* – using information from the investigations to develop the topic.
- *Applying* – creating opportunities for students to carry out further investigations or to engage in writing activities using new ideas developed in earlier phases.

Even on those occasions when students have control of the whole investigation, there can still be value in the use of indirect scaffolding – for example, the 'pupil response sheets' and 'variables tables' described by Watson and Fairbrother (1993). Pupil response sheets are aids to reflection, incorporating questions such as 'What do I know?', 'What do I think will happen, and why?' Variables tables help students to be systematic and careful in their approach to the manipulation of variables by requiring them to set out their strategy in table form.

Embedded in many of these guidelines is the notion of reciprocal teaching, which assumes that students and teachers learn from each other, and that both benefit from an occasional reversal of the usual roles. Indeed, providing opportunities for students to act as teachers can be considered a major Vygotskian strategy. It is, of course, the quality of dialogue during these interactions that is central to good and effective learning. Skilful teachers support their students' attempts to understand by fostering dialogue in which they and their students listen carefully to each other, and they make responses that signal very clearly that serious and careful attention has been paid to what every speaker has said. While the good teacher's comments may sometimes be highly critical, they are always supportive and 'contingently responsive' (Wells and Chang-Wells 1992) to the needs of the learner. Thus, effective teaching is located in careful attention to argument – thoughtful presentation of the teacher's argument and responsive critique of students' arguments – and the fostering of trustful and respectful relationships among students, and between students and teacher. It is not overly concerned with ensuring the 'right answer'. Good teachers act as models of rational inquiry, exhibit the characteristics, practices and values of good inquiry in all aspects of their teaching and seek to provide finely tuned, learner-sensitive guidance and support to their students as they move towards intellectual independence.

Because the outcomes cannot be guaranteed, and because traditional forms of authority and control are not applicable, the approaches suggested in this book can be liberating for some teachers and threatening for others. For some, feelings of competence are rooted in quite narrow definitions of classroom control. Teacher modelling and student-led investigations can both impact severely on this view of class control. When students make their own decisions, ask questions and challenge teachers, and when lesson planning cannot be conducted with precision and certainty of outcome, some teachers may feel that their authority is being challenged, or even undermined. Developing alternative perceptions of what it means to be 'in control' of student learning is an essential part of effecting a shift of emphasis towards science education as enculturation. Some teachers will feel insecure, or feel that they are failing in their responsibility to the students and their parents, if they are unable to ensure coverage of a large and predetermined body of scientific content. However, the very uncertainty of student-led inquiry and honest teacher modelling conveys some important messages:

- learning is uncertain, challenging and sometimes frustrating, but it is also exciting and rewarding;
- teachers are learners too;
- learning is a lifelong process.

Students also come to class with views about what constitutes learning and what constitutes teaching. Any changes that teachers wish to make will need to take account of resistance from those who have a vested interest in current methods because they have previously done very well with them. Students who are accustomed to routine tasks that make few intellectual demands may resist the teacher's attempts to introduce more ambiguous, complex and challenging tasks by trying to 'negotiate the task downwards', failing to comply or generally 'playing up' (Pintrich *et al.* 1993). This point is simply another reminder that if we are to construct good and effective learning experiences we need to take account of *all* factors that impact on the learner. Whatever the activity, it is the nature and timing of teacher intervention that is crucial: deciding how to attend to each learner in a way that is appropriate to her or him, taking into account her or his unique personal framework of understanding, including its affective and social components; and deciding when to encourage and support, when to direct or instruct and when to involve others. Knowing when, where, how much and what type of guidance, critical feedback and support are needed to facilitate effective learning and the development of good learning behaviours is a matter of professional judgement, deriving from experience and thoughtful reflection on it. Too much guidance can interfere with students' thought processes, act to frustrate problem-solving and lead to premature closure; too little guidance can leave students unable to make satisfactory progress and lead to feelings of frustration, and even alienation. To be effective, teacher guidance and assistance need to be pitched slightly beyond the current level of unaided performance – that is, in the zone of proximal development. Constant dialogue between teachers and students is essential if good intervention decisions are to be made. It is, of course, the nature of the language used by the teacher during these exchanges that establishes the interpretive framework within which students are able to make scientific sense of whatever is being studied. Again, there is an issue of fine professional judgement: neither imposing meaning nor permitting students to construct whatever meaning happens to suit them, for whatever reasons.

To achieve intellectual independence, students must eventually take responsibility for their own learning and for the planning, executing and reporting of their own inquiries. In other words, learning as assisted performance must enable students (eventually) to go beyond what they have learned and to use knowledge in creative ways in solving novel problems and building new understanding. In addition to its role in facilitating understanding, collaborative talk between teacher and students serves a further scaffolding function. It empowers students by negotiating this transfer of responsibility. It encourages and supports students in taking increasing responsibility for aspects of the particular task in hand and, eventually, for learning and inquiry in general.

A closer look at group learning

Learning is not a solitary activity. It involves interactions between the learner and other people, including the teacher and other students, and it involves interaction with learning materials through experiences organized by the teacher. In other words, the learning environment comprises multiple, interdependent and interacting social contexts, each of which is impregnated with sociocultural knowledge and reflects particular interests and values. As discussed in Chapter 7, any or all of these social contexts may influence both a student's motivation to learn and the direction of whatever learning results.

Johnson and Johnson (1985) postulate three types of goal structure that organize interpersonal behaviour: *cooperative, competitive* and *individualistic*. In cooperative situations, there is a positive correlation among goal attainments: individuals can only achieve their goals if other participants achieve theirs. Hence, each individual seeks an outcome that is beneficial to all group members. In a competitive social situation, there is a negative correlation among goal attainments: individuals can only achieve their goals if other participants fail to achieve theirs. Hence, each individual seeks outcomes that are personally beneficial but detrimental to others in the group. In an individualistic situation there is no correlation among goal attainments: whether an individual achieves his or her goals has no influence on whether other participants achieve theirs. Hence, each person seeks an outcome that is personally beneficial, ignoring as irrelevant the effects on others.

If Johnson and Johnson's (1985) analysis is correct, participants within cooperative situations benefit from facilitating each other's efforts to achieve, while participants in competitive situations benefit from obstructing each other's efforts. As a consequence, cooperative groups will create more facilitative, encouraging interactions, and so are likely to foster more positive interpersonal relationships, create a sense of belonging, enhance self-esteem and, therefore, lead to enhanced learning. By contrast, competition engenders poor interpersonal relationships and may hinder learning. In individualistic situations, the efforts of others are irrelevant, of course, so participants may as well cooperate as not. Slavin (1985, 1995) states that, after cooperative learning experiences, students express ideas and feelings more readily in class and listen more attentively to teachers. He reports a positive effect on self-esteem and claims that students more frequently, and more strongly, express feelings of belonging and being supported. Each of these effects can contribute to better learning behaviour by assisting a shift to an internal locus of control.

Constructivists claim that group-based discussion promotes higher quality cognitive processes because of the opportunity for participants to confront diverse views. Whether good learning results from controversies and conflicts arising within the group depends, in part, on how the teacher manages them and, in part, on what social skills and negotiating techniques the students already possess and can utilize to good effect. When managed constructively, controversy promotes an active search for more knowledge and better understanding to clarify the precise nature of the dispute. When poorly managed, disputes can soon become destructive.[1] Sometimes one member of a group will have knowledge or skills that can be passed on to others, and sometimes collaborative action can solve a problem that couldn't be solved by a student working alone. On other occasions, students will need to consult the teacher and/or some other source of knowledge or information. For the teacher, it is a question of judging how much help is needed – a few hints that enable the group to work it out for themselves, some clear guidelines on where/how to search for the knowledge they need or some more substantial and detailed teacher input. To make this judgement, the teacher needs to engage in constant and sensitive monitoring of individual and group progress – as a co-participant, by careful reading of student logbooks and personal journals or through feedback from regular class meetings and conferences.

There are, of course, major management problems associated with all forms of group learning: setting time limits and deadlines; pacing the activities; deciding when to move on; signalling the need for winding-up; and so on. Careful record keeping is essential to ensure that each group member experiences a sufficiently wide range of learning activities and engages in a sufficiently varied range of tasks. Making decisions about when and in what way to intervene with new knowledge, new skills or alternative lines of inquiry involves close monitoring of each learner's progress. As indicated previously, careful negotiation between teacher and learner is essential if teacher or peer intervention is to be appropriately located in the student's zone of proximal development. Finding sufficient time for such finely tuned dialogue, and at the particular time it is needed, is a considerable logistical problem. However, the more experienced students become in working in cooperative groups, the more capable they are of assuming responsibility for some of the more routine management tasks, thus freeing the teacher to attend to urgent matters.

The different patterns of activity across groups, and the optimum scheduling of group meetings, have to be coordinated with whole-class activities. If each group has been covering a different aspect of the same general inquiry (a common way of organizing group work, especially in primary schools), regular conferences and class meetings become important learning opportunities for students. They provide a chance for all students to see how the various elements fit together; they may trigger new ideas and new lines of inquiry; they act as a powerful stimulus to reflection on learning progress, and on the nature of scientific inquiry. Reflection might also be extended to a consideration of social, economic, environmental, moral-ethical and aesthetic issues arising directly or indirectly from scientific inquiry and scientific and technological innovation. It is this confrontation of controversial issues, sometimes located in a variety of sociocultural contexts (Chapters 1 and 2), that helps students to develop the 'multiple realities' that assist smooth border crossings.

Conferences are also good opportunities to reflect on how the group functioned. Did everyone feel involved? Did everyone get a chance to do something? Did everyone feel that his or her contribution was recognized and valued? What should be changed about the way the group worked and organized itself? Student self-evaluations also play an important role. Students can be encouraged to identify their successes and set new goals for their future learning by responding to questions such as: 'Which parts of your investigation did you find most enjoyable, and most difficult?', 'If you were starting again, what would you do differently?', 'If you had more time, what would you do next?', 'Did you feel that you worked well, both alone and with others?' These reflections emphasize the reciprocal relationship between product and process: what students learn depends on how they conduct the inquiry, and what they currently know and understand determines the way in which they conduct the next inquiry. In other words, students are reminded of the theory-dependence of inquiry.

Teachers contemplating group work generally have two major concerns. First is the question of maintaining accountability within the group – that is, ensuring that everyone remains on task, avoiding fragmentation into 'leaders and led' and finding working procedures that are goal-oriented without being overly restrictive or directive. Second is the often thorny issue of assessment. Teachers often worry about assigning a common grade for group-based work. One primary concern is that students who feel that a common grade is unjust, because they perceive the workload was not evenly distributed, for example, might withdraw from active involvement in group efforts. Research evidence indicates that, before experiencing cooperative learning, most students believe that competitive grading is best, but afterwards, when given the same grade, they feel that a common grade is fairer (Slavin 1995).

Advocates of group learning have devised a wide range of approaches to encourage different styles of working and the adoption of different roles and responsibilities. This literature will not be reviewed here, save to note that students used to a more standardized diet of competitive learning and whole-class experiences may sometimes resist the introduction of cooperative learning. This is especially noticeable among high achievers. After all, they have done well in school under the existing arrangements, and so have a vested interest in maintaining continuity. It is not easy for them to redefine their role, or the teacher's, even though it may be educationally and socially beneficial for them to do so. In addition, cooperative learning methods introduced in isolation lack social meaning for these students, and so may not be treated seriously. To be effective, they need to be an integral part of regular curriculum provision.

A plea for variety

The foregoing discussion should not be interpreted as a plea for the adoption of an unrelieved diet of cooperative learning based on small groups. It is equally important to create opportunities for students to work individually, and to follow their own interests now and again without having to negotiate with others. It is crucial that students are given time and opportunity to reflect on their own understanding and to explore and develop their own ideas through 'inner dialogue'. Individual reading and writing activities play a key role here. It is also beneficial for students to experience whole-group learning. Listening to a gifted story-teller or a talented lecturer, observing and participating in a skilful teacher demonstration, watching a well made movie in the company of others: each provides a rich blend of intellectual and emotional stimulation that cannot be provided in other ways. Similarly, class field trips and excursions furnish experiences that are of inestimable value.

My own preference, therefore, is for variety: a mix of individual learning, small group work and whole-class experience, with choice on any one occasion being determined by subject matter, availability of resources and facilities, and the style of learning experience in which students have most recently engaged. Of course, students need extensive practice to develop the ability to shift easily between groups of different size and composition, while retaining the capacity to work alone when directed or invited to do so. Through experience, however, they learn to select appropriate strategies, behaviours and language for the changing interpersonal environments in which they work. Eventually, they are comfortable in all circumstances, though they may legitimately retain a preference for a particular style of working and should be encouraged to exercise it.

This suggestion for constant change must be further justified. Unless it could be argued convincingly that regular change would help to prepare students for an uncertain world in which the pace of change is constantly accelerating, and that this is of greater benefit to students than the creation of an island of stability, teachers should not subscribe to a philosophy of change simply for the sake of change. However, there is a more convincing, twofold argument for the kind of variety advocated here. First, different *styles* of learning foster different *kinds* of learning. Second, breadth of experience is essential if students are to make meaningful and realistic choices within a system that affords them a measure of self-determination with regard to learning methods and assessment procedures. A choice made in ignorance of experience is no choice at all. In addition, through these varied experiences, students are learning much more than science. They are learning to be flexible and adaptable, and to participate in a variety of roles – co-worker, leader, friend, teacher and critic, for example. They are learning skills of self-direction and skills of negotiation and cooperation. They are learning to value the uniqueness of the individuals with whom they work – experiencing and appreciating the range of attributes, skills, abilities and aptitudes that a group of students possesses, as well as recognizing and valuing differences in personality, gender, ethnicity, life experiences and home circumstances. Above all, they are learning to play an active role in the establishment and maintenance of a learning community.

The case for variety should be extended to assessment and evaluation procedures. Replacing contrived and restricted tests by a negotiated collection of authentic learning tasks (a portfolio) enables students to *use* knowledge in exploring and developing their personal framework of understanding. A portfolio might include, for example, a letter to Grandma, a personalized concept map, a multiple choice test paper, a poem, a drawing, a collection of newspaper cuttings, an essay or two, even a video clip. Some items might be individually produced, others might be group products. Each portfolio would be unique, reflecting a particular student's response to the various learning experiences provided, thus giving the teacher valuable insight into the student's personal framework of understanding. The use of portfolios is a logical extension of an inquiry-oriented classroom culture. Used appropriately, portfolios play a significant role in the democratization and personalization of the classroom. In contrast with more traditional assessment practice, this kind of assessment is *educative*, in the sense that it enhances and promotes learning by engaging students in activities that are interesting, challenging and significant learning experiences in themselves. Too often, assessment in school science is seen to begin only at the point where learning has stopped and, more significantly, learning is seen to stop at the point when assessment begins. Moreover, setting up special 'assessment occasions' raises anxiety levels and creates a damaging barrier between teacher and learner.

Building a learning community

Making the kinds of curriculum changes advocated in this book requires an educational environment somewhat different from the traditional. Restructuring one's understanding is a risky venture; previous certainty is challenged and, possibly, is abandoned in favour of new and unfamiliar ways of thinking. Many schools do not provide a sufficiently supportive climate to sustain students through such an emotionally demanding undertaking. Nor do schools always ensure a safe, open and supportive forum in which students can express their views, give and take criticism and test out their tentative understanding. Relationships that are socially and emotionally important to students, and are continuously supportive throughout these challenging and uncertain activities, are crucial for learning, because they generate the finely tuned dialogues necessary for sustaining the exploration and development of ideas. We need to prioritize both the affective and the social!

Fraser (1990) reports that teachers commonly hold more favourable views about the learning environment than do their students, and that the actual environment of most classes falls well short of that preferred by either students or teachers. The four dimensions of learning environment included in his analysis were: *personalization* (the degree of emphasis on opportunities for individual students to interact with the teacher and on concern for the personal welfare and social growth of the individual); *participation* (the extent to which students are encouraged to participate rather than be passive listeners); *order and organization* (the degree of emphasis on students behaving in an orderly, quiet and polite manner, and on the overall organization of classroom activities); and *task orientation* (the extent to which it is important to complete planned activities and to stay on-task and within designated subject matter). Interestingly, in the context of the present discussion, it is in the first two categories that the greatest discrepancies were found. Clearly, there is a need to pay much closer attention to developing a greater sense of inclusion and participation for students.

Ravetz (1971) likens the scientific enterprise to cathedral building: a range of specialists with a common goal and shared values contributing, in mutually supportive ways, to a whole that is more than the sum of its individual parts. There is much to be gained by regarding the educational enterprise in a similar light. A class of students and their teacher can be seen as a 'learning community', as a group of individuals with shared values acting in mutually supportive ways in pursuit of the common purpose of effective learning for all. When students feel that they are members of a mutually supportive and caring community, they have more confidence to tackle demanding tasks, they acquire a more positive self-image and they develop a sense of responsibility for their own learning, the learning and well-being of other students and the smooth functioning of the community as a whole.

But a learning community doesn't just happen. It has to be built and it has to be supported. It is built through modelling and by example; it is supported and maintained by the continuing guidance of a skilled and caring teacher, use of curriculum activities and assessment strategies that require students to work cooperatively and adoption of appropriate administrative and organizational structures. The ways in which a teacher interacts with individual students and groups, asks and responds to questions, organizes laboratory work and field trips, manages discussions, anticipates concerns and difficulties, responds to requests, deals with disciplinary matters and so on become the model for the community. These actions shape the overall classroom climate and establish the codes of practice that determine the quality of interpersonal relationships. It is important, for example, that students know that what they say will be listened to, by the teacher and by other students. Teachers can and should model careful listening behaviour: first, by not pre-judging a student's contribution on the grounds of previous history, either good or bad; second, by trying to hear the message behind the particular words employed. When teachers listen carefully and respond appropriately, and are clearly seen to do so, students are encouraged to follow suit, especially when such behaviour is acknowledged and commended. Similarly, if collaboration and respect for others' beliefs and points of view are to become part of the community's established code of practice, they need to be consistently modelled by the teacher, expected of every other member of the community and commended when they are exhibited. Curriculum, class management and organizational structures play an important role in reinforcing the behaviours, expectations and values modelled by the teacher. The simple message is: be consistent. It would be absurd, for example, to encourage collaborative learning, yet to utilize assessment and evaluation procedures based solely on competitive, norm-referenced tests.

One of the keys to consolidating the modelled behaviour is engaging students in a wide range of other roles: teacher (through peer tutoring), discussion chair, evaluator, facilitator, coordinator, reporter and the like. When students have experienced these roles themselves they can more readily empathize with others who are struggling to fulfil them, act as constructive critics and provide the necessary support that helps the novice to develop expertise. Because their experiences of learning a new role are more recent, students are sometimes more skilled than teachers at locating their support and intervention in the zone of proximal development of the novice (Tudge 1990). In addition, they can frequently illuminate a point by making reference to common experiences and utilizing language that is more familiar and accessible than the teacher's. When students work with numerous other students acting in a variety of roles, they develop flexibility and understanding of different ways of approaching these tasks. By negotiating different ways of organizing and coordinating their work with a variety of other people, they improve their communication skills, learn tolerance and acquire sensitivity to the moods and needs of others. Moreover, they become more able and willing to accept shared responsibility for ensuring that community practice and community codes of behaviour and values are observed.

Being serious about the notion of a learning community means extending it beyond the immediate classroom by involving the whole school and the wider community. Visits and field trips, invitations to guest speakers, collaborative ventures with other schools and community groups (perhaps extending to other countries via the Internet) all have a role to play. While strictly outside the scope of this book, it is worth noting that opportunities for student groups to be involved in community affairs and to exercise responsibility for such things as fund raising, organizing educational and recreational visits, landscaping of the school grounds, furnishing and decorating the classroom, editing journals and newsletters and monitoring the school's energy consumption are invaluable for fostering intellectual independence and critical scientific literacy, developing a sense of community and an awareness of the needs, interests and aspirations of others, establishing a sense of ownership and responsibility for self-directed learning, sensitizing students to moral and ethical issues and cultivating environmental and sociopolitical awareness.

The skills of working cooperatively with others, and the values and attitudes that underpin the notion of a learning community, are, as argued above, built up over time through modelling, negotiating and acknowledging the contributions of others, not by laying down a set of rules. While rules may be useful in facilitating the efficient execution of tasks with clear, predetermined and expected outcomes, they are of little value in the pursuit of more diffuse goals relating to continuing learning, personal development and intellectual independence, and may actually hinder them. For such an enterprise, the strict rules often found in schools have to be replaced by a commitment to negotiate the most supportive and facilitative climate for the particular participants. In a learning community, teacher–student interaction is viewed as a process of negotiating and co-constructing meaning, not imposing it. This applies just as much to the meanings that underpin ways of organizing classroom learning as it does to the learning itself. As an aside, it is worth mentioning that a particularly powerful enabling tool for the maintenance of a learning community is the Computer Supported Intentional Learning Environment (CSILE), through which participants use a database to compile notes and critical comments on the topic under discussion (Scardamalia and Bereiter 1994).

Given the authoritarian and hierarchical system typical of most schools, it is inevitable that children will learn that power and status are the most significant features of human relationships. Curriculum decisions and matters of school organization are invariably in the hands of teachers; students are rarely, if ever, consulted. Many teachers use their power to enforce learning styles that may not be appropriate for some students. Often there is an almost unrelieved diet of instruction-based teaching and worksheet-driven practical work. Not only is this practice pedagogically unsound, but it reinforces those implicit messages about power and authority. Moreover, since senior positions in most schools are held by white males, there is an additional powerful message relating status and power to ethnicity and gender.[2] A more democratic school system and more democratic classroom organization could project a different set of messages: mutual tolerance, respect and value for all, the importance of conflict resolution through negotiation and compromise. Needless to say, a more equitable distribution of senior posts would project a significantly different message about ethnicity, gender, status and power. Recommendations on appointments and on alternative styles of school government (such as the collegial system operated within the Rudolph Steiner schools) fall outside the scope of this book, but recommendations for alternative teaching and learning methods and alternative forms of curriculum organization do not. Above all, there needs to be a much greater emphasis on mutual responsibility, negotiation and the fostering of community spirit.

Implications for teacher education

If the principles of learning set out in the later chapters of this book are valid, they apply just as much to teachers as they do to students, and they apply just as much to pre-service and in-service teacher education as they do to school science education. In other words, teacher education can be regarded as enculturation into the conceptual and procedural knowledge, language, codes of conduct, attitudes and values of the community of teachers. Adoption of the apprenticeship model advocated for student learning of science leads to the proposal that student teachers learn about teaching, and learn to teach, by working alongside a skilled practitioner acting as model, guide, critic and support. Those teachers with experience develop their expertise towards connoisseurship through critical reflection on existing practice, informed by reading, writing, classroom research, discussion with colleagues and consultation with more expert teachers acting as change agents. This view of teacher education is more about commitment to continued learning than about implementation of a set of previously acquired skills.

Teaching effectively in the style described here, making on-the-spot decisions about when and how to intervene in ways that enable *all* students to negotiate border crossings into the subcultures of science and school science, requires not only deep and robust understanding of a wide range of scientific and educational matters, but also a sensitivity to the knowledge, experiences, aspirations, attitudes and values of people from many different sociocultural groups, and a capacity to learn through critical reflection on current practice. This demanding set of attributes can best be achieved by extending the notion of a community of inquiry to the twin tasks of teacher education and curriculum development through the adoption of an action research approach. It could also be argued that if teachers are to implement these principles of learning, and teach successfully in the inquiry mode, they need to have experienced this sort of learning themselves. Action research provides such an opportunity.

A fundamental principle of action research is that all curriculum knowledge should be regarded as problematic, and open to scrutiny, critical appraisal and revision. Nothing should be taken for granted, whether it be goals, content, teaching and learning activities, or assessment and evaluation strategies. Nothing should be accepted unquestioningly, just because it is handed down from the Ministry of Education, local education authority or school board. Also underpinning the action research approach is recognition that teacher development, however desirable, cannot be achieved by trying to compel or even to exhort teachers to change. Nor can the precise nature and extent of change be predetermined. Control of the direction and pace of development must rest with teachers. Indeed, in discussing *emancipatory* action research, Kemmis (1988: 47) advises teachers to work alone, without interference even from researchers and developers, in order to free themselves from 'irrational or unjust habits, customs, precedents, coercion, or bureaucratic systemization'. Outsiders, says Kemmis, are unnecessary.

My own view is that outsiders *are* necessary, and that there is an important role for a change agent acting as a facilitator, critic and support for a group of teachers engaged in curriculum renewal. Through dialogue with the change agent, attention is focused on criticizing, challenging, modifying and changing teachers' beliefs, understandings, attitudes, skills, values and relationships, rather than on providing 'curriculum information'. This approach assumes that teachers can acquire the expertise necessary for effective curriculum development by refining and extending the practical professional knowledge they already possess through critical collaborative activity supported by change agents (or researcher/facilitators), whose work involves fostering critical awareness, enhancing curriculum problem-solving skills and assisting the group in working through conflicts by the provision of whatever research-based, theoretical knowledge may be appropriate, in whatever form is appropriate (Pedretti and Hodson 1995; Bencze and Hodson 1998; Hodson and Bencze 1998).

Teaching is a complex and uncertain business, but we get better at it by critical reflection on practice and on the arguments for different approaches. Those who claim that there is only one way to teach science, or that there is one best way, mistake the nature of the enterprise. Teachers need the courage to be wrong and to make mistakes, but they also need the commitment to learn from their mistakes. When we expect to make mistakes, we can use them to inform our thinking. In other words, the key to professional development, as to any form of intellectual independence, is to have a mastery or learning orientation rather than a performance orientation, and a commitment to learn, a commitment to seek better, more appropriate, more effective ways to teach science. Of course, this necessitates a shift in the way in which teachers are appraised and evaluated. There is no room for predetermined checklists of teacher behaviours. The guarantee of good and improving educational provision is not the strict application of a rigorous form of teacher appraisal in relation to a prespecified list of approved behaviours, but teacher commitment to trying to find the wisest way to proceed in the circumstances. It is this commitment that constitutes the ethical drive of the connoisseur teacher.

Notes

1 Rudduck and Cowie (1988) give advice on how to manage learning groups and how to teach students the skills of self-management that enable groups to function more effectively.
2 'Most schools' refers to schools in those countries with which I am most familiar: the UK, Canada, the USA, New Zealand and Australia.

References

Abelson, R.P. (1986) Beliefs are like possessions, *Journal for the Theory of Social Behavior*, 16: 223–50.

Abdullah, A. and Scaife, J. (1997) Using interviews to assess children's understanding of science concepts, *School Science Review*, 78(285): 79–83.

Abruscato, J. (1988) *Teaching Children Science*, 2nd edn. Englewood Cliffs, NJ: Prentice Hall.

Abt-Perkins, D. and Pagnucci, G. (1993) From tourist to storyteller: reading and writing science. In S. Tchudi (ed.) *The Astonishing Curriculum: Integrating Science and Humanities through Language*. Urbana, IL: National Council of Teachers of English.

Aikenhead, G.S. (1990) Scientific/technological literacy, critical reasoning, and classroom practice. In S.P. Norris and L.M. Phillips (eds) *Foundations of Literacy Policy in Canada*. Calgary: Detselig.

Aikenhead, G. (1994) Consequences to learning science through STS: a research perspective. In J. Solomon and G. Aikenhead (eds) *Science–Technology–Society Education: International Perspectives on Reform*. New York: Teachers College Press.

Aikenhead, G. (1996) Science education: border crossing into the subculture of science, *Studies in Science Education*, 27: 1–52.

Aikenhead, G.S. (1997) Toward a First Nations cross-cultural science and technology curriculum, *Science Education*, 81: 217–38.

American Association for the Advancement of Science (1989) *Science for All Americans*. A Project 2061 Report on Literacy Goals in Science, Mathematics, and Technology. Washington, DC: AAAS.

American Association for the Advancement of Science (1993) *Benchmarks for Scientific Literacy*. Oxford: Oxford University Press.

Ames, C. (1992) Classrooms: goals, structures, and student motivation, *Journal of Educational Psychology*, 84: 261–71.

Appleton, K. (1993) Using theory to guide practice: teaching science from a constructivist perspective, *School Science and Mathematics*, 93: 269–74.

Arons, A.B. (1983) Achieving wider scientific literacy, *Daedalus*, 112: 91–122.

Atwater, M.M. (1996) Social constructivism: infusion into the multicultural science education research agenda, *Journal of Research in Science Teaching*, 33: 821–37.

Ausubel, D.P. (1968) *Educational Psychology: A Cognitive View*. New York: Holt, Rinehart & Winston.

Ausubel, D.P., Novak, J.D. and Hanesian, H. (1978) *Educational Psychology: A Cognitive View*, 2nd edn. New York: Holt, Rinehart & Winston.

Baird, J.R. (1986) Improving learning through enhanced metacognition: a classroom study, *European Journal of Science Education*, 8: 263–82.

Baird, J.R. and Mitchell, I.J. (eds) (1986) *Improving the Quality of Teaching and Learning: An Australian Case Study – the PEEL Project*. Clayton, Victoria: Monash University.

Baird, J.R. and Northfield, R.J. (eds) (1992) *Learning from the PEEL Experience*. Clayton, Victoria: Monash University.

Bajracharya, H. and Brouwer, W. (1997) A narrative approach to science teaching in Nepal, *International Journal of Science Education*, 19: 429–46.

Baker, D. and Taylor, P.C.S. (1995) The effect of culture on the learning of science in non-western countries: the results of an integrated research review, *International Journal of Science Education*, 17: 695–704.

Bakhtin, M.M. (1981) *The Dialogic Imagination: Four Essays*. Austin, TX: University of Texas Press.

Bakhtin, M.M. (1986) *Speech Genres and Other Late Essays*. Austin, TX: University of Texas Press.

Barker, M. and Carr, M.D. (1989) Photosynthesis: can our pupils see the wood for the trees?, *Journal of Biological Education*, 23: 41–4.

Barlex, D. and Carre, C. (1985) *Visual Communication in Science*. Cambridge: Cambridge University Press.

Barnes, D. (1988) Oral language and learning. In S. Hynds and D. Rubin (eds) *Perspectives on Talk and Learning*. Urbana, IL: National Council of Teachers of English.

Barrass, R. (1984) Some misconceptions and misunderstandings perpetuated by teachers and textbooks of biology, *Journal of Biological Education*, 18: 201–6.

Bell, B.F. (1981) When is an animal not an animal?, *Journal of Biological Education*, 15: 213–18.

Bell, B. (collator) (1995) *Responses to 'Challenging NZ Science Education' by Michael R. Matthews*. Hamilton: University of Waikato.

Bencze, J.L. (1996) Correlational studies in school science: breaking the science–experiment–certainty connection, *School Science Review*, 78(282): 95–101.

Bencze, L. and Hodson, D. (1998) Coping with uncertainty in elementary school science: a case study in collaborative action research, *Teachers and Teaching: Theory and Practice*, 4: 77–94.

Bereiter, C. and Scardamalia, M. (1987) *The Psychology of Written Composition*. Hillsdale, NJ: Erlbaum.

Bettencourt, A. (1992) On what it means to understand science. In S. Hills (ed.) *The History and Philosophy of Science in Science Education*, vol. I. Kingston, ON: Queen's University.

Bhaskara Rao, D. (1992) Scientific attitude in secondary school pupils. In S. Hills (ed.) *The History and Philosophy of Science in Science Education*, vol. II. Kingston, ON: Queen's University.

Biddulph, F. and Osborne, R.J. (1984) *Making Sense of Our World: An Interactive Teaching Approach*. Hamilton, New Zealand: University of Waikato.

Black, P.J. and Lucas, A.M. (eds) (1993) *Children's Informal Ideas in Science*. London: Routledge.

Bloom, B.S. (1976) *Human Characteristics and School Learning*. New York: McGraw Hill.

Bloom, J.W. (1992) Contexts of meaning and conceptual integration: how children understand and learn. In R.A. Duschl and R.J. Hamilton (eds) *Philosophy of Science*,

Cognitive Psychology, and Educational Theory and Practice. Albany: State University of New York Press.

Bloom, J.W. (1995) Assessing and extending the scope of children's contexts of meaning: context maps as a methodological perspective, *International Journal of Science Education*, 17: 167–87.

Bridgman, P.W. (1950) *Reflections of a Physicist.* New York: Philosophical Library.

British Council (1997) Science across the world, *Science Education Newsletter*, 134 (October): 7–8.

Bronfenbrenner, U. (1979) *The Ecology of Human Development.* Cambridge, MA: Harvard University Press.

Brown, J.S., Collins, A. and Duguid, P. (1989) Situated cognition and the culture of learning, *Educational Researcher*, 18: 32–42.

Bruner, J.S. (1971) *The Relevance of Education.* Harmondsworth: Penguin.

Bruner, J.S. (1983) *Child's Talk: Learning to Use Language.* Oxford: Oxford University Press.

Bruner, J.S. (1985) Vygotsky: a historical and conceptual perspective. In J.V. Wertsch (ed.) *Culture, Communication and Cognition: Vygotskian Perspectives.* Cambridge: Cambridge University Press.

Bruner, J.S. (1990) *Acts of Meaning.* Cambridge, MA: Harvard University Press.

Brusic, S.A. (1992) Achieving STS goals through experiential learning, *Theory into Practice*, 20: 60–70.

Burbules, N.C. and Linn, M.C. (1988) Response to contradiction: scientific reasoning during adolescence, *Journal of Educational Psychology*, 80: 67–75.

Carey, S. (1986) Cognitive science and science education, *American Psychologist*, 41: 123–30.

Carraher, T.N., Carraher, D.W. and Schliemann, A.D. (1985) Mathematics in the streets and in schools, *British Journal of Developmental Psychology*, 3: 21–9.

Carraher, T.N., Carraher, D.W. and Schliemann, A.D. (1987) Written and oral mathematics, *Journal for Research in Mathematics Education*, 18: 83–97.

Carraher, T.N., Schliemann, A.D. and Carraher, D.W. (1988) Mathematical concepts in everyday life. In G.B. Saxe and M. Gearhart (eds) *Children's Mathematics.* San Francisco: Jossey Bass.

Cassels, J.R.T. and Johnstone, A.H. (1985) *Words that Matter in Science.* London: Royal Society of Chemistry.

Cawthron, E.R. and Rowell, J.A. (1978) Epistemology and science education, *Studies in Science Education*, 5: 31–59.

Chalmers, A.F. (1980) *What Is This Thing Called Science?* Milton Keynes: Open University Press.

Chambers, D.W. (1982) Stereotypic images of the scientist: the draw-a-scientist test, *Science Education*, 67: 255–65.

Champagne, A.B., Gunstone, R.F. and Klopfer, L.E. (1985) Effecting changes in cognitive structures among physics students. In L.H.T. West and A.L. Pines (eds) *Cognitive Structure and Conceptual Change.* Orlando, FL: Academic Press.

Cheek, D.W. (1992) *Thinking Constructively about Science, Technology and Society Education.* Albany: State University of New York Press.

Chinn, C.A. and Brewer, W.F. (1993) The role of anomalous data in knowledge acquisition. A theoretical framework and implications for science instruction, *Review of Educational Research*, 63: 1–49.

Cho, H-H., Kahle, J. and Norland, F. (1985) An investigation of high school biology textbooks as sources of misconceptions and difficulties in genetics and some suggestions for teaching genetics, *Science Education*, 69: 707–19.

Clark, H. (1985) Thoughts on the epistemological effects of conceptual change teaching, cited as personal communication by M. Watts and D. Bentley (1987) Constructivism in the classroom: enabling conceptual change by words and deeds, *British Educational Research Journal*, 13: 121–35.

Claxton, G. (1989) Cognition doesn't matter if you're scared, depressed or bored. In P. Adey, J. Bliss, J. Head and M. Shayer (eds) *Adolescent Development and School Science*. Lewes: Falmer Press.

Claxton, G. (1990) *Teaching to Learn: A Direction for Education*. London: Cassell.

Claxton, G. (1991) *Educating the Inquiring Mind: The Challenge for School Science*. New York: Harvester Wheatsheaf.

Claxton, G. (1993) Minitheories: a preliminary model for learning science. In P.J. Black and A.M. Lucas (eds) *Children's Informal Ideas in Science*. London: Routledge.

Cobern, W.W. (1991) *World View Theory and Science Education Research*. NARST monograph no. 3. Cincinnati, OH: National Association for Research in Science Teaching.

Cobern, W.W. (1993) Contextual constructivism: the impact of culture on the learning and teaching of science. In K. Tobin (ed.) *The Practice of Constructivism in Science Education*. Hillsdale, NJ: Erlbaum.

Cobern, W.W. (1995) Science education as an exercise in foreign affairs, *Science and Education*, 4: 287–302.

Cobern, W.W. (1996) Worldview theory and conceptual change in science education, *Science Education*, 80: 579–610.

Cole, M. and Scribner, S. (1978) Introduction. In L.S. Vygotsky, *Mind in Society*. Cambridge, MA: Harvard University Press.

Cosgrove, M., Osborne, R.J. and Tasker, R. (1982) *Towards Generative Learning*, LISP working paper no. 205. Hamilton, New Zealand: University of Waikato.

Costa, V.B. (1995) When science is 'another world': relationships between worlds of family, friends, school, and science, *Science Education*, 79: 313–33.

Danserau, D.F. (1985) Learning strategy research. In J. Segal, S. Chipman and R. Glaser (eds) *Thinking and Learning Skills: Vol. 1. Relating Instruction to Research*. Hillsdale, NJ: Erlbaum.

Davies, F. and Greene, T. (1984) *Reading for Learning in the Sciences*. Edinburgh: Oliver & Boyd.

Deci, E.L. and Ryan, R.M. (1985) *Intrinsic Motivation and Self-determination in Human Behavior*. New York: Plenum Press.

Delamont, S., Beynon, J. and Atkinson, P. (1988) In the beginning was the Bunsen: the foundations of secondary school science, *Qualitative Studies in Education*, 1: 315–28.

Demastes, S.S., Good, R.G. and Peebles, P. (1995) Students' conceptual ecologies and the process of conceptual change in evolution, *Science Education*, 79: 637–66.

Demastes, S.S., Good, R.G. and Peebles, P. (1996) Patterns of conceptual change in evolution, *Journal of Research in Science Teaching*, 33: 407–31.

Department of Education and Science (1975) *A Language for Life* (the Bullock Report). London: HMSO.

Diener, C.I. and Dweck, C.S. (1978) An analysis of learned helplessness: ongoing changes in performance, strategy, and achievement cognition following failure, *Journal of Personality and Social Psychology*, 36: 451–62.

Diener, C.I. and Dweck, C.S. (1980) An analysis of learned helplessness: II. The processing of success, *Journal of Personality and Social Psychology*, 39: 940–52.

di Sessa, A. (1982) Unlearning Aristotelian physics: a case study of knowledge-based learning, *Cognitive Science*, 6: 37–75.

Dixon, B. (1973) *What Is Science For?* London: Collins.

Domingos, A.M. (1989) Conceptual demand of science courses and social class. In P. Adey, J. Bliss, J. Head and M. Shayer (eds) *Adolescent Development and School Science*. Lewes: Falmer Press.

Driver, R. (1983) *The Pupil as Scientist?* Milton Keynes: Open University Press.

Driver, R. (1989) Changing conceptions. In P. Adey, J. Bliss, J. Head and M. Shayer (eds) *Adolescent Development and School Science*. Lewes: Falmer Press.

Driver, R., Asoko, H., Leach, J., Mortimer, E. and Scott, P. (1994a) Constructing scientific knowledge in the classroom, *Educational Researcher*, 23: 5–12.

Driver, R. and Bell, B. (1986) Students' thinking and the learning of science: a constructivist view, *School Science Review*, 67(240): 443–56.

Driver, R. and Erickson, G. (1983) Theories-in-action: some theoretical and empirical issues in the study of students' conceptual frameworks in science, *Studies in Science Education*, 10: 37–60.

Driver, R., Guesne, E. and Tiberghien, A. (eds) (1985) *Children's Ideas in Science*. Milton Keynes: Open University Press.

Driver, R., Squires, A., Rushworth, P. and Wood-Robinson, V. (1994b) *Making Sense of Secondary Science: Research into Children's Ideas*. London: Routledge.

Duhem, P. (1962) *The Aim and Structure of Physical Theory*. New York: Atheneum Press.

Durojaiye, M.O.A. (1980) *The Contribution of African Universities to the Reform of Education*. Paris: UNESCO.

Dweck, C.S. (1986) Motivational processes affecting learning, *American Psychologist*, 41: 1040–8.

Dweck, C.S., Davidson, W., Nelson, S. and Enna, B. (1978) Sex differences in learned helplessness: (II) The contingencies of evaluative feedback in the classroom: (III) An experimental analysis, *Developmental Psychology*, 14: 268–76.

Edwards, D. and Mercer, N. (1987) *Common Knowledge: the Development of Understanding in the Classroom*. London: Methuen.

Eisenhart, M., Finkel, E. and Marion, S.F. (1996) Creating the conditions for scientific literacy: a re-examination, *American Educational Research Journal*, 33: 261–95.

Elstgeest, J. (1985) Encounter, interaction, dialogue. In W. Harlen (ed.) *Primary Science: Taking the Plunge*. London: Heinemann.

Entwistle, N. (1981) *Styles of Learning and Teaching*. Chichester: John Wiley.

Eylon, B. and Linn, M. (1988) Learning and instruction: an examination of four research perspectives in science education, *Review of Educational Research*, 58: 251–301.

Faire, J. and Cosgrove, M. (1988) *Teaching Primary Science*. Hamilton, New Zealand: Waikato Education Centre.

Fensham, P.J. (1989) Theory into practice: how to assist teachers to teach constructively. In P. Adey, J. Bliss, J. Head and M. Shayer (eds) *Adolescent Development and School Science*. Lewes: Falmer Press.

Fensham, P.J. (1994) Science education. In K. Wiltshire, M. McMeniman and T. Tolhurst (eds) *Shaping the Future, vol. 2*. Brisbane: Queensland Government Printer.

Fensham, P.J. (1998) Science education and sub-cultural border crossing. In D. Hodson (ed.) *Science and Technology Education and Ethnicity: An Aotearoa/New Zealand Perspective*. Wellington: The Royal Society of New Zealand.

Fensham, P.J. and Kass, H. (1988) Inconsistent or discrepant events in science instruction, *Studies in Science Education*, 15: 1–16.

Feyerabend, P.K. (1962) Explanation, reduction and empiricism, *Minnesota Studies in the Philosophy of Science*, 3: 28–97.

Flanders, N. A. (1970) *Analysing Teaching Behavior*. Reading, MA: Addison-Wesley.

Fleming, R. (1986) Adolescent reasoning in socio-scientific issues. Part I: Social cognition, *Journal of Research in Science Teaching*, 23: 677–87; Part II: Nonsocial cognition, *Journal of Research in Science Teaching*, 23: 689–98.

Flick, L.B. (1995) Navigating a sea of ideas: teacher and students negotiate a course toward mutual relevance, *Journal of Research in Science Teaching*, 32: 1065–82.

Fraser, B.J. (1990) Students' perceptions of their classroom environments. In K. Tobin, J.B. Kahle and B.J. Fraser (eds) (1990) *Windows into Science Classrooms: Problems Associated with Higher-level Cognitive Learning*. London: Falmer Press.

Fuller, S. (1988) *Social Epistemology*. Bloomington, IN: Indiana University Press.

Furnham, A. (1992) Lay understanding of science: young people and adults' ideas of scientific concepts, *Studies in Science Education*, 20: 29–64.

Galbraith, P.L., Carss, M.C., Grice, R.D., Endean, L. and Warry, M. (1997) Towards scientific literacy for the third millennium: a view from Australia, *International Journal of Science Education*, 19: 447–67.

Galili, I. and Bar, V. (1992) Motion implies force: where to expect vestiges of the misconceptions, *International Journal of Science Education*, 14: 63–81.

Gardner, H. (1984) *Frames of Mind: The Theory of Multiple Intelligences*. London: Heinemann.

Gauld, C.F. and Hukins, A.A. (1980) Scientific attitudes: a review, *Studies in Science Education*, 7: 129–61.

Gayford, C. (1992) Patterns of group behaviour in open-ended problem-solving in science classes of 15-year-old students in England, *International Journal of Science Education*, 14: 41–9.

Gazzaniga, M. (1988) *Mind Matters*. Boston: Houghton Mifflin.

Geddis, A.N. (1992) Using truth strategies to develop a more adequate view of observation for the science classroom. In S. Hills (ed.) *History and Philosophy of Science in Science Education, vol. 1*. Kingston, ON: Queen's University.

George, J.M. (1995) Health education challenges in a rural context: a case study, *Studies in Science Education*, 25: 239–62.

George, J. and Glasgow, J. (1988) Street science and conventional science in the West Indies, *Studies in Science Education*, 15: 109–18.

Gilbert, J.K. and Watts, D.M. (1983) Concepts, misconceptions and alternative conceptions: changing perspectives in science education, *Studies in Science Education*, 10: 61–98.

Gil-Perez, D. (1996) New trends in science education, *International Journal of Science Education*, 18: 889–901.

Gil-Perez, D. and Carrascosa-Alis, J. (1985) Science learning as a conceptual and methodological change, *European Journal of Science Education*, 7: 231–6.

Gil-Perez, D. and Carrascosa-Alis, J. (1994) Bringing pupils' learning closer to a scientific construction of knowledge: a permanent feature of innovations in science teaching, *Science Education*, 78: 301–15.

Giroux, H. (1992) *Border Crossings: Cultural Workers and the Politics of Education*. New York: Routledge.

Glynn, S.M. and Muth, D. (1994) Reading and writing to learn science: achieving scientific literacy, *Journal of Research in Science Teaching*, 31: 1057–73.

Gott, R. and Duggan, S. (1995) *Investigative Work in the Science Curriculum*. Buckingham: Open University Press.

Gott, R. and Duggan, S. (1996) Practical work: its role in the understanding of evidence in science, *International Journal of Science Education*, 18: 791–806.

Gough, N. (1993) *Laboratories in Fiction: Science Education and Popular Media*. Geelong, Victoria: Deaking University Press.

Groisman, B., Shapiro, B. and Willinsky, J. (1991) The potential of semiotics to inform understanding of events in science education, *International Journal of Science Education*, 13: 217–26.

Guesne, E. (1985) Light. In R. Driver, E. Guesne and A. Tiberghien (eds) *Children's Ideas in Science*. Milton Keynes: Open University Press.

Gunstone, R.F. (1988) Learners in science education. In P.J. Fensham (ed.) *Development and Dilemmas in Science Education*. Lewes: Falmer Press.

Gunstone, R.F. (1991) Restructuring theory from practical experience. In B.E. Woolnough (ed.) *Practical Science: The Role and Reality of Practical Work in School Science*. Buckingham: Open University Press.

Gunstone, R.F. (1994) The importance of specific science content in the enhancement of metacognition. In P.J. Fensham, R.F. Gunstone and R.T. White (eds) *The Content of Science: A Constructivist Approach to its Teaching and Learning*. London: Falmer Press.

Gunstone, R.F., Mitchell, I.J. and the Monash Children's Science Group (1988) Two teaching strategies for considering children's science. In *What Research Says to the Science Teacher*. ICASE Yearbook no. 2.

Gunstone, R. and White, R. (1981) Understanding gravity, *Science Education*, 65: 291–9.

Hammer, D. (1994) Students' beliefs about conceptual knowledge in introductory physics, *International Journal of Science Education*, 16: 385–403.

Harlen, W. (1992) *The Teaching of Science*. London: David Fulton.

Hashweh, M.Z. (1986) Toward an explanation of conceptual change, *European Journal of Science Education*, 8: 229–49.

Hatano, G. and Inagaki, K. (1992) Desituating cognition through the construction of conceptual knowledge. In P. Light and G. Butterworth (eds) *Context and Cognition: Ways of Learning and Knowing*. New York: Harvester Wheatsheaf.

Hawkins, J. and Pea, R.D. (1987) Tools for bridging the cultures of everyday and scientific thinking, *Journal of Research in Science Teaching*, 24: 291–307.

Helms, J.V. (1998) Science and/in the community: context and goals in practical work, *International Journal of Science Education*, 20: 643–53.

Hennessy, S. (1993) Situated cognition and cognitive apprenticeship: implications for classroom learning, *Studies in Science Education*, 22: 1–41.

Hewson, P.W. (1981) A conceptual change approach to learning science, *European Journal of Science Education*, 3: 383–96.

Hewson, P.W. and Hewson, M.G. (1984) The role of conceptual conflict in conceptual change and the design of science instruction, *Instructional Science*, 13: 1–13.

Hewson, P.W. and Thorley, N.R. (1989) The conditions of conceptual change in the classroom, *International Journal of Science Education*, 11: 541–3.

Hicks, D. (1988) *Education for Peace: Issues, Principles and Practice*. London: Routledge.

Hidi, S. (1990) Interest and its contribution as a mental resource for learning, *Review of Educational Research*, 60: 549–71.

Hills, G.L. (1989) Students' 'untutored' beliefs about natural phenomena: primitive science or common sense? *Science Education*, 73: 155–86.

Hodson, D. (1982) Science – the pursuit of truth? Part I, *School Science Review*, 63: 643–52; Part II, *School Science Review*, 64: 23–30.

Hodson, D. (1986) Rethinking the role and status of observation in science education, *Journal of Curriculum Studies*, 18: 381–96.

Hodson, D. (1988) Experiments in science and science teaching, *Educational Philosophy and Theory*, 20: 53–66.

Hodson, D. (1990) A critical look at practical work in school science, *School Science Review*, 70: 33–40.

Hodson, D. (1992) Assessment of practical work: some considerations in philosophy of science, *Science and Education*, 1: 115–44.

Hodson, D. (1993a) In search of a rationale for multicultural science education, *Science Education*, 77: 685–711.

Hodson, D. (1993b) Philosophic stance of secondary school teachers, curriculum experiences, and children's understanding of science: some preliminary findings, *Interchange*, 1 and 2: 41–52.

Hodson, D. (1993c) Re-thinking old ways; towards a more critical approach to practical work in school science, *Studies in Science Education*, 22: 85–142.

Hodson, D. (1993d) Teaching and learning about science: considerations in the philosophy and sociology of science. In D. Edwards, E. Scanlon and D. West (eds) *Teaching, Learning and Assessment in Science Education*. London: Paul Chapman/Open University.

Hodson, D. (1994) Seeking directions for change: the personalisation and politicisation of science education, *Curriculum Studies*, 2: 71–98.

Hodson, D. (1998) Personalizing, de-mythologizing and politicizing: critical multiculturalism in science and technology education. In S. May (ed.) *Critical Multiculturalism: Rethinking Multicultural and Antiracist Education*. Lewes: Falmer Press.

Hodson, D. and Bencze, L. (1998) Becoming critical about practical work: changing views and changing practice through action research, *International Journal of Science Education*, 20: 683–94.

Hodson, D. and Prophet, B. (1986) A bumpy start to science education, *New Scientist*, 1521: 25–8.

Hodson, D. and Reid, D. (1988) Science for all: motives, meanings and implications. *School Science Review*, 69: 653–61.

Hodson, J. (1996) The effects of peer collaboration on writing performance and attitudes towards writing of male and female standard 3/4 students. Unpublished MA thesis, University of Auckland.

Hofstein, A. and Kempa, R.F. (1985) Motivating strategies in science education: attempt at an analysis, *European Journal of Science Education*, 7: 221–9.

Holman, J. (ed.) (1986) *Science and Technology in Society: Teaching Units and Teacher's Guide*. Hatfield: Association for Science Education.

Holton, G. (1978) *The Scientific Imagination: Case Studies*. Cambridge: Cambridge University Press.

Holton, G. (1986) *The Advancement of Science and Its Burdens*. Cambridge: Cambridge University Press.

Howe, A.C. and Thompsen, P. (1989) Overview of the seminar. In P. Adey, J. Bliss, J. Head and M. Shayer (eds) *Adolescent Development and School Science*. Lewes: Falmer Press.

Hughes, M. and Grieve, R. (1983) On asking children bizarre questions. In M. Donaldson, R. Grieve and C. Pratt (eds) *Early Childhood Development and Education*. Oxford: Blackwell.

Hume, D. (1854) Of the understanding. In *Philosophical Works, vol. 1*. Edinburgh: Adam and Charles Black (reprinted by Scientia Verlag, 1964).

Hunt, A. (ed.) (1990) *SATIS 16–19*. Hatfield: Association for Science Education.

Hynd, C.R., McWhorter, J.Y., Phares, V.L. and Suttles, C.W. (1994) The role of instructional variables in conceptual change in high school physics topics, *Journal of Research in Science Teaching*, 31: 933–46.

Jegede, O. (1995) Collateral learning and the eco-cultural paradigm in science and mathematics education in Africa, *Studies in Science Education*, 25: 97–137.

Jegede, O. (1998) Worldview presuppositions and science and technology education. In D. Hodson (ed.) *Science and Technology Education and Ethnicity: An Aotearoa/New Zealand Perspective*. Wellington: The Royal Society of New Zealand.

Jenkins, E.W. (1990) Scientific literacy and school science education, *School Science Review*, 71: 43–51.

Jenkins, E.W. (1992) School science education: towards a reconstruction, *Journal of Curriculum Studies*, 24: 229–46.

Johnson, D.W. and Johnson, R.T. (1985) The internal dynamics of cooperative learning groups. In R. Slavin, S. Sharan, S. Kagan, R. Hertz-Lazarowitz, C. Webb and R. Schmuck (eds) *Learning to Cooperate, Cooperating to Learn*. New York: Plenum Press.

Johnson, D.W. and Johnson, R.T. (1994) *Learning Together and Alone: Cooperative, and Individualistic Learning*, 4th edn. Boston: Allyn & Bacon.

Johnson, P. and Gott, R. (1996) Constructivism and evidence from children's ideas, *Science Education*, 80: 561–77.

Johnstone, A.H. and Wham, A.J.B. (1982) The demands of practical work, *Education in Chemistry*, 19: 71–3.

Jones, A. (1985) Which girls are learning to lose? Gender, class, race in the classroom, *New Zealand Women's Studies Journal*, August, 15–27.

Jones, A.T. and Kirk, C.M. (1990) Introducing technological applications into the physics classroom: Help or hindrance to learning?, *International Journal of Science Education*, 12: 481–90.

Juell, P. (1985) The course journal. In A. Ruggles Gere (ed.) *Roots in the Sawdust: Writing to Learn across the Disciplines*. Urbana, IL: National Council of Teachers of English.

Kawasaki, K. (1996) The concepts of science in Japanese and Western education, *Science and Education*, 5: 1–20.

Kelly, A. (1987) The construction of masculine science. In A. Kelly (ed.) *Science for Girls?* Milton Keynes: Open University Press.

Kelly, G.A. (1955) *The Psychology of Personal Constructs*. New York: Norton.

Kelly, G.J. (1997) Research traditions in comparative context: a philosophical challenge to radical constructivism, *Science Education*, 81: 355–75.

Kemmis, S. (1988) Action research. In J.P. Keeves (ed.) *Educational Research, Methodology and Measurement: An International Handbook*. London: Pergamon Press.

Kempa, R.F. and Ayob, A. (1991) Learning interactions in group work in science, *International Journal of Science Education*, 13: 341–54.

Kempa, R.F. and Ayob, A. (1995) Learning from group work in science, *International Journal of Science Education*, 17: 743–54.

Kempa, R.F. and Diaz, M.M. (1990) Motivational traits and preferences for different instructional modes in science. Parts 1 and 2, *International Journal of Science Education*, 12: 195–203; 205–16.

King, A.R. and Brownell, J.A. (1966) *The Curriculum and the Disciplines of Knowledge: A Theory of Curriculum Practice*. New York: John Wiley.

Kirkwood, V.M. (1989) Energy for a change: teaching and learning about the energy concept in New Zealand secondary school junior science classrooms. Unpublished DPhil thesis. University of Waikato.

Kirschner, P.A. and Huisman, W. (1998) 'Dry laboratories' in science education: computer-based practical work, *International Journal of Science Education*, 20: 665–82.

Knorr-Cetina, K.D. (1983) The ethnographic study of scientific work. In K.D. Knorr-Cetina and M. Mulkay (eds) *Science Observed*. London: Sage.

Kozulin, A. (1990) *Vygotsky's Psychology: A Biography of Ideas*. Cambridge, MA: Harvard University Press.

Kruglanski, A.W. (1989) *Lay Epistemics and Human Knowledge: Cognitive and Motivational Bases*. New York: Plenum.

Krugly-Smolska, E. (1995) Cultural influences in science education, *International Journal of Science Education*, 17: 45–58.

Krugly-Smolska, E. (1996) Scientific culture, multiculturalism and the science classroom, *Science and Education*, 5: 21–9.

Kuhn, D. (1989) Children and adults as intuitive scientists, *Psychological Review*, 56: 674–89.

Kuhn, T.S. (1970) *The Structure of Scientific Revolutions*. Chicago: University of Chicago Press.

Kuhn, T.S. (1977) *The Essential Tension*. Chicago: University of Chicago Press.

Kyle, W.C. (1996) Editorial: the importance of investing in human resources, *Journal of Research in Science Teaching*, 33: 1–4.

Lakatos, I. (1978) *The Methodology of Scientific Research Programmes*. Cambridge: Cambridge University Press.

Larkin, J.H. (1983) The role of problem representation in physics. In D. Gentner and A.L. Stevens (eds) *Mental Models*. Hillsdale, NJ: Lawrence Erlbaum.

Larson, J.O. (1995) Fatima's rules and other elements of an unintended chemistry curriculum. Conference paper, AERA Annual Meeting, San Francisco.

Lave, J. (1988) *Cognition in Practice: Mind, Mathematics and Culture in Everyday Life*. New York: Cambridge University Press.

Lave, J. (1991) Situating learning in communities of practice. In L.B. Resnick, J.M. Levine and S.D. Teasley (eds) *Perspectives on Socially Shared Cognition*. Washington, DC: American Psychological Association.

Lave, J. and Wenger, E. (1991) *Situated Learning: Legitimate Peripheral Participation*. Cambridge: Cambridge University Press.

Layton, D. (1986) Revaluing science education. In P. Tomlinson and M. Quinton (eds) *Values Across the Curriculum*. Lewes: Falmer Press.

Layton, D., Jenkins, E., Macgill, S. and Davey, A. (1993) *Inarticulate Science?* Driffield: Studies in Education.

Lemke, J.L. (1987) Social semiotics and science education, *American Journal of Semiotics*, 5: 217–32.

Lemke, J.L. (1990) *Talking Science: Language, Learning and Values*. Norwood, NJ: Ablex.

Leont'ev, A.N. (1981) The problem of activity in psychology. In J.V. Wertsch (ed.) *The Concept of Activity in Soviet Psychology*. Armonk, NY: Sharpe.

Longino, H. (1994) The fate of knowledge in social theories of science. In F.T. Schmitt (ed.) *Socializing Epistemology: the Social Dimensions of Knowledge*. Lanham, MD: Rowman and Littlefield.

Loving, C. (1997) From the summit of truth to its slippery slopes: science education's journey through positivist-postmodern territory, *American Educational Research Journal*, 34: 421–52.

Lucas, A.M. (1991) 'Infotainment' and informal sources for learning science, *International Journal of Science Education*, 13: 495–504.

Lunzer, E. and Gardner, K. (1979) *Learning from the Written Word*. Edinburgh: Oliver & Boyd.

McClelland, G. (1983) Discussion in science lessons, *School Science Review*, 65: 129–33.

McCombs, B.L. and Pope, J.E. (eds) (1994) *Motivating Hard to Reach Students*. Washington, DC: American Psychological Association.

McLellan, H. (ed.) (1996) *Situated Learning Perspectives*. Englewood Cliffs, NJ: Educational Technology Publications.

McNairy, M.R. (1985) Sciencing: science education for early childhood, *School Science and Mathematics*, 85: 383–93.

McRobbie, C. and Tobin, K. (1997) A social constructivist perspective on learning environments, *International Journal of Science Education*, 19: 193–208.

Mallow, J.V. (1991) Reading science, *Journal of Reading*, 34: 324–8.

Martin, N. (1976) Language across the curriculum: a paradox and its potential for change, *Educational Review*, 2: 206–19.

Maslow, A. (1970) *Motivation and Personality*. New York: Harper & Row.

Maslow, A.H. (1971) *The Farther Reaches of Human Nature*. New York: Viking.

Matthews, M.R. (1993a) Constructivism and science education: some epistemological problems, *Journal of Science Education and Technology*, 2: 359–70.

Matthews, M.R. (1993b) Curriculum reform degrades sciences, *The New Zealand Herald*, 26 August, 8.

Matthews, M.R. (1994) *Science Teaching: The Role of History and Philosophy of Science*. New York: Routledge.

Matthews, M.R. (1995) *Challenging New Zealand Science Education*. Palmerston North: Dunmore Press.

Matthews, M.R. (1997) Introductory comments on philosophy and constructivism in science education, *Science and Education*, 6: 5–14.

May, S. (1994) *Making Multicultural Education Work*. Clevedon: Multilingual Matters.

Mayer, E. (1988) *Toward a New Philosophy of Biology*. Cambridge, MA: Harvard University Press.

Medawar, P.B. (1967) *The Art of the Soluble*. London: Methuen.

Medawar, P.B. (1969) *Induction and Intuition in Scientific Thought*. London: Methuen.

Meyer, K. and Woodruff, E. (1997) Consensually driven explanation in science teaching, *Science Education*, 81: 173–92.

Millar, R. (1989) Constructive criticisms, *International Journal of Science Education*, 11: 587–96.

Miller, J.P. (1993) *The Holistic Teacher*. Toronto: OISE Press.

Ministry of Education (Alberta) (1990) *STS Education: Unifying the Goals of Science Education*. Edmonton: Alberta Government Printer.

Ministry of Education (New Zealand) (1989) *Forms 1–5 Science Syllabus: Draft*. Wellington: Learning Media (in 1989, it was the Department of Education).

Ministry of Education (New Zealand) (1992) *Science in the National Curriculum: Draft*. Wellington: Learning Media.

Ministry of Education (New Zealand) (1993) *Science in the New Zealand Curriculum*. Wellington: Learning Media.

Mitchell, J.A. and Mitchell, I.J. (1992) Some classroom procedures. In J.R. Baird and J.R. Northfield (eds) *Learning from the PEEL Project*. Clayton, Victoria: Monash University.

Moje, E.B. (1995) Talking about science: an interpretation of the effects of teacher talk in a high school science classroom, *Journal of Research in Science Teaching*, 32: 349–71.

Mortimer, E.F. (1995) Conceptual change or conceptual profile change? *Science and Education*, 4: 267–85.

Mulkay, M. (1979) *Science and the Sociology of Knowledge*. London: Allen and Unwin.

Munby, H. (1980) Analyzing teaching for intellectual independence. In H. Munby, G. Orpwood and T. Russell (eds) *Seeing Curriculum in a New Light: Essays from Science Education*. Toronto: OISE Press.

Muthukrishna, N., Carmine, D., Grossen, B. and Miller, S. (1993) Children's alternative frameworks: should they be directly addressed by science instruction?, *Journal of Research in Science Teaching*, 30: 233–48.

Nadeau, R. and Desautels, J.F. (1984) *Epistemology and the Teaching of Science: A Discussion Paper*. Ottawa: Science Council of Canada.

Nersessian, N.J. (1989) Conceptual change in science and in science education, *Synthese*, 80: 163–83.

Newman, D., Griffin, P. and Cole, M. (1989) *The Construction Zone: Working for Cognitive Change in School*. Cambridge: Cambridge University Press.

Newton-Smith, W.H. (1981) *The Rationality of Science*. London: Routledge and Kegan Paul.

Nicholls, J.G. (1984) Achievement motivation: conceptions of ability, subjective experience, task choice, and performance, *Psychological Review*, 91: 328–46.

Nicholls, J.G. (1989) *The Competitive Ethos and Democratic Education*. Cambridge, MA: Harvard University Press.

Nickerson, R.S. (1986) Reasoning. In R.F. Dillon and R.J. Sternberg (eds) *Cognition and Instruction*. New York: Academic Press.

Norris, S.P. (1997) Intellectual independence for nonscientists and other content-transcendent goals of science education, *Science Education*, 81: 239–58.

Nott, M. and Smith, R. (1995) 'Talking your way out of it', 'rigging', and 'conjuring': what science teachers do when practicals go wrong, *International Journal of Science Education*, 17: 399–410.

Nott, M. and Wellington, J. (1996) When the black box springs open: practical work in school science and the nature of science, *International Journal of Science Education*, 18: 807–18.

Novak, J.D. (1989) The use of metacognitive tools to facilitate meaningful learning. In P. Adey, J. Bliss, J. Head and M. Shayer (eds) *Adolescent Development and School Science*. Lewes: Falmer Press.

Novak, J.D. (1990) Concept maps and Vee diagrams: two metacognitive tools for science and mathematics education, *Instructional Science*, 19: 29–52.

Nussbaum, J. (1985) The particulate nature of matter in the gaseous phase. In R. Driver, E. Guesne and A. Tiberghien (eds) *Children's Ideas in Science*. Milton Keynes: Open University Press.

Nussbaum, J. and Novick, S. (1982) Alternative frameworks, conceptual conflict and accommodation: toward a principled teaching strategy, *Instructional Science*, 11: 183–200.

Oakeshott, M. (1962) *Rationalism in Politics and Other Essays*. London: Methuen.

Ogawa, M. (1995) Science education in a multi-science perspective, *Science Education*, 79: 583–93.

Ogunniyi, M.B., Jegede, O.J., Ogawa, M., Yandila, C.D. and Oladele, F.K. (1995) Nature of worldview presuppositions among science teachers in Botswana, Indonesia, Japan, Nigeria and the Philippines, *Journal of Research in Science Teaching*, 32: 817–31.

O'Loughlin, M. (1992) Rethinking science education: beyond Piagetian constructivism toward a sociocultural model of teaching and learning, *Journal of Research in Science Teaching*, 29: 791–820.

Osborne, J.F. (1996) Beyond constructivism, *Science Education*, 80: 53–82.

Osborne, J.F. (1997) Practical alternatives, *School Science Review*, 78(285): 61–6.

Osborne, R.J., Bell, B.F. and Gilbert, J.K. (1983) Science teaching and children's views of the world, *European Journal of Science Education*, 5: 1–14.

Osborne, R. and Cosgrove, M. (1983) Children's conceptions of the change of state of water, *Journal of Research in Science Teaching*, 20: 825–38.

Osborne, R. and Freyberg, P. (1985) *Learning in Science: The Implications of Children's Science.* Auckland: Heinemann.

Osborne, R. and Wittrock, M. (1985) The generative learning model and its implications for science education, *Studies in Science Education*, 12: 59–87.

Palincsar, A.S. and Brown, A.L. (1984) Reciprocal teaching of comprehension-fostering and monitoring activities, *Cognition and Instruction*, 1: 117–75.

Paris, S.G., Cross, D.R. and Lipson, M.Y. (1984) Informed strategies for learning: a program to improve children's reading awareness and comprehension, *Journal of Educational Psychology*, 76: 1239–52.

Paris, S.G., Saarnio, D.A. and Cross, D.R. (1986) A metacognitive curriculum to promote children's reading and learning, *Australian Journal of Psychology*, 38: 107–23.

Pearson, P.D., Roehler, L.R., Dole, J.A. and Duffy, G.G. (1992) Developing expertise in reading comprehension. In S.J. Samuels and A.E. Farstup (eds) *What Research Has to Say About Reading Instruction*, 2nd edn. Newark, DE: International Reading Association.

Pedretti, E. and Hodson, D. (1995) From rhetoric to action: implementing STS education through action research, *Journal of Research in Science Teaching*, 32: 463–85.

Pella, M.O., O'Hearn, G.T. and Gale, C.W. (1966) Referents to scientific literacy, *Journal of Research in Science Teaching*, 4: 199–208.

Perkins, D.N. and Salomon, G. (1989) Are cognitive skills context-bound?, *Educational Researcher*, 18: 16–25.

Pfundt, H. and Duit, R. (1994) *Bibliography: Students' Alternative Frameworks and Science Education*, 4th edn. Kiel: IPN, University of Kiel.

Phelan, P., Davidson, A.L. and Cao, H.T. (1991) Students' multiple worlds: negotiating the boundaries of family, peer, and school cultures, *Anthropology and Education Quarterly*, 22: 224–50.

Pintrich, P.R., Marx, R.W. and Boyle, R.A. (1993) Beyond cold conceptual change: the role of motivational beliefs and classroom contextual factors in the process of conceptual change, *Review of Educational Research*, 63: 167–99.

Polanyi, M. (1958) *Personal Knowledge: Towards a Post-Critical Philosophy.* London: Routledge and Kegan Paul.

Pomeroy, D. (1994) Science education and cultural diversity: mapping the field, *Studies in Science Education*, 24: 49–73.

Popper, K.R. (1968) *The Logic of Scientific Discovery.* London: Hutchinson.

Popper, K.R. (1972) *Objective Knowledge.* Oxford: Oxford University Press.

Posner, G.J., Strike, K.A., Hewson, P.W. and Gertzog, W.A. (1982) Accommodation of a scientific conception: toward a theory of conceptual change, *Science Education*, 66: 211–27.

Prawat, R.S. (1993) The value of ideas: problems versus possibilities in learning, *Educational Researcher*, 22: 5–16.

Pugh, M. and Lock, R. (1989) Pupil talk in biology practical work – a preliminary study, *Research in Science and Technological Education*, 7: 15–26.

Raffini, J.P. (1993) *Winners without Losers: Structures and Strategies for Increasing Student Motivation to Learn.* Needham Heights, MA: Allyn & Bacon.

Raper, G. and Stringer, J. (1987) *Encouraging Primary Science: An Introduction to the Development of Science in Primary Schools.* London: Cassell.

Ravetz, J.R. (1971) *Scientific Knowledge and Its Social Problems.* Harmondsworth: Penguin.

Riding, R., Burton, D., Rees, G. and Sharratt, M. (1995) Cognitive style and personality in 12 year old children, *British Journal of Educational Psychology*, 65: 113–24.

Rivard, L.P. (1994) A review of writing to learn in science: implications for practice and research, *Journal of Research in Science Teaching*, 31: 969–83.

Roberts, D.A. (1988) What counts as science education? In P. Fensham (ed.) *Development and Dilemmas in Science Education*. Lewes: Falmer Press.

Roberts, M. (1998) Indigenous knowledge and Western science: perspectives from the Pacific. In D. Hodson (ed.) *Science and Technology Education and Ethnicity: An Aotearoa/New Zealand Perspective*. Wellington: The Royal Society of New Zealand.

Rogoff, B. (1990) *Apprenticeship in Thinking: Cognitive Development in Social Context*. New York: Oxford University Press.

Rogoff, B. (1991) Social interaction as apprenticeship in thinking: guidance and participation in spatial planning. In L.B. Resnick, J.M. Levine and S.D. Teasley (eds) *Perspectives on Socially Shared Cognition*. Washington, DC: American Psychological Association.

Rokeach, M. (1960) *The Open and Closed Mind*. New York: Basic Books.

Rosenthal, R. and Jacobson, L. (1968) *Pygmalion in the Classroom: Teacher Expectation and Pupils' Intellectual Development*. New York: Holt, Rinehart & Winston.

Ross, K. and Sutton, C. (1982) Concept profiles and the cultural context, *European Journal of Science Education*, 4: 311–23.

Roth, K. and Anderson, C. (1988) Promoting conceptual change learning from science textbooks. In P. Ramsden (ed.) *Improving Learning: New Perspectives*. London: Kogan Page.

Roth, W.-M. and Alexander, T. (1997) The interaction of students' scientific and religious discourses: two case studies, *International Journal of Science Education*, 19: 125–46.

Roth, W.-M. and Roychoudhury, A. (1993) The development of science process skills in authentic contexts, *Journal of Research in Science Teaching*, 30: 127–52.

Rowe, M.B. (1973) *Teaching Science as Continuous Inquiry*. New York: McGraw Hill.

Rowe, M.B. (1974) Wait-time and rewards as instructional variables, their influence on language, logic and fate control, *Journal of Research in Science Teaching*, 11: 81–94.

Rowell, J., Dawson, C. and Lyndon, H. (1990) Changing misconceptions: a challenge in science education, *International Journal of Science Education*, 12: 167–75.

Rudduck, J. and Cowie, H. (1988) An introduction to cooperative group work, *Educational and Child Psychology*, 5: 91–102.

Rumelhart, D.E. and Norman, D.A. (1981) Accretion, tuning and restructuring: three modes of learning. In R.L. Klatzky and J.W. Cotton (eds) *Semantic Factors in Cognition*. Hillsdale, NJ: Lawrence Erlbaum.

Saunders, W.L. (1992) The constructivist perspective: implications and teaching strategies for science, *School Science and Mathematics*, 92: 136–41.

Saxe, G.B. (1991) *Culture and Cognitive Development: Studies in Mathematical Understanding*. Hillsdale, NJ: Lawrence Erlbaum.

Scardamalia, M. and Bereiter, C. (1994) Computer support for knowledge-building communities, *Journal of the Learning Sciences*, 3: 265–83.

Schank, R. (1990) *Tell Me a Story: A New Look at Real and Artificial Memory*. New York: Macmillan.

Schibeci, R.A. (1984) Attitudes to science: an update, *Studies in Science Education*, 11: 26–59.

Schibeci, R.A. (1987) Helping students work independently: using projects in science teaching, *Australian Science Teachers Journal*, 33: 91–4.

Schliemann, A.D. and Carraher, D.W. (1992) Proportional reasoning in and out of school. In P. Light and G. Butterworth (eds) *Context and Cognition: Ways of Learning and Knowing*. New York: Harvester Wheatsheaf.

Scottish Consultative Council on the Curriculum (1996) *Science Education in Scottish Schools: Looking to the Future*. Broughty Ferry: SCCC.

Scribner, S. (1984) Studying working intelligence. In B. Rogoff and J. Lave (eds) *Everyday Cognition*. Cambridge, MA: Harvard University Press.

Selby, D. (1995) *Earthkind: A Teachers' Handbook on Humane Education*. Stoke-on-Trent: Trentham Books.

Shahn, E. (1988) On science literacy, *Educational Philosophy and Theory*, 20: 42–52.

Shapiro, B.L. (1988) What children bring to light. In P.J. Fensham (ed.) *Development and Dilemmas in Science Education*. Lewes: Falmer Press.

Shapiro, B.L. (1992) A life of science learning: an approach to the study of personal, social and cultural features in the initiation to school science. In G.L.C. Hills (ed.) *History and Philosophy of Science in Science Education, vol. II*. Kingston, ON: Queen's University.

Shapiro, B.L. (1994) *What Children Bring to Light: A Constructivist Perspective on Children's Learning in Science*. New York: Teachers College Press.

Shipstone, D. (1985) Electricity in simple circuits. In R. Driver, E. Guesne and A. Tiberghien (eds) *Children's Ideas in Science*. Milton Keynes: Open University Press.

Shuell, T.J. (1990) Phases of meaningful learning, *Review of Educational Research*, 60: 531–47.

Slavin, R.E. (1985) An introduction to cooperative learning research. In R. Slavin, S. Sharan, S. Kagan, R. Hertz-Lazarowitz, C. Webb and R. Schmuck (eds) *Learning to Cooperate, Cooperating to Learn*. New York: Plenum Press.

Slavin, R.E. (1995) *Cooperative Learning: Theory, Research and Practice*, 2nd edn. Boston: Allyn and Bacon.

Slezak, P. (1994) Sociology of scientific knowledge and scientific education: part 1, *Science and Education*, 3: 265–94.

Smolicz, J.J. and Nunan, E.E. (1975) The philosophical and sociological foundations of science education: the demythologizing of school science, *Studies in Science Education*, 2: 101–43.

Solomon, J. (1987) Social influences on the construction of pupils' understanding of science, *Studies in Science Education*, 14: 63–82.

Solomon, J. (1989) A study of behaviour in the teaching laboratory, *International Journal of Science Education*, 11: 317–26.

Solomon, J. (1991) School laboratory life. In B.E. Woolnough (ed.) *Practical Science: The Role and Reality of Practical Work in School Science*. Milton Keynes: Open University Press.

Solomon, J. (1993) The social construction of children's scientific knowledge. In P.J. Black and A.M. Lucas (eds) *Children's Informal Ideas in Science*. London: Routledge.

Solomon, J. (1996) Student learning on a GNVQ science course: motivation and self-esteem, *School Science Review*, 78(280): 37–44.

Solomon, J. and Aikenhead, G. (eds) (1994) *STS Education: International Perspectives on Reform*. New York: Teachers College Press.

Stanley, W.B. and Brickhouse, N.W. (1994) Multiculturalism, universalism, and science education, *Science Education*, 78: 387–98.

Staver, J.R. and Lumpe, A.T. (1995) Two investigations of students' understanding of the mole concept and its use in problem solving, *Journal of Research in Science Teaching*, 32: 177–93.

Stead, B.F. (1980) Living. Working paper no. 15, Learning in Science Project. Hamilton, New Zealand: University of Waikato.

Stipek, D.J. (1993) *Motivation to Learn: From Theory to Practice*, 2nd edn. Needham Heights, MA: Allyn and Bacon.

Strike, K.A. and Posner, G.J. (1985) A conceptual change view of learning and understanding. In L. West and A.L. Pines (eds) *Cognitive Structure and Conceptual Change*. New York: Academic Press.

Strike, K.A. and Posner, G.J. (1992) A revisionist theory of conceptual change. In R.A. Duschl and R.J. Hamilton (eds) *Philosophy of Science, Cognitive Psychology, and Educational Theory and Practice*. Albany: State University of New York Press.

Suchting, W.A. (1992) Constructivism deconstructed, *Science and Education*, 1: 223–54.

Sutton, C. (1992) *Words, Science and Learning*. Buckingham: Open University Press.

Sutton, C. (1996) Beliefs about science and beliefs about language, *International Journal of Science Education*, 18: 1–18.

Swift, J.N. and Gooding, C.T. (1983) Interaction of wait time, feedback and questioning instruction on middle school science teaching, *Journal of Research in Science Teaching*, 20: 721–30.

Tendencia, C. (ed.) (1987) *Science and Technology Education towards Informed Citizenship*. Proceedings of the 5th ACASE-Asian Symposium. Penang: RECSAM.

Tharp, R. and Gallimore, R. (eds)(1988) *Rousing Minds to Life: Teaching, Learning and Schooling in Social Context*. Cambridge: Cambridge University Press.

Theobald, D.W. (1968) *An Introduction to the Philosophy of Science*. London: Methuen.

Thomas, E.L. and Robinson, H.A. (1972) *Improving Reading in Every Class: A Sourcebook for Teachers*. Boston: Allyn and Bacon.

Thorley, N.R. and Stofflett, R.T. (1996) Representation of the conceptual change model in science teacher education, *Science Education*, 80: 317–39.

Timm, J. (1992) *Self-esteem is for Everyone (SEE) Program*. Tampa, FL: Learning Advantages.

Toulmin, S.E. (1972) *Human Understanding*. Princeton, NJ: Princeton University Press.

Tudge, J. (1990) Vygotsky, the zone of proximal development, and peer collaboration: Implications for classroom practice. In L.C. Moll (ed.) *Vygotsky and Education: Instructional Implications and Applications of Sociohistorical Psychology*. Cambridge: Cambridge University Press.

Tunnicliffe, S.D. (1989) Challenge based science. In B.N. Honeyman (ed.) *Science Education and the Quality of Life*. ICASE Yearbook. Australian Science Teachers Association/International Council of Associations for Science Education.

Tyson, L.M., Venville, G.J., Harrison, A.G. and Treagust, D.F. (1997) A multidimensional framework for interpreting conceptual change events in the classroom, *Science Education*, 81: 387–404.

von Glasersfeld, E. (1987) *Construction of Knowledge*. Salinas, CA: Intersystems Publications.

von Glasersfeld, E. (1989) Cognition, construction of knowledge, and teaching, *Synthese*, 80: 121–40.

von Glasersfeld, E. (1992) Constructivism reconstructed: a reply to Suchting, *Science and Education*, 1: 379–84.

Vroom, V.H. (1964) *Work and Motivation*. New York: John Wiley.

Vygotsky, L.S. (1962) *Thought and Language*. Cambridge, MA: MIT Press.

Vygotsky, L.S. (1978) *Mind in Society: The Development of Higher Psychological Processes*. Cambridge, MA: Harvard University Press.

Vygotsky, L.S. (1987) *The Collected Works of L. S. Vygotsky: Problems of General Psychology*. New York: Plenum Press.

Wallace, J. (1986) Social interactions within second year groups doing practical science. Unpublished MSc thesis, University of Oxford (cited by Solomon, 1987).

Watson, R. and Fairbrother, B. (1993) Open-ended work in science (OPENS) project: managing investigations in the laboratory, *School Science Review*, 75(271): 31–8.

Watts, D.M. and Alsop, S. (1995) Questioning and conceptual understanding: the quality of pupils' questions in science, *School Science Review*, 76(277): 91–5.

Watts, D.M. and Bentley, D. (1987) Constructivism in the classroom: enabling conceptual change by words and deeds, *British Educational Research Journal*, 13: 121–35.

Watts, D.M. and Bentley, D. (1994) Humanizing and feminizing school science: reviving anthropomorphic and animistic thinking in constructivist science education, *International Journal of Science Education*, 16: 83–97.

Webb, N. (1984) An analysis of group interaction and mathematical errors in heterogeneous ability groups, *British Journal of Educational Psychology*, 50: 266–76.

Weck, M.A. (1995) Are today's models tomorrow's misconceptions? In F. Finley, D. Allchin, D. Rhees and S. Fifield (eds) *Third International History, Philosophy, and Science Teaching Conference, vol. 2*. Minneapolis: University of Minnesota.

Wellington, J.J. (1989) Skills and processes in science education: an introduction. In J.J. Wellington (ed.) *Skills and Processes in Science Education*. London: Routledge.

Wells, G. (1993) Text, talk and inquiry: schooling as semiotic apprenticeship. Conference paper, the Language in Education Conference, Hong Kong.

Wells, G. and Chang-Wells, G.L. (1992) *Constructing Knowledge Together: Classrooms as Centers of Inquiry and Literacy*. Portsmouth, NH: Heinemann.

West, L.H.T. and Pines, A.L. (1983) How 'rational' is rationality?, *Science Education*, 67: 37–9.

White, R.T. (1991) Episodes and the purpose and conduct of practical work. In B.E. Woolnough (ed.) *Practical Science: The Role and Reality of Practical Work in School Science*. Buckingham: Open University Press.

White, R.T. (1996) The link between the laboratory and learning, *International Journal of Science Education*, 18: 761–74.

White, R.T. and Gunstone, R.F. (1989) Metalearning and conceptual change, *International Journal of Science Education*, 11: 577–86.

White, R.T. and Mitchell, I.J. (1994) Metacognition and the quality of learning, *Studies in Science Education*, 23: 21–37.

Wood, D. (1991) Aspects of teaching and learning. In P. Light, S. Sheldon and M. Woodhead (eds) *Learning to Think*. London: Routledge.

Wood, D., Bruner, J.S. and Ross, G. (1976) The role of tutoring in problem solving, *Journal of Child Psychology and Psychiatry*, 17: 89–100.

Woolnough, B. and Allsop, T. (1985) *Practical Work in Science*. Cambridge: Cambridge University Press.

Yager, R.E. (ed.) (1996) *Science/Technology/Society as Reform in Science Education*. Albany: State University of New York Press.

Young, R.M. (1987) Racist society, racist science. In D. Gill and L. Levidow (eds) *Antiracist Science Teaching*. London: Free Association Books.

Zilbersztain, A. and Gilbert, J. (1981) Does practice in the laboratory fit the spirit?, *Australian Science Teachers Journal*, 27: 39–44.

Index

Aikenhead, G.S., 1, 3, 63, 105, 112, 135, 139–40, 163
anthropomorphism, 30, 134
apprenticeship, 95, 106, 115, 118, 123–4, 149–51, 156, 179–80
assessment and evaluation, 43, 70, 73, 103, 138, 164, 173, 175, 177
Ausubel, D.P., 26, 37, 91, 131

Bakhtin, M.M., 108
Bell, B.F., 28, 29, 49, 56
Bloom, J.W., 54, 134, 138
border crossing, 100, 102, 112, 125, 128–9, 131, 133, 135–42, 163–4, 167
Bruner, J.S., 87–8, 97, 163

children's science, 26–31, 36–7, 40, 50, 104
citizenship (science education for), 1, 29, 159
classroom language, see language of classroom
Claxton, G., 38, 49, 58–60, 76, 78, 89
Cobern, W.W., 135–6, 139
collateral learning, 137, 141
common sense, 32, 45, 48, 52, 89–90, 95–6, 104, 116–17, 121, 128–31
community of scientists, 16, 19, 20, 46–7, 52–3, 55, 88, 92–3, 95–9, 102, 112, 115, 118, 121, 123, 141, 144, 158, 166

concept maps, 26, 35, 42, 133, 138–9, 162
conceptual change (reorganization), 37–42, 49, 52–6, 71, 74, 113, 115, 131
conceptual structures, 6, 11–12, 17–18, 25, 27, 90–2, 154
connoisseurship, 19–20, 98, 115, 150, 152, 177, 179–80
consensus, 16, 53, 74, 92
correlational studies, 22, 106, 119, 123, 148, 152
Costa, V.B., 104–6

DARTs, 160–1, 164
Demastes, S.S., 113, 136, 142
demonstrations, see teacher demonstrations
doing science, 5, 11, 60, 117–20, 143–4, 148–9, 151–2, 161, 166–7, 168
Driver, R., 26, 33–4, 37, 47, 49, 130, 146
Dweck, C.S., 63–5

economic issues, 1, 2, 16, 17
emotional climate, 5, 35, 54–5, 58–9, 78, 97, 175–9
empowerment, 21–2, 88
environmental issues, 1, 3, 4, 6, 21, 178
episodic knowledge, 35, 147–8
epistemological profile, 132

ethnicity (gender and class), 5, 6, 54, 59, 81–2, 103–5, 112, 125, 135–7, 163, 175, 178
everyday understanding, *see* common sense
experiments, 11, 13–15, 18–19, 22, 25, 37, 48, 94, 106, 118, 123, 130, 141, 149, 152

feminist science, 20, 141
Fensham, P.J., 1, 35, 37, 146

gender (ethnicity and class), 5, 6, 54, 59, 81–2, 103–5, 112, 125, 135–7, 163, 175, 178
Gil-Perez, D., 48, 130, 139
goals of science education, 1, 29, 128, 132, 135, 145, 151, 162
group work, 35–6, 40, 43, 76–82, 98–9, 121–3, 157, 171–4
Gunstone, R.F., 25, 35, 37–8, 42, 69, 147

Hewson, P.W., 37, 39, 42, 131, 142
Hodson, D., 4, 13, 17, 20, 21, 47, 50, 92, 104, 118, 140–1, 144, 148, 153, 180

induction, 12–14, 19, 141
inquiry-based learning, 120–3
intellectual independence, 3, 9, 36, 88, 94, 132–3, 151, 160, 169, 171, 178, 180
intuition, 19, 20, 53, 62, 83
issues-based curriculum/learning, 4, 7, 21–2, 137

Jegede, O., 135–7, 141
Johnson, D.W., 78, 171

King, A.R., 140–1
Kruglanski, A.W., 67, 70
Kuhn, D., 94–5, 130
Kuhn, T.S., 14–15, 115

language of classroom, 67, 81, 102–3, 108–10, 169
language of science, 15, 23–4, 28–9, 31, 46, 51–2, 55, 82, 90–1, 103, 123–5, 141, 159

Lave, J., 31, 95–6, 114, 150
Layton, D., 4, 21, 114
learner control, 79–80, 97, 107, 109, 129, 133, 144–5, 149–52, 168, 171
learning about science, 5, 92–5, 102, 117–20, 129–31, 135, 143–4, 148–9, 151–2, 161, 168
learning goals, 64–71, 97, 110, 180
learning science, 5, 41, 48, 60, 75, 91, 117–20, 143–4, 145–8, 151–2, 161, 168
Lemke, J.L., 52, 103, 124, 159
Leont'ev, A.N., 88
Longino, H., 93

Maslow, A., 61–2
mastery goals, *see* learning goals
Matthews, M.R., 44–6, 48, 56–7, 66, 90–2, 130
metacognition, 42, 67–8, 71–2, 83, 94, 98, 132–4, 138, 142
modelling, 67, 73, 88, 96, 98, 106, 121, 149–52, 169–70, 176–7, 179
models, 18, 50, 52, 132, 146
moral-ethical issues, 17, 21
motivation, 43, 60–4, 67–70, 78–82, 96, 97, 99, 133, 143–4, 168, 171
myths of science, 141

Nadeau, R., 106, 136
Nicholls, J.G., 64, 70
normal science, 14–15, 113, 125

observation, 10–15, 17–19, 23–5, 27, 31, 37, 45, 47–8, 92, 94, 118, 130, 141, 145, 149, 152
O'Loughlin, M., 109, 125
Osborne, J.F., 47, 92, 162
Osborne, R.J., 27, 30, 32, 34–5, 42
ownership, 21–2, 36, 115, 120, 178

PEEL project, 43, 134
Pella, M.O., 2
performance goals, 64–71, 97, 110, 180
personal framework of understanding, 27, 49–57, 67, 70, 74–5, 82–3, 85, 95, 98, 106, 112, 113, 115, 121, 127–9, 131, 134–7, 138, 142, 154, 158, 162, 166, 170, 172
Phelan, P., 100, 104, 137

Piaget, J., 37, 86, 88, 116
P-O-E (predict-observe-explain), 37, 147
politicization, 3, 4, 6, 21, 22, 70, 125, 137
Pomeroy, D., 81, 137, 139
Popper, K.R., 14, 99
portfolios, 43, 167, 175
Posner, G.J., 39, 42, 52–4, 95, 113, 116, 133, 142
power (issues of), 53, 76–7, 102, 106–7, 110, 125, 178
prediction, 13, 14, 25, 37, 147
problem solving, 6, 148
processes of science, 24, 25, 118–19, 141, 143, 150

questions/questioning, 35–6, 55, 96, 107–9, 121, 122, 138–9, 149, 154–5

radical constructivism, 45–8
Ravetz, J.R., 150, 176
reading, 155, 159–61, 166–7, 174
realism, 45, 50, 95, 132
reflection, 40, 41–3, 73, 75, 149, 151, 169–70, 173, 179
relativism, 46, 66, 95
Rowell, J., 9, 40

scaffolding, 67, 86–7, 96–8, 102, 121, 133, 145, 159, 169, 171
science education goals/purpose, see goals of science education
Science for all Americans, 2, 3
scientific classification, 24–5
scientific community, see community of scientists
scientific investigation/inquiry, 4, 6, 9, 11–12, 19, 23–5, 36, 46–7, 94, 118–20, 123, 141, 147, 151–2, 165
scientific observation, see observation
scientific practice, 5, 94, 103

scientific revolutions, 14–16, 113, 125
scientific theory, 11, 15, 18, 24, 48, 50, 52, 128, 146
scientific truth, 14, 18, 45, 47
self-esteem, 36, 59–62, 64, 66, 69, 73, 78, 97, 99, 101, 137, 172, 176
Shapiro, B.L., 37, 42–3, 78, 83
situated cognition, 31, 50, 95–6, 114–18
Slavin, R.E., 78, 172–3
Smolicz, J.J., 93–4
social and environmental action, 4, 21, 22
Solomon, J., 1, 64, 74, 76–8, 80
Stead, B.F., 28, 29, 49, 56
STS (science-technology-society), 1, 3, 4, 21, 115
Sutton, C., 51, 57, 160, 162–3

tacit knowledge, 19, 83, 120
talking, 5, 80, 85–6, 102, 121–5, 147, 154–9, 166–7
teacher demonstrations, 35, 37, 40, 174
teacher questions, see questions/questioning
theory-building, 18, 28–30, 46, 50, 75, 91, 118, 131, 143, 159
Toulmin, S.E., 134, 142

von Glasersfeld, E., 46–7, 56–7
Vroom, V.H., 62–3
Vygotsky, L.S., 71, 84–9, 96, 98, 123, 129, 132, 144–5

Wells, G., 123, 156, 169
White, R.T., 35, 41, 43, 129, 133–4, 147
worldview, 41, 135–7, 139, 163–4
writing, 35, 36, 155, 161–7, 174

ZPD (zone of proximal development), 71, 86–7, 97, 106, 123, 129, 132–3, 144, 168, 170, 172, 177